THE STORY WE NEED TO KNOW

We've all heard at least some version of the story of the *Mayflower*, how in 1620 the Pilgrims sailed to the New World in search of religious freedom; how after drawing up the Mayflower Compact, they landed at Plymouth Rock and befriended the local Wampanoag Indians, who taught them how to plant corn and whose leader, or sachem, Massasoit, helped them celebrate the First Thanksgiving.

But the story of the Pilgrims does not end with the First Thanksgiving. When we look at how the Pilgrims and the Wampanoags maintained more than fifty years of peace and how that peace suddenly erupted into King Philip's War, one of the deadliest wars ever fought on American soil, the real history of Plymouth Colony becomes something altogether new, rich, troubling, and complex. Instead of the story we already know, it becomes the story we *need* to know. . . .

OTHER BOOKS YOU MAY ENJOY

Around the World in Eighty Days	Jules Verne
Code Talker	Joseph Bruchac
Deadweather and Sunrise	Geoff Rodkey
The Great Wide Sea	M. H. Herlong
Revenge of the Whale	Nathaniel Philbrick
Treasure Island	Robert Louis Stevenson

THE

Mayflower

AND THE

PILGRIMS' NEW WORLD

A Mapp of New ENGLAND by John Seller Hydrographer To the King And are to bee Sold at his Shop at the Hermitage in Wapping And by Iohn Hills In Exchange Alley in Cornhill London
Ornat.mo Prudent.mo Domino ROBERTO THOMSON Armigero Hanc Novæ Angliæ Tabulam D.D.D. Johannes Seller.
N E W
C O N E C T I C U T
C O L O N Y
E N G
N E W E N G L A N D
Conecticut River
New Albanie
The Conecticuts Country
The Waoranacks Country
The Mohiegans Country
Nutcrofs Country
The Sounds
L O N G I S L A N D
New Yorke
Staten Isle
Archipelage
Hemsted
Amersford
Gardiners Isle
Shelters Island
Fishers Isle

LACONA or the province of MAIN
S E T S
NOR
FOLK
The Wippanaps
ESS
EX
MIDLE
SEX
Cape Ann
Boon Island
Isle of Shoales
Masachusets Bay
SUF
FOLK
CAPE COD
Barstable
Bay
Pokanoket
Country
King
Philips
Naragansett Bay
Rode Island
Newport
the
Naragan-
sets
Elizabeth Isle
Block Isle

NATHANIEL PHILBRICK

THE Mayflower AND THE PILGRIMS' NEW WORLD

PUFFIN BOOKS
An Imprint of Penguin Group (USA)

PUFFIN BOOKS
Published by the Penguin Group
Penguin Group (USA) LLC
375 Hudson Street
New York, New York 10014

USA * Canada * UK * Ireland * Australia
New Zealand * India * South Africa * China

penguin.com
A Penguin Random House Company

First published in the United States of America by G. P. Putnam's Sons,
a division of Penguin Putnam Books for Young Readers, 2008
Published by Puffin Books, a division of Penguin Young Readers Group, 2009

THE LIBRARY OF CONGRESS HAS CATALOGED THE G. P. PUTNAM'S SONS EDITION AS FOLLOWS:
Philbrick, Nathaniel.
The Mayflower and the Pilgrims' New World / by Nathaniel Philbrick.
p. cm.
Adaptation of: Mayflower : a story of courage, community, and war. New York : Viking, 2006. Includes index.
ISBN 978-0-399-24795-8 (hardcover)
1. Pilgrims (New Plymouth Colony)—Juvenile literature.
2. Massachusetts—History—New Plymouth, 1620–1691—Juvenile literature.
3. Bradford, William, 1590–1657—Juvenile literature. 4. Church, Benjamin, 1639–1718—Juvenile literature.
5. Indians of North America—Wars—1600–1750—Juvenile literature. I. Philbrick, Nathaniel. Mayflower.
II. Title. F68.P445 2008 978.2'2—dc22 2007030669

Puffin Books ISBN 978-0-14-241458-3

Designed by Richard Amari

Printed in the United States of America

7 9 10 8 6

To Melissa

◆ ◆ ◆

THE MAYFLOWER AND THE PILGRIMS' NEW WORLD

CONTENTS

◆ ◆ ◆

PART III

WAR

◆ ◆ ◆

LIST OF CHARACTERS

◆ ◆ ◆

First Settlers and Their Affiliates

William Bradford • governor of Plymouth Colony after John Carver dies; writes *Of Plymouth Plantation*

John Robinson • pastor and leader of the English Separatists in Leiden before they leave for America

Elder William Brewster • Pilgrims' leading lay minister

John Carver • first governor of Plymouth Colony

Robert Cushman • helped organize voyage to America

Thomas Weston • leading Adventurer from London

Christopher Jones • *Mayflower*'s master

Robert Coppin • Jones's mate and pilot

Captain Miles Standish • (wife Rose) Pilgrims' leading military officer

Christopher Martin • *Mayflower* governor, original purchasing agent

Stephen Hopkins • Stranger who may have been to Jamestown before boarding the *Mayflower*

Edward Winslow • leading Pilgrim diplomat who also served as governor

John Howland • indentured servant who eventually became a leading citizen of the colony

John Billington • head of what Bradford called the "profanest family" on the *Mayflower;* sons John and Francis

Thomas Morton • leader of Merrymount

John Sanders • leader of Wessagussett settlement

Phineas Pratt • another leader of Wessagussett settlement

John Hamden • English gentleman who spent winter of 1623 with the Pilgrims

Native Americans

Massasoit • Pokanoket sachem

Canonicus • Narragansett sachem

Squanto • Pilgrims' interpreter, originally from Patuxet (Plymouth Harbor)

Epenow • sachem from Martha's Vineyard

Samoset • sachem from Pemaquid Point, Maine

Passaconaway • sachem and powwow from Merrimack River in southern New Hampshire

Aspinet • Nauset sachem

Canacum • Manomet sachem

Iyanough • Cummaquid sachem

Corbitant • Mattapoisett sachem

Hobbamock • Pokanoket pniese

Obtakiest • Massachusetts sachem

Pecksuot • Massachusetts pniese

Wituwamat • Massachusetts warrior

Uncas • Mohegan sachem, pledged loyalty to Puritans during Pequot War

Miantonomi • Narragansett sachem

The Next Generation Settlers

Thomas Prence • Plymouth governor
Thomas Willett • founder of Wannamoisett and friend of Alexander (Wamsutta)
Major William Bradford Jr. • William Bradford's son
John Miles • Swansea minister whose house became Miles garrison
James Cudworth • army commander from Scituate
Benjamin Church • carpenter and leading captain during King Philip's War
Alice Church • Benjamin Church's wife
Josiah Winslow • son of Edward; first governor of Plymouth Colony born in the New World
Samuel Moseley • leading captain during King Philip's War; known for his hatred of Indians
Captain Roger Goulding • mariner who rescued Church's men at the Pease Field Fight and was present at death of Philip
Captain Thomas Lathrop • leader at Bloody Brook
Major Robert Treat • led Connecticut forces at Great Swamp Fight
John Eliot • leading Puritan missionary to the Praying Indians
Captain Daniel Gookin • superintendent to Praying Indians
Major Samuel Appleton • commander of Massachusetts forces
John Gorham • led Plymouth forces with William Bradford at Great Swamp Fight
Captain Samuel Wadsworth • led rescue of Lancaster
Mary Rowlandson • (son Joseph, daughters Mary and Sarah) captured by Indians at Lancaster
John Rowlandson • Mary Rowlandson's husband, minister of Lancaster
Captain Michael Pierce • from Scituate, killed with most of his men at Blackstone River
Captain George Denison • led Connecticut force with Mohegans, Pequots, Niantics that captured Canonchet
John Hoar • from Concord, negotiated ransom and release of Mary Rowlandson
Captain William Turner • led attack on Indians at Connecticut River
Pastor John Cotton • Plymouth minister
John Leverett • Massachusetts governor

Native Americans

Wamsutta/Alexander • Massasoit's eldest son
Weetamoo • Alexander's wife, female Pocasset sachem
Metacom/Philip • Alexander's younger brother, "King Philip"
Tuspaquin • Amie's husband, "Black Sachem" of Nemasket
John Sassamon • interpreter for Alexander and Philip; one of John Eliot's pupils
Awashonks • (son Peter) female Sakonnet sachem
Tobias • one of Philip's senior counselors, accused of murdering John Sassamon
Totoson • sachem from Buzzard's Bay, attacked Dartmouth and Clark's garrison
Nimrod • one of Philip's leading warriors
Canonchet • Narragansett sachem
Quinnapin • Narragansett sachem and Weetamoo's husband during King Philip's War, Mary Rowlandson's master
Annawon • Philip's principal captain
Job Kattenanit • Praying Indian, becomes spy for English
Sagamore Sam • Nipmuck sachem, bargains with English for ransom of Mary Rowlandson

PREFACE

The Story We Need to Know

◆ ◆ ◆

WE'VE ALL HEARD at least some version of the story of the *Mayflower*, how in 1620 the Pilgrims sailed to the New World in search of religious freedom; how after drawing up the Mayflower Compact, they landed at Plymouth Rock and befriended the local Wampanoag Indians, who taught them how to plant corn and whose leader, or sachem, Massasoit, helped them celebrate the First Thanksgiving.

But the story of the Pilgrims does not end with the First Thanksgiving. When we look at how the Pilgrims and the Wampanoags maintained more than fifty years of peace and how that peace suddenly erupted into King Philip's War, one of the deadliest wars ever fought on American soil, the real history of Plymouth Colony becomes something altogether new, rich, troubling, and complex. Instead of the story we already know, it becomes the story we *need* to know.

◆ ◆ ◆ It was King Philip who led me to the Pilgrims. Philip was the son of Massasoit, the Wampanoag leader who formed an alliance with the Pilgrims in 1621. I was researching the history of my adopted home, Nantucket Island, when I encountered a reference to Philip in the town's records. In attempting to answer the question of why Philip—whose headquarters were in modern Bristol, Rhode Island—had traveled more than sixty-five miles across the water to Nantucket, I realized that I had to begin with Philip's father, Massasoit, and the Pilgrims.

My first impression of the period consisted of two conflicting ideas: the time-honored tradition of how the Pilgrims came to symbolize all that is good about America, and the now equally familiar modern tale of how the evil Europeans killed the innocent Native Americans. I soon learned that the real-life Indians and English of the seventeenth century were too smart, too generous, too greedy, too brave—in short, too human—to behave so predictably.

Without Massasoit's help, the Pilgrims would never have survived their first year in America, and they remained supporters of the sachem to the very end. For his part, Massasoit realized almost from the start that his own fortunes were linked to those of the English. In this respect, there is a surprising amount of truth in the traditional story of the First Thanksgiving.

But the Indians and English of Plymouth Colony did not live in perfect harmony. It was fifty-five years of struggle and compromise—a difficult process of give-and-take. As long as both sides recognized that they needed each other, there was peace. The moment any of them gave up on the difficult work of living with their neighbors, they risked losing everything. It was a lesson that the first generation of Plymouth Colony had learned over the course of more than three long decades. That it could be so quickly forgotten by their children remains a lesson for us today.

King Philip's War lasted only fourteen months, but it changed the face of New England. After fifty-five years of peace, the lives of Native and English peoples had become so closely intertwined that when fighting broke out in June 1675, many of the region's Indians found themselves, in the words of a contemporary writer, "in a kind of maze, not knowing what to do."

Some Indians chose to support Philip; others joined the colonial forces; still others attempted to stay out of the conflict altogether. When the English authorities decided that all Indians—no matter whose side they said they were on—were now their enemies, the violence quickly spread. Soon, the entire region was a terrifying war zone. By the end of the fighting, a third of the hundred or so towns in New England had been burned and abandoned.

When violence and fear grip a society, there is an almost overpowering temptation to demonize the enemy, and both Indians and English began to view their former neighbors as subhuman and evil. But even in the midst of one of the deadliest wars in American history, there were Englishmen who believed the Indians were not naturally evil, and there were Indians who believed the same about the English. They remembered to treat each other like human beings and to keep learning from each other, just as their parents had done fifty years before. Unfortunately, this was not enough to prevent war from destroying the promise of the First Thanksgiving.

◆ ◆ ◆ The story of the *Mayflower* ends in tragedy, but it begins with a ship on a wide and blustery sea.

PART I
DISCOVERY

ONE
They Knew They Were Pilgrims

FOR SIXTY-FIVE DAYS, the *Mayflower* had sailed through storms and headwinds, her bottom covered with seaweed and barnacles, her leaky decks spewing salt water onto her passengers' heads. There were 102 of them—104 if you counted the two dogs, a spaniel and a giant, slobbery mastiff.

They were nearly ten weeks into a voyage that was supposed to have been completed during the warm days of summer. But they had started late, and it was now November. Winter was coming on fast. They had long since run out of firewood, and they were reaching the slimy bottoms of their water barrels. Of even greater concern, they were down to their last casks of beer. Due to the terrible quality of the drinking water in seventeenth-century England, beer was considered essential to a healthy diet. And sure enough, with the rationing of their beer came the signs of scurvy: bleeding gums, loosening teeth, and foul-smelling breath. So far only two had died—a sailor and a young servant—but if they didn't reach land soon, many more would follow.

They were a most unusual group of colonists. Instead of noblemen, craftsmen, and servants—the types of people who had founded the Jamestown colony in Virginia—these were, for the most part, families—men, women, and children who were willing to endure almost anything if it meant they could worship God as they pleased. The motivating force behind the voyage had come from a congregation of approximately four hundred English Puritans living in Leiden, Holland.

Like all Puritans, these English exiles believed that the Church of

• *Photograph of the* Mayflower II, *a replica of the seventeenth-century ship, built in England in the 1950s and now at Plimoth Plantation.*

England had been corrupted. But unlike most English Puritans, they believed it was necessary to leave the Church of England if they were to worship God properly—an illegal act at the time. Known as Separatists, they represented the radical fringe of the Puritan movement. In 1608, they had decided to do as several groups of English Separatists had done before them and move to the more religiously tolerant country of Holland.

They settled in Leiden, a university town that could not have been more different from the rolling, sheep-dotted fields of their native England. Leiden was a redbrick maze of building-packed streets and carefully engineered canals, a city overrun with refugees from all across Europe. Under the leadership of their charismatic minister, John Robinson, their congregation had more than tripled in size.

But once again, it had become time for them to leave. As foreigners in Holland, many of them had been forced to work backbreaking jobs in the cloth industry, and their health had suffered. Worse yet, their children were becoming Dutch. While the congregation had rejected the Church of England, the vast majority of its members were still proudly English. By sailing to the New World, they hoped to re-create the English village life they so dearly missed while remaining far from King James and his bishops.

It was a stunningly brave plan. With the exception of Jamestown, all other attempts to establish a permanent English settlement on the North American continent had so far failed. And Jamestown, founded in 1607, could hardly be called a success. During the first year, 70 of 108 settlers had died. The following winter came the "starving time," when 440 of 500 settlers were buried in just six months.

In addition to starvation and disease, there was the threat of Indian attack. At the university library in Leiden were terrifying accounts left by earlier explorers and settlers, telling how the Indians "delight to torment men in the most bloody manner that may be; flaying some alive with the shells of fishes, cutting off the members and joints of others by piecemeal and broiling on the coals."

But in the end, all arguments for and against sailing to America ended with the conviction that God wanted them to go. These English Separatists believed it was their spiritual duty to found an English plantation in the New World. "We verily believe and trust the Lord is with us," John Robinson and William Brewster, a leading member of the congregation, wrote, "and that He will graciously prosper our endeavors according to the simplicity of our hearts therein."

Their time in Leiden, they now realized, had been a mere rehearsal for the real adventure. Because of the extraordinary spiritual connection they had developed as exiles, they were prepared for whatever lay ahead. "[I]t is not with us as with other men," Robinson and Brewster confidently insisted, "whom small things can discourage, or small discontentments cause to wish themselves home again." Or, as one of their number, a thirty-year-old corduroy worker named William Bradford, later wrote, "They knew they were pilgrims."

◆ ◆ ◆ Taking Bradford's lead, we refer to them today as the Pilgrims, a name that is as good as any to describe a people who were almost always on the move. Eventually, Bradford became their leader, and if not for his steady, often forceful leadership, it is doubtful whether there ever would have been a colony at all. Without his *Of Plymouth Plantation*, certainly the greatest book written in seventeenth-century America, there would be almost no information about the voyage with which it all began. For William Bradford, however, the true voyage had begun close to twenty years before.

William Bradford was born in the tiny farming town of Austerfield, Yorkshire, deep in northern England. Although he came from a family of well-to-do farmers, Bradford had experienced more than his share of troubles. By the time he turned twelve, he had lost not only his father, his mother, and a sister, but also the grandfather who had raised him. Soon after moving in with his two uncles, he was struck by a mysterious illness that prevented him from working in the fields. Bradford later claimed that his "long sickness" had saved him from "the vanities of youth, and made him the fitter for what he was afterwards to undergo." Most important, his illness gave him the opportunity to read.

Lonely and intelligent, he looked to the Bible for consolation and guidance. For a boy in need of instruction, the Geneva Bible, translated in the previous century by a small team of English ministers and equipped with helpful notes, was just the thing. There was also John Foxe's *Book of Martyrs*, an account of the Protestants killed by Queen Elizabeth's Catholic predecessor on the throne, "Bloody Mary." Foxe insisted that England was, like Israel before it, God's chosen nation. This had a deep and lasting influence on Bradford, and as Foxe made horrifyingly clear, to be a godly Englishman sometimes required a person to make the ultimate sacrifice.

Bradford was just twelve years old when he became uneasy with the way God was worshipped in Austerfield. He eventually found what he was looking for when he met William Brewster, the postmaster in a neighboring town called Scrooby. At Brewster's home, a group of Separatist Puritans gathered every Sunday to worship in secret under the direction of two ministers, one of whom was the young John Robinson.

At the turn of the seventeenth century, there were a lot of debates about the proper way for a Christian to worship God. Puritans believed

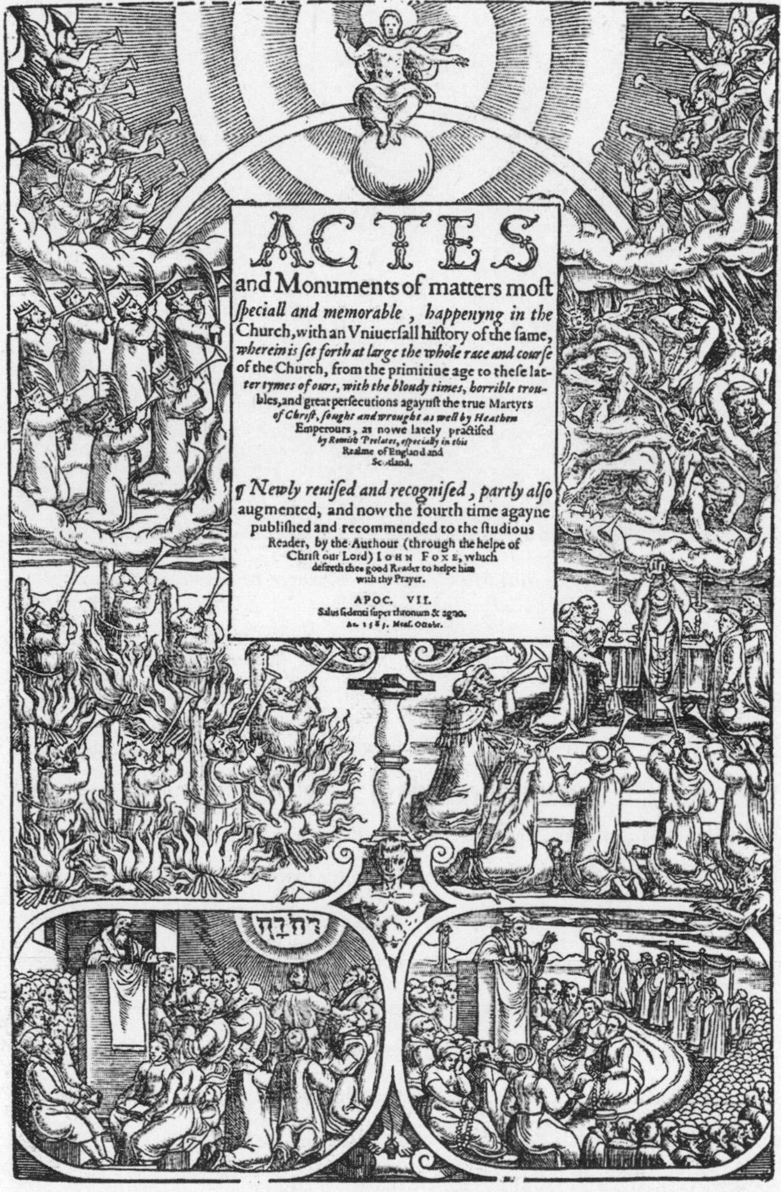

ACTES
and Monuments of matters most
speciall and memorable, happenyng in the
Church, with an Vniuersall history of the same,
wherein is set forth at large the whole race and course
of the Church, from the primitiue age to these lat-
ter tymes of ours, with the bloudy times, horrible trou-
bles, and great persecutions agaynst the true Martyrs
of Christ, sought and wrought as well by Heathen
Emperours, as nowe lately practised
by Romish Prelates, especially in this
Realme of England and
Scotland.

¶ *Newly reuised and recognised, partly also*
augmented, and now the fourth time agayne
published and recommended to the studious
Reader, by the Authour (through the helpe of
Christ our Lord) IOHN FOXE, which
desireth thee good Reader to helpe him
with thy Prayer.

APOC. VII.
Salus sedenti super thronum & agno.
An. 1583. Mens. Octobr.

◆ *Title page of a 1583 edition of John Foxe's* Book of Martyrs.

◆ *St. Helena's Church in Austerfield, Yorkshire, where Bradford worshipped as a young boy.*

it was necessary to go back to the absolute beginning of Christianity, before the church had been corrupted by man. To them, the New Testament provided the only reliable account of Christ's time on earth, while the Old Testament contained a rich storehouse of truths. If something was not in the scriptures, it was a man-made distortion of what God intended. The Puritans had chosen to turn away from thousands of years of tradition in favor of a text that gave them a direct and personal connection to God.

A Puritan had no use for the Church of England's Book of Common Prayer, since it tampered with the original meaning of the Bible. Even more importantly, Puritans saw no reason for the system of bishops that ran the Church of England. The only biblically acceptable organizational unit was the individual congregation.

Taking their cue from the apostle Paul's words to "come out among them, and be separate," the Separatists were Puritans who had determined that the Church of England was not a true church of Christ. If they were to remain true to their faith, they must form a church of what were known as "visible Saints," members who supported each other in the proper worship of God. If members of the congregation strayed from the true path, they were criticized; if they failed to correct themselves, they were forced to leave the congregation. A Separatist congregation shared in an intense bond of spirituality and discipline that touched every aspect of everyone's life.

King James viewed all Puritans as troublemakers, and at a gathering of religious leaders at his palace in Hampton Court, he angrily declared, "I shall harry them out of the land!" The congregation that met at Brewster's house knew that it was only a matter of time before the authorities found them out.

Sometime in 1607, the bishop of York became aware of the meetings at Brewster's manor house. Some members of the congregation were thrown in prison; others discovered that their houses were being watched. It was time to leave. But if King James had vowed to "harry" the Puritans out of England, he was unwilling to provide them with a legal means of leaving the country. A person needed official permission to voyage to the Continent, something the authorities refused to grant the Separatists. If they were to sail for Holland, they must do it secretly.

For a group of farmers, most of whom had rarely, if ever, ventured beyond the Nottinghamshire-Yorkshire region, it was a scary prospect. But for seventeen-year-old William Bradford, who would lose the people upon whom he had come to depend if he did not follow them to Holland, there was little choice in the matter. Despite the protests of his friends and relatives, who must have pointed out that he was due to receive a comfortable inheritance at age twenty-one, he decided to sail with John Robinson and William Brewster to a new land.

◆ ◆ ◆ Their escape from England did not go well. The first ship captain they hired turned out to be a traitor and a thief who surrendered them to the authorities. After their leaders spent several months in jail, they tried again. This time they hired a trustworthy Dutch captain, but they had not yet loaded all the men or any women and children onto the vessel when the local militia appeared. Fearing capture, the captain set sail for Amsterdam, leaving the women and children weeping as their husbands looked on from the deck of the departing ship. It was several months before they were all reunited in Holland.

Once in Amsterdam, the Separatists found themselves thrust into conflict with other English Separatists who had come before them. Not wanting to get involved in their debates or worship, they moved on. Showing the firmness, sensitivity, and judgment that came to characterize his ministry in the years ahead, John Robinson led his congregation to the neighboring city of Leiden, where they were free to establish themselves on their own terms.

In Leiden, Robinson found a house not far from the Pieterskerk, one of the city's largest churches. In the garden behind Robinson's home, they created a miniature village of close to a dozen houses. Even though approximately half the congregation lived in houses elsewhere in the city, what was known as De Groene Poort, meaning the green lane or alley, came to represent the ideal of a Christian village they would aspire to for the rest of their lives.

William Bradford soon emerged as one of the leading members of the

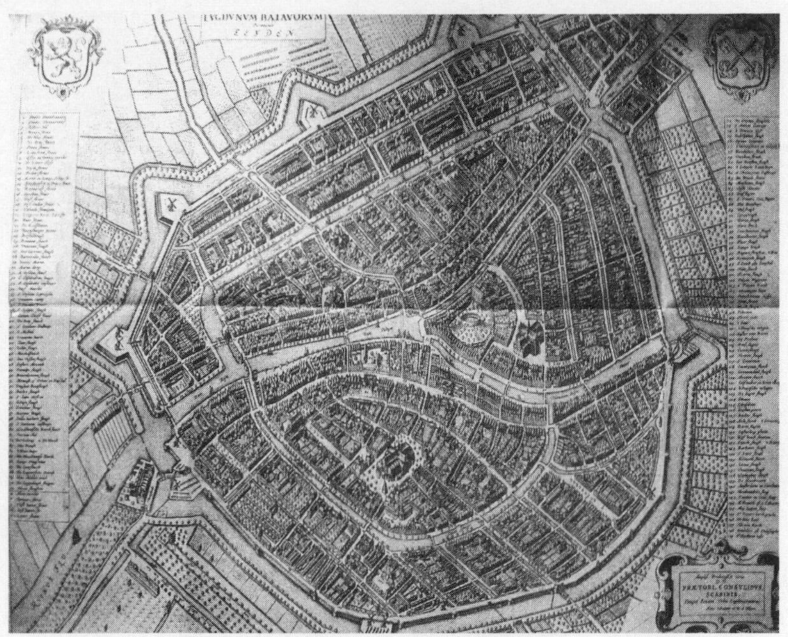

◆ *A map of Leiden, Holland, in the early seventeenth century.*

congregation. When he turned twenty-one in 1611, he sold the property he had inherited in England and used the money to buy a small house in Leiden. A fustian, or corduroy worker, Bradford became a citizen of Leiden in 1612 in recognition of his high standing in the community. In 1613, he married Dorothy May, and four years later they had a son, John.

Leiden was a thriving city of forty thousand, but it was also a commercial center that required its people to work at a pace that must have come as a shock to farmers from Nottinghamshire and Yorkshire. A life of farming involved periods of intense labor, but its seasonal rhythms left long stretches of relative inactivity. In Leiden, on the other hand, men, women, and even children were expected to work from

◆ *Edward Winslow, painted in England, 1651.*

dawn to dusk, six days a week, with a bell sounding in the tower of the yarn market to announce when work was to begin and end. As the years of ceaseless labor began to add up and their children began to lose touch with their English ancestry, the Pilgrims decided it was time to start over again.

It began badly when William Brewster got in trouble with the English government. In Leiden, he had established a printing press, which he ran with the help of the twenty-three-year-old Edward Winslow. In 1618 Brewster and Winslow published a religious tract critical of the English king and his bishops. King James ordered Brewster's arrest, and when the king's agents in Holland came to seize the Pilgrim elder, Brewster was forced into hiding just as preparations to depart for America entered their most important phase. More than anyone else, with the possible exception of Pastor Robinson, Elder Brewster was the person upon whom the congregation depended for guidance and support. But as they wrestled with the many details of planning a voyage to America, Brewster was, at least for now, lost to them.

◆ ◆ ◆ By the beginning of the seventeenth century, it had become clear that the colonization of North America was essential to England's future prosperity. France, Holland, and especially Spain had already taken advantage of the seemingly limitless resources of the New World. But the British government lacked the money to fund a major colonization effort of its own. Seeing it as an opportunity to add to their already considerable personal wealth, two groups of noblemen—one based in London, the other to the west in Plymouth—were eager to finance British settlements in America. They issued special grants known as patents, which gave the settlers the right to attempt to found a colony in five to seven years' time. After that, they could apply for a new patent that gave them permanent ownership of the land.

With Brewster in hiding, the Pilgrims looked to their deacon, John Carver, probably in his midthirties, and fellow pilgrim Robert Cushman, forty-one, to carry on negotiations with the officials in London. By June 1619, Carver and Cushman had succeeded in securing a patent from what had become the Virginia Company. But the Pilgrims' plans were still far from complete. They had a patent but had not, as of yet, figured out how they were going to pay for their journey. Still, William Bradford's faith in the mission was so strong that he sold his house in the spring of 1619.

The members of Robinson's congregation knew each other wonderfully well, but when it came to the outside world, they could sometimes run into trouble. They were so focused on their own inner lives, they failed to notice the true motives of people who did not share in their beliefs. Time and time again during their preparations to sail for America, the Pilgrims demonstrated an extraordinary talent for getting duped.

To pay for the voyage, the Pilgrims threw in their lot with a smooth-talking merchant from London named Thomas Weston. Weston represented a group of investors known as the Adventurers—about seventy London merchants who viewed the colonization of America as both a way "to plant religion" and a way to make money. And even though the Pilgrims had secured a patent the year before, the Adventurers obtained a patent of their own for a settlement at the mouth of the Hudson River.

In the beginning, Weston seemed perfect—a man sympathetic to their religious goals who also claimed to have the means to make their dreams come true. The Adventurers would put up most of the money with the expectation that, once they were settled in America, the Pilgrims would quickly begin to make a profit, primarily through codfishing and the fur trade. The Pilgrims would each be given a small share in the company. For the next seven years, they would work four days a week for the company and two days a week for themselves, with the Sabbath reserved for worship. At the end of the seven years, the profits would be divided among all of them, with the Pilgrims owning their houses free and clear.

As the spring of 1620 approached, about 125 people (a third of their total congregation) were ready to depart for the New World, with the rest to follow soon after. Pastor Robinson, it was decided, would stay for now in Leiden with the majority of his flock, with Elder Brewster attending to the religious needs of those in America.

But as the Pilgrims prepared to depart in the spring of 1620, Weston's true nature began to reveal itself. He now claimed that circumstances

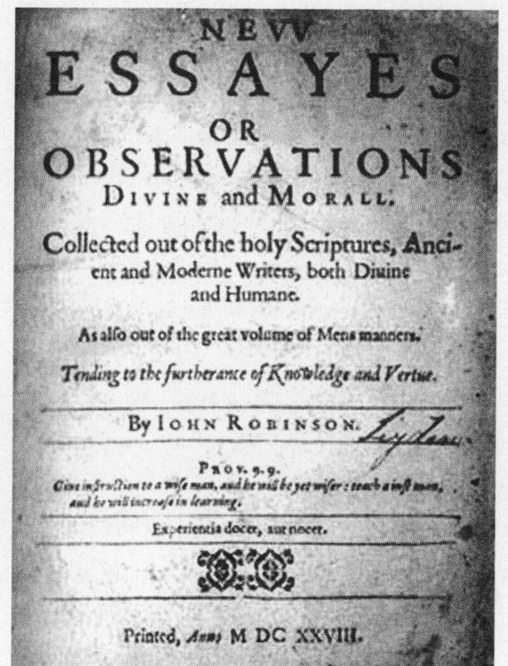

NEVV
ESSAYES
OR
OBSERVATIONS
DIVINE and MORALL.

Collected out of the holy Scriptures, Ancient and Moderne Writers, both Diuine and Humane.

As also out of the great volume of Mens manners.

Tending to the furtherance of Knowledge and Vertue.

By IOHN ROBINSON.

PROV. 9.9.
Giue instruction to a wise man, and he will be yet wiser: teach a iust man, and he will increase in learning.

Experientia docet, aut nocet.

Printed, *Anno* M DC XXVIII.

◆ *Title page of Pastor John Robinson's book,* **Observations Divine and Moral.**

had changed so that instead of having two days a week for themselves, they would have to spend every minute laboring for the Adventurers. Robinson and the Pilgrims in Leiden objected, claiming that the new terms were "fitter for thieves and bondslaves than honest men."

In June they discovered that, incredibly, Weston had not yet arranged any transportation to America. If they had any hope of reaching the mouth of the Hudson River before winter, they needed to depart as soon as possible. While Weston hunted up a ship in London, the Pilgrims decided to purchase a small sailing vessel of their own in Holland. Not only would it be used to transport some of them across the Atlantic, it would be useful for both fishing and exploring the coast once they were in America. And if the worst should happen, it would provide a means for the survivors to return to England.

Adding to the Pilgrims' growing sense of alarm was the fact that the Adventurers had insisted on bringing along some non-Separatists from London. Some had strong ties to the group in Leiden, but others were completely unknown to them. How they would get along with these "Strangers" was of deep concern, especially since one of them, a man named Christopher Martin, was already proving to be a most difficult personality.

The Adventurers named Martin as a purchasing agent, which meant that he, along with Cushman and Carver, was to secure supplies and provisions: beer, wine, hardtack, salted beef and pork, dried peas, fishing supplies, muskets, armor, clothing, tools, and trade goods for the Indians. But Martin refused to work with Carver and Cushman. While the Pilgrim agents collected provisions in London and Canterbury, Martin did as he pleased in Southampton, a major port in the south of England. Soon, no one really knew where matters stood when it came to provisions. "[W]e are readier to dispute than to set forward a voyage," Cushman complained on June 10.

Despite the chaotic nature of the preparations in England, the Pilgrims in Leiden moved ahead, purchasing a sixty-ton vessel named the *Speedwell.* Less than fifty feet in length, she was considered large enough for a voyage across the Atlantic; earlier expeditions had successfully completed the crossing in vessels that were less than half the *Speedwell*'s size. The Pilgrims hired a master to captain the ship and a crew who agreed to stay on for at least a year in America and who undoubtedly oversaw the fitting out of the vessel with two new and larger masts. The refitting of the *Speedwell* may have seemed like an insignificant matter at the time. As it turned out, however, this misnamed vessel and her master, known to us only as "Mr. Reynolds," would have a disastrous impact on the voyage ahead.

◆ ◆ ◆ By the end of July, the Pilgrims, accompanied by a large number of family and friends, had made their way to Delfshaven, the small Dutch port where the *Speedwell* was waiting. The plan was to sail for Southampton in England, where they would meet whatever ship Weston had secured in London. "[T]hey went aboard and their friends with them," Bradford wrote, "where truly doleful was the sight of that sad and mournful parting, to see what sighs and sobs and prayers did sound amongst them, what tears did gush from every eye, and pithy speeches pierced each heart."

For William Bradford and his wife, Dorothy, the parting in Delfshaven was particularly painful. They had decided to leave their three-year-old son, John, behind in Holland, perhaps with Dorothy's parents in Amsterdam. It was certainly safer for the child, but the emotional cost, especially for the boy's mother, would become difficult to bear.

When the tide turned in their favor, it was time to depart. Pastor Robinson fell down to his knees on the *Speedwell*'s deck, as did everyone present, and "with watery cheeks commended them with most fervent prayers to the Lord and His blessing." It was a remarkable display of "such love as indeed is seldom found on earth." Years later, the residents of Delfshaven were still talking about the departure of the Pilgrims in July 1620.

◆ ◆ ◆ By the time the Leideners left Delfshaven, Weston had hired an old and reliable ship named the *Mayflower,* which after taking aboard passengers in London, sailed to Southampton to meet up with the *Speed-*

◆ **Departure of the Pilgrims from Delfshaven** *by Adam Willaerts, 1620.*

well. The *Mayflower* was a typical merchant vessel of her day. Rated at 180 tons (meaning that her hold was capable of accommodating 180 casks, or "tuns," of wine), she was approximately three times the size of the *Speedwell* and about one hundred feet in length.

The *Mayflower*'s master was Christopher Jones. About fifty years old, he was also a part owner of the ship. Records indicate that Jones had been master of the *Mayflower* for the last eleven years, sailing back and forth across the Channel with English wool cloth to France and returning to London with French wine. Wine ships such as the *Mayflower* were known as "sweet ships," since the inevitable spillage of the acidic wine helped to

temper the stench of the bilge. In addition to wine and wool, Jones had transported hats, hemp, Spanish salt, hops, and vinegar to Norway and may even have taken the *Mayflower* on a whaling voyage to Greenland. He and his wife, Josian, had had five children.

Serving as Jones's first mate and pilot was Robert Coppin, who, unlike Jones, had been to America before. Also serving as pilot was John Clark, forty-five, who'd delivered some cattle to Jamestown the previous year. Giles Heale was the ship's surgeon. In the days ahead, as sickness spread through the passengers and crew, he would become one of the most sought-after officers of the *Mayflower*.

Another important position was that of the cooper, who was in charge of maintaining all barreled supplies and provisions. In Southampton, Jones secured the twenty-one-year-old cooper John Alden, who because of his youth and skills was already being encouraged by the Pilgrims to remain in America at the completion of the crossing. In addition, there were somewhere between twenty and thirty sailors, whose names have not survived.

In Southampton, the Leideners met up with the family and friends who had first boarded the *Mayflower* in London and would be continuing on with them to America. The most notable of the group was Elder William Brewster, who had been hiding out in Holland and perhaps even England for the last year. Also joining them in Southampton were Robert Cushman and John Carver, who was traveling with his wife, Katherine, and five servants.

Along for the journey as well was Captain Miles Standish. Although not a member of the congregation, Standish was well known to the Leideners. Standish had served as an English mercenary in Holland and would be handling the colony's military matters in America.

It was in Southampton that they met the so-called Strangers—passengers recruited by the Adventurers to take the places of those who had chosen to remain in Holland. Besides Christopher Martin, who had been designated the "governor" of the *Mayflower* by the Adventurers and was traveling with his wife and two servants, there were four additional families. Stephen Hopkins was making his second trip to America. Eleven years earlier, in 1609, he had sailed on the *Sea Venture* for Virginia, only to become shipwrecked in Bermuda—an incident that became the basis for Shakespeare's play *The Tempest.* While on Bermuda, Hopkins had been part of an attempted mutiny and been sentenced to hang, but pleading tearfully for his life, he was spared at the last minute. Hopkins spent two years in Jamestown before returning to England and was now accompanied by his pregnant wife, Elizabeth; his son, Giles; and daughters Constance and Damaris, along with two servants, Edward Doty and Edward Leister.

◆ *A steeple-crowned beaver hat attributed to Constance Hopkins.*

In addition to the Mullinses, Eatons, and Billingtons (whom Bradford later called "one of the profanest families amongst them"), there were four unaccompanied English children: Ellen, Jasper, Richard, and Mary More. They had been sent to London by their father, who had paid for their passage to America. Ellen, eight years old, had been assigned to Edward and Elizabeth Winslow; Jasper, seven, to the Carvers; and both Richard, five, and Mary, four, to William and Mary Brewster, who were accompanied by their evocatively named sons Love and Wrestling.

In the meantime, matters were coming to a head between the Leideners and Thomas Weston. Robert Cushman had signed the revised agreement to work full-time with the merchants in London, but the Leideners refused to honor it. Weston stalked off in a huff, insisting that "they must then look to stand on their own legs." As Cushman knew better than anyone, this was not in their best interests. They didn't have enough provisions to last a year. Without Weston to provide them with the necessary funds, they were forced to sell off some of their precious provisions, including more than two tons of butter, before they could sail from Southampton.

Adding to the turmoil and confusion was the behavior of Christopher Martin. The *Mayflower*'s governor was, according to Cushman, a monster. "[H]e insulteth over our poor people, with such scorn and contempt," Cushman wrote, "as if they were not good enough to wipe his shoes. . . . If I speak to him, he flies in my face as mutinous, and saith no complaints shall be heard or received but by himself." In a letter hastily written to a friend in London, Cushman saw only doom and disaster ahead. "Friend, if ever we make a plantation God works a miracle, especially considering how scant we shall be of victuals, and most of all un-united amongst ourselves and devoid of good tutors and regiment. Violence will break all. Where is the meek and humble spirit of Moses?"

When it finally came time to leave Southampton, Cushman made sure he was with his friends aboard the *Speedwell*. He was now free of Martin but soon found that the *Speedwell* was anything but speedy. "[S]he is as open and leaky as a sieve," he wrote. Several days after clearing the Isle of Wight off England's southern coast, it was decided the *Speedwell* needed repairs, and both vessels sailed for Dartmouth, a port only seventy-five miles to the west of Southampton.

It was now August 17. The repairs were quickly completed, but this time the wind refused to cooperate. People were beginning to panic—and with good reason. "Our victuals will be half eaten up, I think, before we go from the coast of England," Cushman wrote.

The months of tension had caught up with Cushman. For the last two weeks he had felt a searing pain in his chest—"a bundle of lead as it were, crushing my heart." He was sure this would be his last good-bye: "[A]lthough I do the actions of a living man yet I am but as dead. . . . I pray you prepare for evil tidings of us every day. . . . I see not in reason how we shall escape even the passing of hunger-starved persons; but God can do much, and His will be done."

They finally departed from Dartmouth and were more than two hundred miles beyond the southwestern tip of England at Land's End when the *Speedwell* sprang another leak. It was now early September, and they had no choice but to give up on the *Speedwell.* It was a devastating turn of events. Not only had the vessel cost them a lot of money, but she had been considered vital to the future success of the settlement.

They stopped at Plymouth, about fifty miles to the west of Dartmouth. If they were to continue, they had to crowd as many passengers as would fit into the *Mayflower* and sail on alone. To no one's surprise, Cushman gave up his place to someone else. And despite his fear of imminent death, he lived another five years.

It was later learned that the *Speedwell*'s master, Mr. Reynolds, had been secretly working against them. In Holland, the vessel had been fitted with new and larger masts and—as any sailor knew, when a ship's masts were too tall, the added strain opened up the seams between the planks, causing the hull to leak. By overmasting the *Speedwell,* Reynolds had provided himself with an easy way to deceive the Pilgrims. He might shrug his shoulders and scratch his head when the vessel began to take on water, but all he had to do was reduce sail and the *Speedwell* would stop leaking. Soon after the *Mayflower* set out across the Atlantic, the *Speedwell* was sold, refitted, and, according to Bradford, "made many voyages . . . to the great profit of her owners."

In early September, the wind began to blow west across the North Atlantic. The provisions, already low when they first set out from Southampton, had shrunk even further by more than a month of delays. The passengers, cooped up aboard ship for all this time, were in no shape for a long journey. But on September 6, 1620, the *Mayflower* set out from Plymouth with what Bradford called "a prosperous wind."

◆ ◆ ◆ By the time the *Mayflower* left Plymouth, the group from Leiden had been reduced by more than a quarter. The original plan had been to

10° 00'
05° 00'
55° 00'
Belfast
Isle of Man
IRELAND
Dublin
Irish Sea
Atlantic Ocean
50° 00'
Plymouth
Dartmouth
Land's End

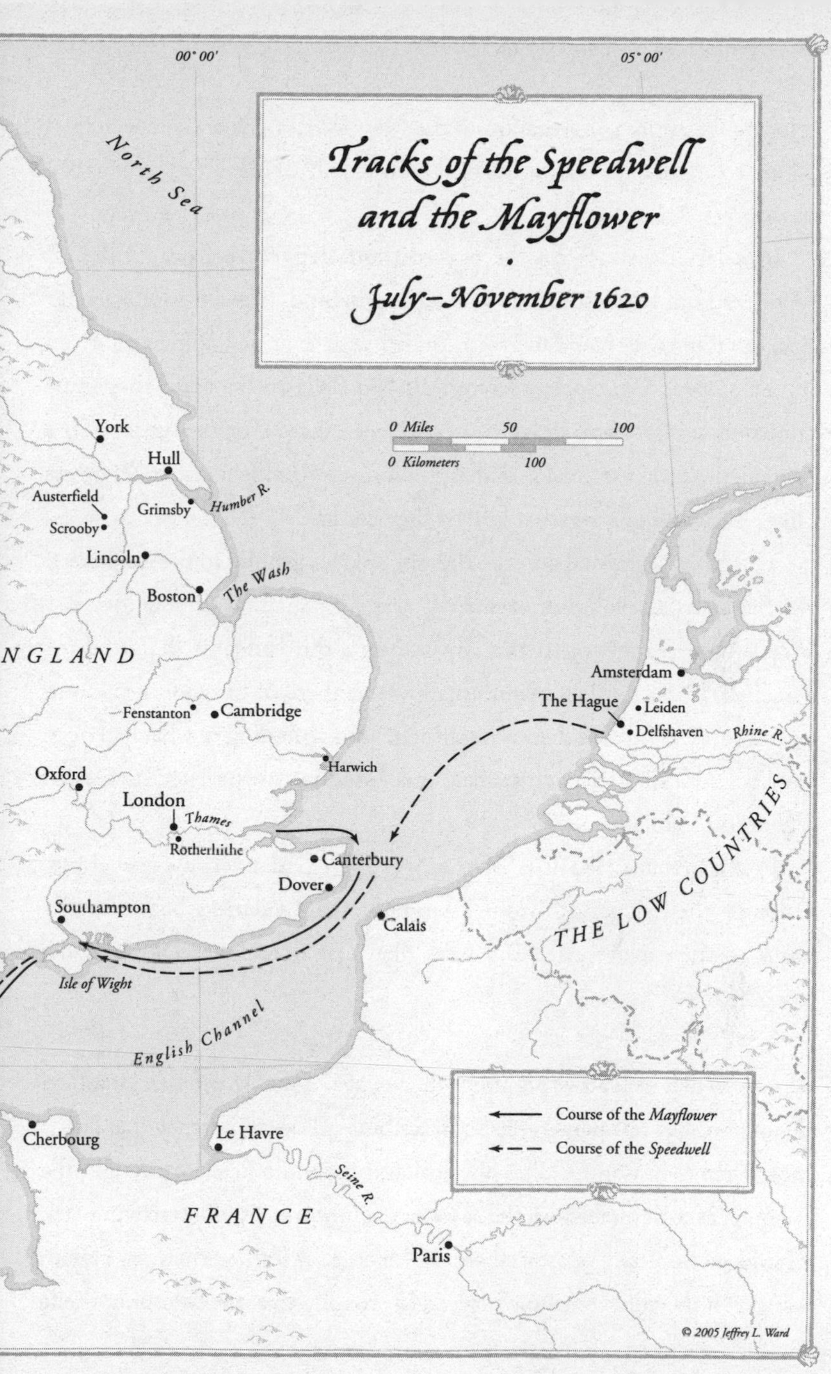

00° 00'
05° 00'
Tracks of the Speedwell and the Mayflower
July–November 1620
North Sea
0 Miles 50 100
0 Kilometers 100
York
Hull
Austerfield
Grimsby
Humber R.
Scrooby
Lincoln
Boston
The Wash
ENGLAND
Amsterdam
The Hague
Leiden
Delfshaven
Rhine R.
Fenstanton
Cambridge
Harwich
Oxford
London
Thames
Rotherhithe
Canterbury
Dover
THE LOW COUNTRIES
Southampton
Calais
Isle of Wight
English Channel
Course of the Mayflower
Course of the Speedwell
Cherbourg
Le Havre
Seine R.
FRANCE
Paris
© 2005 Jeffrey L. Ward

relocate the entire congregation to the New World. Now there were just 50 or so of them, making up only about half of the *Mayflower*'s 102 passengers.

In a letter written on the eve of their departure from Holland, Minister John Robinson, who was staying behind, urged his followers to do everything they could to avoid conflict with their new shipmates. Even if men such as Christopher Martin pushed them to the edge, they must control any impulse to judge and condemn others. For the future of the settlement, it was essential that all the colonists—Leideners and Strangers alike—learn to live together as best they could.

This nonjudgmental attitude did not come naturally to the Leideners. As Separatists, a sense of exclusivity was fundamental to how they saw themselves in the world. But, by the time the Pilgrims departed for America, Robinson had begun to allow members of his congregation to attend services outside their own church. This softening of what had once been an inflexible Separatist ideal was essential to the later success of Plymouth Plantation.

In this regard, the loss of the *Speedwell* had been a good thing. Prior to their departure from Plymouth, the Leideners had naturally stuck to their own vessel. But now, like it or not, they were all in the same boat.

◆ ◆ ◆ When he later wrote about the voyage of the *Mayflower*, Bradford devoted only a few paragraphs to describing an ocean journey that lasted more than two months. The physical and psychological torture that the passengers experienced on the sea was made worse by the terrifying lack of information they possessed about America. All they knew for certain was that if they did somehow succeed in crossing this three-thousand-mile

◆ MAYFLOWER CROSS-SECTION KEY ◆

A ◆ Round House
B ◆ Ship's Bell
C ◆ Great Cabin
D ◆ Whipstaff
E ◆ Steerage
F ◆ Capstan
G ◆ Forecastle
H ◆ Lower Deck or 'Tween Decks
I ◆ Gunroom or Cannon
J ◆ Hold
K ◆ Windlass

stretch of ocean, no one—except perhaps for some hostile Indians—would be there to greet them.

Most of their provisions and equipment were kept in the hold in the lower part of the ship. The passengers were in the between (or 'tween) decks—a dank, airless space about seventy-five feet long and not even five feet high that separated the hold from the upper deck. The 'tween decks was more of a crawl space than a place to live, made even more claustrophobic by the passengers' attempts to provide themselves with some privacy. They built a number of thin-walled cabins, creating a crowded series of rooms that overflowed with people and their possessions: chests of clothing, casks of food, chairs, pillows, rugs, and omnipresent chamber pots. There was even a small boat—cut into pieces for later assembly—that some passengers used as a bed.

Soon after departing from Plymouth, the passengers began to suffer the effects of seasickness. As often happens at sea, the sailors took great delight in mocking the Pilgrims' sufferings. There was one sailor in particular, "a proud and very profane young man," Bradford remembered, who "would always be contemning the poor people in their sickness and cursing them daily with grievous execrations." The sailor even had the nerve to say that "he hoped to help to cast half of them overboard before they came to their journey's end."

As it turned out, however, this strong and arrogant sailor was the first to die. "But it pleased God," Bradford wrote, "before they came half seas over, to smite this young man with a grievous disease, of which he died in a desperate manner, and so was himself the first that was thrown overboard." Bradford claimed "it was an astonishment to all his fellows for they noted it to be the just hand of God upon him."

Throughout the voyage, there were terrible storms, and in midocean an especially large wave exploded against the old ship's side, cracking a large wooden beam like a chicken bone. Master Jones considered turning back to England. But Jones had to give his passengers credit. Despite all they had so far suffered—agonizing delays, seasickness, cold, and the scorn and ridicule of the sailors—they did everything in their power to help the carpenter repair the fractured beam. They had brought along a screw jack—a mechanical device used to lift heavy objects—to assist them in constructing houses in the New World. With the help of the screw jack, they lifted the beam into place, and once the carpenter had hammered in a post for support, the *Mayflower* was able to continue on.

Several times during the passage, the conditions grew so bad that even though it meant he would lose many hard-won miles, Jones was forced to "lie ahull"—to roll up the sails, and let the waves take his 180-ton ship. At one point, as the *Mayflower* lay ahull, a young servant named John Howland grew restless down below. He saw no reason why he could not venture out of the 'tween decks for just a moment. After more than a month as a passenger ship, the *Mayflower* was no longer a "sweet ship," and Howland wanted some air. So he climbed a ladder to one of the hatches and stepped onto the deck.

Howland quickly discovered that the deck of a storm-tossed ship was no place for a landsman. Even if the ship rode the waves with ease, the gale continued to rage with astonishing violence around her. The shriek of the wind through the rope rigging was terrifying, as was the sight of all those towering waves. The *Mayflower* lurched suddenly, Howland staggered to the ship's rail and tumbled into the sea.

That should have been the end of him. But dangling over the side and trailing behind the ship was the topsail halyard, the rope used to raise and lower the upper sail. Howland was in his midtwenties and strong. When his hand found the halyard, he gripped the rope with such desperation that even though he was pulled down more than ten feet below the ocean's surface, he never let go. Several sailors hauled Howland back in, finally snagging him with a boat hook and dragging him up onto the deck.

When William Bradford wrote about this incident more than a decade later, John Howland was not only alive and well, but he and his wife, Elizabeth, were on their way to raising ten children, who would, in turn, produce an astounding eighty-eight grandchildren. A Puritan believed that everything happened for a reason. Whether it was the salvation of John Howland or the death of the profane young sailor, it occurred because God had made it so. If something good happened to the

◆ *Cross-staff: navigational instrument used to measure latitude. By pointing at the sun and sliding the vane along the notched staff, a sailor could calculate the angles to arrive at latitude.*

Pilgrims, it was inevitably interpreted as a sign of God's approval. But if something bad happened, it didn't necessarily mean that God disapproved; it might mean that he was testing them for a higher purpose. And as all aboard the *Mayflower* knew, the true test was yet to come.

◆ ◆ ◆ Unknown to Jones and any other sailor of the day was the presence of the Gulf Stream—a current of warm water flowing up from the Caribbean along the North American coast, across the Atlantic, and past the British Isles. Sailing against the Gulf Stream would slow down any voyage, and the *Mayflower* had managed an average speed of just two miles an hour since leaving England back in September.

Jones had a cross-staff, a three-foot-long stick that enabled him to calculate his latitude, or north-south position, within a few miles. But he had no reliable way of determining his longitude, or east-west position. This meant that after all the bad weather they'd encountered, Jones had only the vaguest idea of how far he was from land.

He knew the *Mayflower* was well north of her destination, the mouth of the Hudson River. But at this late stage in the voyage, with disease beginning to appear among the passengers and crew, Jones needed to find his way to the coast as quickly as possible. So he made a run for it, sailing west along a latitude that would lead him to the sandy peninsula known to most sailors of the time as Cape Cod. Reaching out to them like an upturned arm, the Cape was as good a target as any.

The *Mayflower* pushed on until they were within smelling distance of the shore. Seagulls began to appear in the sky, and the color of the water changed from deep blue to pale green. And then, at daybreak on Thursday, November 9, 1620, after sixty-five days at sea, they saw land.

TWO
The Compact

◆ ◆ ◆

IT WAS A beautiful late-fall morning—clear skies and light winds out of the northwest. There was a thin slice of moon overhead, gradually fading to nothingness as the sun rose behind them in the east. Up ahead to the west was what Jones believed to be the forearm of Cape Cod. This thirty-mile stretch of beach runs from north to south and is edged by dramatic hundred-foot-high cliffs of sand, which must have been instantly recognizable to those of Jones's pilots who had been in this region before. Stretching behind the cliffs were rolling, tree-covered hills.

The *Mayflower*'s passengers were, according to Bradford, "not a little joyful." On a crisp autumn day in New England the colors seem brighter, and the Pilgrims were "much comforted . . . [by] seeing so goodly a land, and wooded to the brink of the sea."

Now they had a decision to make: Where should they go? They were well to the north of their intended destination. And yet there were reasons to consider the region around Cape Cod as a possible settlement site. In the final chaotic months before their departure from England, Weston and others had begun to insist that a more northern site in New England—which was the new name for what are now the states of Massachusetts, Connecticut, Rhode Island, Maine, New Hampshire, and Vermont—was a better place to settle.

As Cape Cod's name indicates, this area was famous for the large schools of codfish that swam by its shores. Come spring, hundreds of codfishing vessels from England, France, Holland, and other European countries fished the waters of New England. A colony established on

The names of those which came over first, in ye year 1620
and were (by the blesing of God) the first beginers, and
(in a sort) the foundation, of all the plantations, and
Colonies, in New-England (and their families)

8 Mr John Carver.
Kathrine his wife.
Desire minter; &
2. man-servants
John Howland
Roger Wilder.
William Latham, a boy.
& a maid servant & a
child yt was put to him
called, Jasper More

6 Mr William Brewster.
Mary his wife, with
2 sons, whose names
were Loue, & Wrasling.
and a boy was put to
him called Richard More; and another of his brothers
the rest of his Children
were left behind & came
over afterwards.

5 Mr Edward Winslow
Elizabeth his wife, &
2 men servants, caled
Georg Sowle, and
Elias Story; also a litle
girle was put to him caled
Ellen, the sister of Richard
More.

2 William Bradford, and
Dorathy his wife, having
but one child, a sone left
behind, who came afterward.

6 Mr Isaack Allerton, and
Mary his wife; with 3. children
Bartholmew
Remember &
Mary. and a servant boy.
John Hooke.

2 Mr Samuell fuller; and
a servant, caled
William Butten. His wife
was behind & a child, which
came afterwards.

2 John Crakston and his sone
John Crakston

2 Captin Myles Standish
and Rose, his wife

4 Mr Christpher Martin,
and his wife; and 2. servants,
Salamon prower, and
John Langemore

5 Mr William Mullines, and his
wife; and 2. Children
Joseph, & priscila; and a servant
Robart Carter.

6 Mr White William White, and
Susana his wife; and one sone
Caled resolved, and one borne
a ship-bord caled perigriene; &
2. servants, named
William Holbeck & Edward Thomson

8 Mr Hopin Steven Hopkins, &
Elizabeth his wife; and 2
Children, caled Giles, and
Constanta a doughter, both
by a former wife. And 2. more
by this wife, caled Damaris, &
Oceanus, the last was borne at
sea. And 2. servants, called
Edward Doty, and Edward Litster.

1 Mr Richard Warren, but his
wife and Children were lefte
behind and came afterwards

4 John Billinton, and Elen his wife;
and 2. sones John, & francis.

4 Edward Tillie, and Ann his wife;
and 2. Children that were their
Cosens; Henery Samson, and Humility Coper

3 John Tillie, and his wife; and
Eelizabeth their doughter

1

◆ *Photograph of William Bradford's passenger list, taken from an 1896 facsimile edition of his handwritten history* Of Plymouth Plantation.

Cape Cod could take advantage of this profitable fishery. But when the *Mayflower* had departed from England, it had been impossible to secure a patent for this region. If they were to settle where they had legally been granted land, they had to sail south for the mouth of the Hudson River 220 miles away.

Unfortunately, there was no reliable English map of the waters between Cape Cod and the Hudson. Little had changed since 1614, when Captain John Smith (of Pocahontas fame) had dismissed all existing maps of the region as "so much waste paper, though they cost me more." Smith's own chart of New England only went as far south as the back side of the Cape—where the *Mayflower* had first sighted land—and provided no help for a voyage south. Except for what knowledge Jones's pilots might have of this coast—which appears to have been minimal—the captain was sailing blind.

For the next five hours, the *Mayflower* sailed easily along. After sixty-five days of storms, it must have been wonderful for the passengers, who crowded onto the chilly, sun-drenched deck to drink in their first view of the New World. But for Master Jones, it was the beginning of the most tense portion of the voyage. Any captain would rather have braved the fiercest North Atlantic storm than risk the danger of an unknown coast. Until the *Mayflower* was quietly at anchor, Jones would get little sleep.

The *Mayflower* sailed south past the future locations of Wellfleet, Eastham, Orleans, and Chatham. Throughout the morning, the tide was in their favor, but around 1 P.M., it began to flow against them. Then the water dropped alarmingly, as did the wind. Suddenly, the *Mayflower* was in the midst of what has been called "one of the meanest stretches of shoal [shallow] water on the American coast"—Pollack Rip.

Pollack Rip is part of a complex and ever-changing maze of sandbars stretching between the elbow of Cape Cod and the tip of Nantucket

Island, fifteen or so miles to the south. The huge volume of water that moves back and forth between the ocean to the east and Nantucket Sound to the west rushes and swirls amid these shoals with a ferocity that is still, almost four hundred years later, terrifying to behold. It's been claimed that half the wrecks along the entire Atlantic and Gulf coasts of the United States have occurred in this area.

The calm waters had suddenly been transformed into a churning sea. And with the wind dying to almost nothing, Jones had no way to get his ship away from the danger, especially since what breeze remained was from the north, pinning the *Mayflower* against the breakers. It was approaching 3 P.M., with only another hour and a half of daylight left.

Just when it seemed that all had been lost, the wind began to change, gradually shifting in a clockwise direction to the south. This, combined with a fair tide, was all Master Jones needed. By sunset at 4:35 P.M., the *Mayflower* had turned around and was well to the northwest of Pollack Rip.

With the wind building from the south, Jones made a historic decision. They weren't going to the Hudson River. They would keep going north, back around Cape Cod to New England.

◆ ◆ ◆ By 5 P.M., it was almost completely dark. Not wanting to run into any more shoals, Jones decided to "heave to," adjusting the sails so that the ship was barely moving—standard procedure on an unknown coast at night. Four or five miles off present-day Chatham, the *Mayflower* drifted with the tide, waiting for dawn.

In the meantime, the news that they were headed to New England instead of the Hudson River put the passengers in an uproar. As they all knew, their patent did not technically apply to a settlement north of the Hudson. Some of the Strangers made "discontented and mutinous

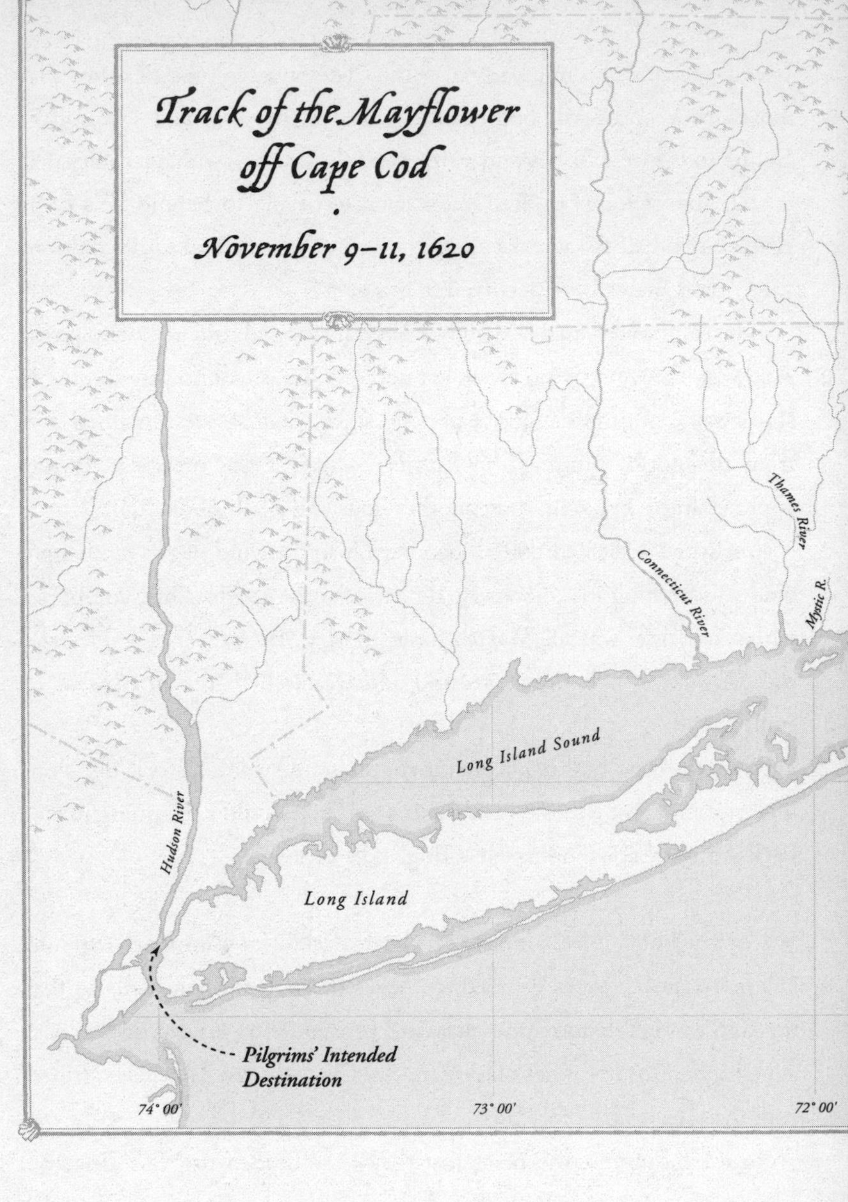

Track of the Mayflower off Cape Cod
November 9–11, 1620
Thames River
Connecticut River
Mystic R.
Long Island Sound
Hudson River
Long Island
Pilgrims' Intended Destination
74° 00'
73° 00'
72° 00'

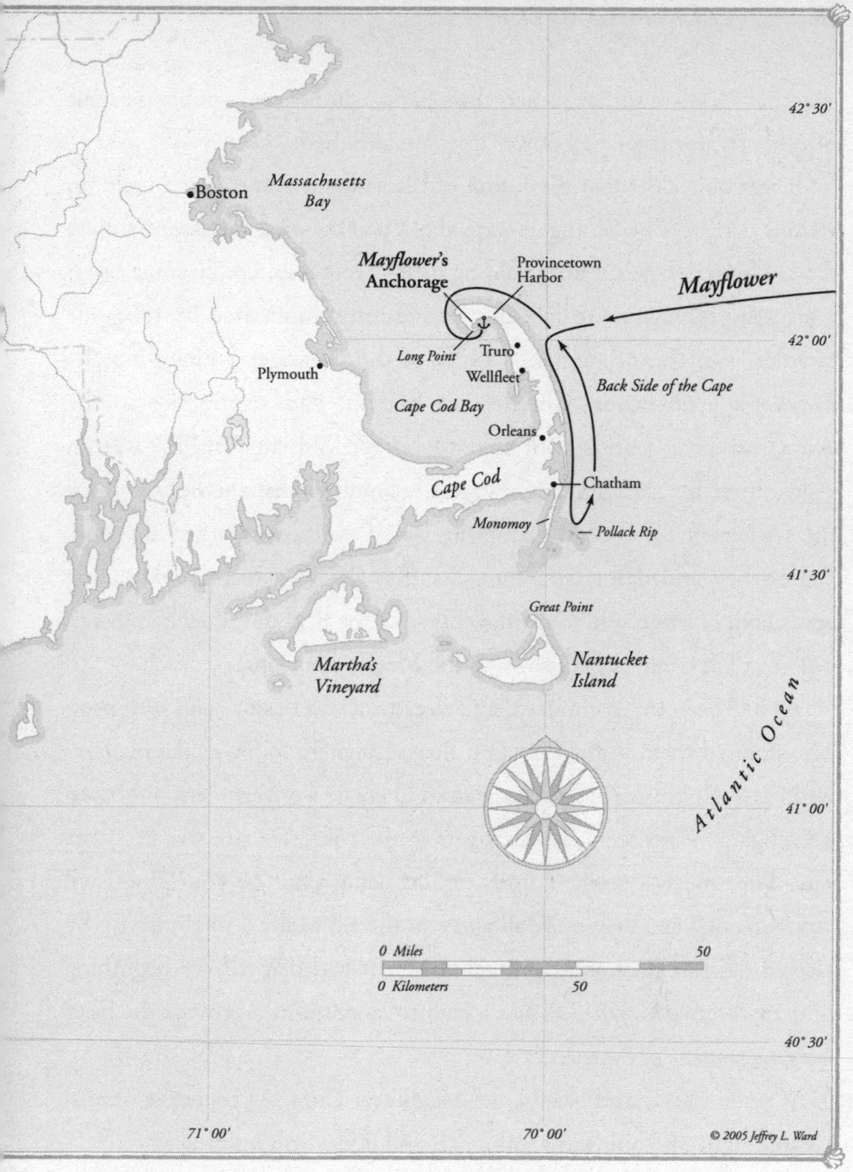

Massachusetts Bay
Boston
Mayflower's Anchorage
Provincetown Harbor
Mayflower
Long Point
Truro
Wellfleet
Plymouth
Back Side of the Cape
Cape Cod Bay
Orleans
Cape Cod
Chatham
Monomoy
Pollack Rip
Great Point
Nantucket Island
Martha's Vineyard
Atlantic Ocean
42° 30'
42° 00'
41° 30'
41° 00'
40° 30'
71° 00'
70° 00'
0 Miles 50
0 Kilometers 50
© 2005 Jeffrey L. Ward

speeches," insisting that "when they came ashore they would use their own liberty, for none had power to command them."

It was now clear that the future of the settlement was, once again, in serious danger. The Strangers were about half the passengers, and unlike the Leideners, they had little holding them together except, in some cases, a growing reluctance to live in a community dominated by religious fanatics. On the other hand, some of the Strangers, including the *Mayflower*'s governor, Christopher Martin, had strong ties to the Adventurers in London; in fact, passenger William Mullins was an Adventurer himself. These Strangers recognized that the only way for the settlement to succeed financially was if everyone worked together. Before they landed, it was essential that they all sign a formal and binding agreement of some sort. Over the course of the next day, they hammered out what has come to be known as the Mayflower Compact.

As had been true for more than a decade, it was Pastor John Robinson who pointed them in the direction they ultimately followed. In his farewell letter, Robinson had seen the need to create a government not based on religion. With so many Strangers in their midst, there was no other way. They must "become a body politic, using amongst yourselves civil government," i.e., they must all agree to submit to the laws drawn up by elected officials. Just as a spiritual covenant had marked the beginning of their congregation in Leiden, a civil covenant would provide the basis for government in America.

Written clearly and briefly, the Mayflower Compact bears the unmistakable signs of Robinson's influence, and it is worth quoting in full:

> Having undertaken, for the glory of God and advancement of the Christian faith and honor of our King and country, a voyage to plant

◆ *A seventeenth-century engraving of the Pilgrims signing the Mayflower Compact on board the* Mayflower.

the first colony in the northern parts of Virginia, do these present solemnly and mutually in the presence of God and one of another, covenant and combine ourselves together into a civil body politic, for our better ordering and preservation, and furtherance of the ends aforesaid; and by virtue hereof to enact, constitute and frame such just and equal laws, ordinances, acts, constitutions and offices, from time to time, as shall be thought most meet and convenient for the general good of the colony, unto which we promise all due submission and obedience.

◆ *A writing cabinet said to have been brought on the* Mayflower *by the White family in 1620.*

They were nearing the end of a long and frightening voyage. They were bound for a place about which they knew nothing. It was almost winter. They didn't have enough food. Some of them were sick, and two had already died. Still others were threatening to leave, which would have probably meant the end of the settlement and, most likely, their deaths. The Leideners might have looked to their military officer, Miles Standish, and ordered him to subdue the rebels. Instead, they put pen to paper and created a document that ranks with the Declaration of Independence and the United States Constitution as an essential American text.

But there was one more critical decision to make. They must choose a leader. The Leideners were barely a majority, but they could be counted on to vote together, guaranteeing that their leader would *not* be the *Mayflower*'s governor, Christopher Martin. The only other person aboard the *Mayflower* who had played a central role in organizing the voyage was deacon John Carver. Carver was, according to one account, "a gentleman of singular piety, rare humility, and great condescendency." He was also wealthy and had contributed much of his personal fortune to the congregation in Leiden and to this voyage. He and his wife, Katherine, who had buried two children in Leiden, had brought five servants on the *Mayflower,* one of whom was John Howland, who had almost died when he fell overboard. John Carver, it was decided, would be their governor.

As the Pilgrims created their compact, Master Jones pointed the

Mayflower north. By nightfall, the ship was nearing the northern tip of Cape Cod. Jones wanted to enter Provincetown Harbor, known to them as Cape Cod Harbor, as close as possible to sunrise so that they'd have most of the day for exploring the surrounding countryside. But before they could set foot on land, every man who was healthy enough to write his name or, if he couldn't write, scratch out an X, had to sign the compact.

They awakened very early on the morning of November 11, 1620. Sunrise was at 6:55 A.M., and the passengers probably met in the *Mayflower*'s great cabin—approximately thirteen by seventeen feet, with two windows in the stern and one on either side. Beginning with John Carver and ending with the servant Edward Leister, a total of forty-one men signed the compact. Only nine adult males did not sign—some had been hired as seamen for only a year, while others were probably too sick to put pen to paper. The ceremony ended with the official selection of a leader. Bradford informs us that "they chose or rather confirmed, Mr. John Carver (a man godly and well approved amongst them) their Governor for that year."

In the meantime, Master Jones guided the *Mayflower* into Provincetown Harbor, one of the largest and safest natural harbors in New England. Tucked within the curled wrist of Cape Cod, the harbor is so large that Jones estimated that it could accommodate at least a thousand ships.

But on the morning of November 11, they were the only vessel in the harbor. Jones found a deep spot with good holding ground for the anchor to grip. No matter from what direction the wind blew, the *Mayflower* was now safely at rest beside what is known today as Long Point.

Many of the passengers knew that Master Jones was already impatient to get them off his ship and head the *Mayflower* back for home. But the land that surrounded them was low and sandy—a most unpromising place for a plantation. Bradford called it "a hideous and desolate wilderness." And then there were the native people of this place, who they feared were "readier to fill their sides full of arrows than otherwise."

Years later, Bradford looked back to that first morning in America with wonder. "But here I cannot stay and make a pause," he wrote, "and stand half amazed at this poor people's present condition. . . . [T]hey had now no friends to welcome them nor inns to entertain or refresh their weatherbeaten bodies; no houses or much less towns to repair to, to seek for succor." And in the next four months, half of them would be dead.

◆ *Nineteenth-century illustration of the Pilgrims landing in the New World.*

But what truly astonished Bradford was that half of them would somehow survive. "What could now sustain them," Bradford wrote, "but the spirit of God and His Grace? May not and ought not the children of these fathers rightly say: 'Our fathers were Englishmen which came over this great ocean, and were ready to perish in this wilderness; but they cried unto the Lord, and He heard their voice and looked on their adversity.'"

It was time to go ashore. They had brought with them an open boat that could be both rowed and sailed, known as a shallop. About thirty-five feet long, it had been cut up into four pieces and stored below—where it had been "much bruised and shattered" over the course of the

voyage. It would take many days for the carpenter to assemble and rebuild it. For the time being, they used the smaller ship's boat. Loaded with sixteen well-armed men, the boat made its way to shore.

It was only a narrow neck of land, but for these sea-weary men, it was enough. "[T]hey fell upon their knees," Bradford wrote, "and blessed the God of Heaven who had brought them over the vast and furious ocean, and delivered them from all the perils and miseries thereof, again to set their feet on the firm and stable earth, their proper element."

They wandered over hills of sand and found birch, holly, ash, and walnut trees. With darkness coming, they loaded their boat with red cedar. The freshly sawed wood "smelled very sweet and strong," and that night aboard the *Mayflower,* for the first time in perhaps weeks, they enjoyed a warm fire.

It had been, for the most part, a reassuring introduction to the New World. Despite the barren landscape, they had found more trees than they would have come across back in Holland and even coastal England. But there had been something missing: Nowhere had they found any people.

THREE
The Plague

◆ ◆ ◆

ABOUT SIXTY MILES southwest of Provincetown Harbor, at a place called Pokanoket at the head of Narragansett Bay in modern Rhode Island, lived Massasoit, the most powerful Native leader, or sachem, in the region. He was in the prime of his life—about thirty-five, strong and imposing, with the quiet dignity that was expected of a sachem.

During the three years that the Pilgrims had been organizing their voyage to America, Massasoit's people, the Pokanokets, had been devastated by disease. It may have been the bubonic plague, introduced by European fishermen in modern Maine. Whatever the disease was, it quickly spread south along the Atlantic seaboard to the eastern shore of Narragansett Bay, killing in some cases as many as 90 percent of the region's inhabitants.

So many died so quickly that there was no one left to bury the dead. Portions of coastal New England that had once been as densely populated as western Europe were suddenly empty of people, with only the whitened bones of the dead to indicate that a community had once existed along these shores.

The Pokanokets had been particularly hard hit. Before the plague, they had numbered about twelve thousand, from which Massasoit could gather three thousand fighting men. After three years of disease, his force had been reduced to a few hundred warriors. Making it even worse was that the plague had not affected the Pokanokets' neighboring enemies, the Narragansetts. Their homeland was on the western portion of the bay, and they numbered about twenty thousand, with five thousand fighting

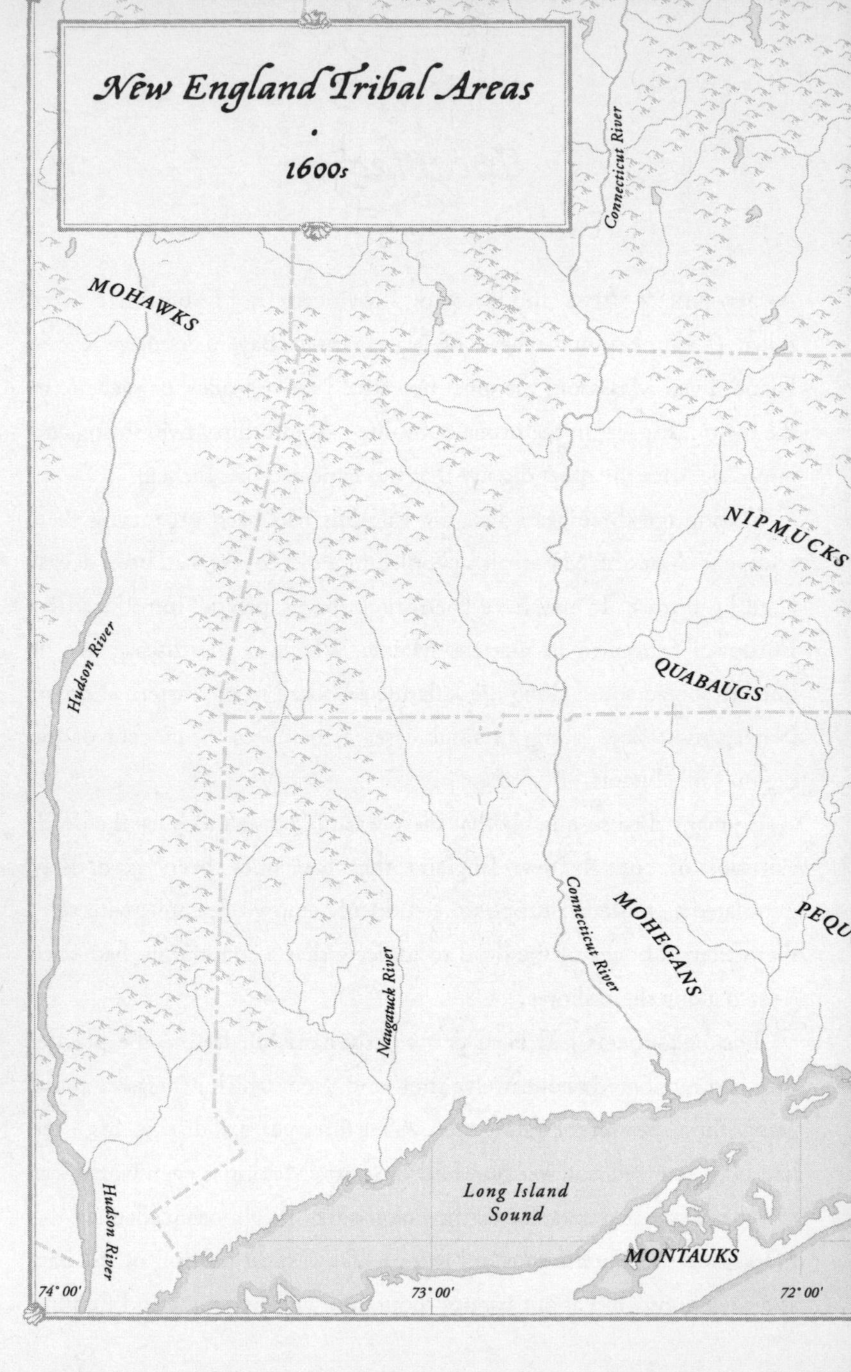
New England Tribal Areas
1600s
Connecticut River
MOHAWKS
NIPMUCKS
Hudson River
QUABAUGS
Connecticut River
MOHEGANS
PEQU
Naugatuck River
Long Island
Sound
Hudson River
MONTAUKS
74° 00'
73° 00'
72° 00'

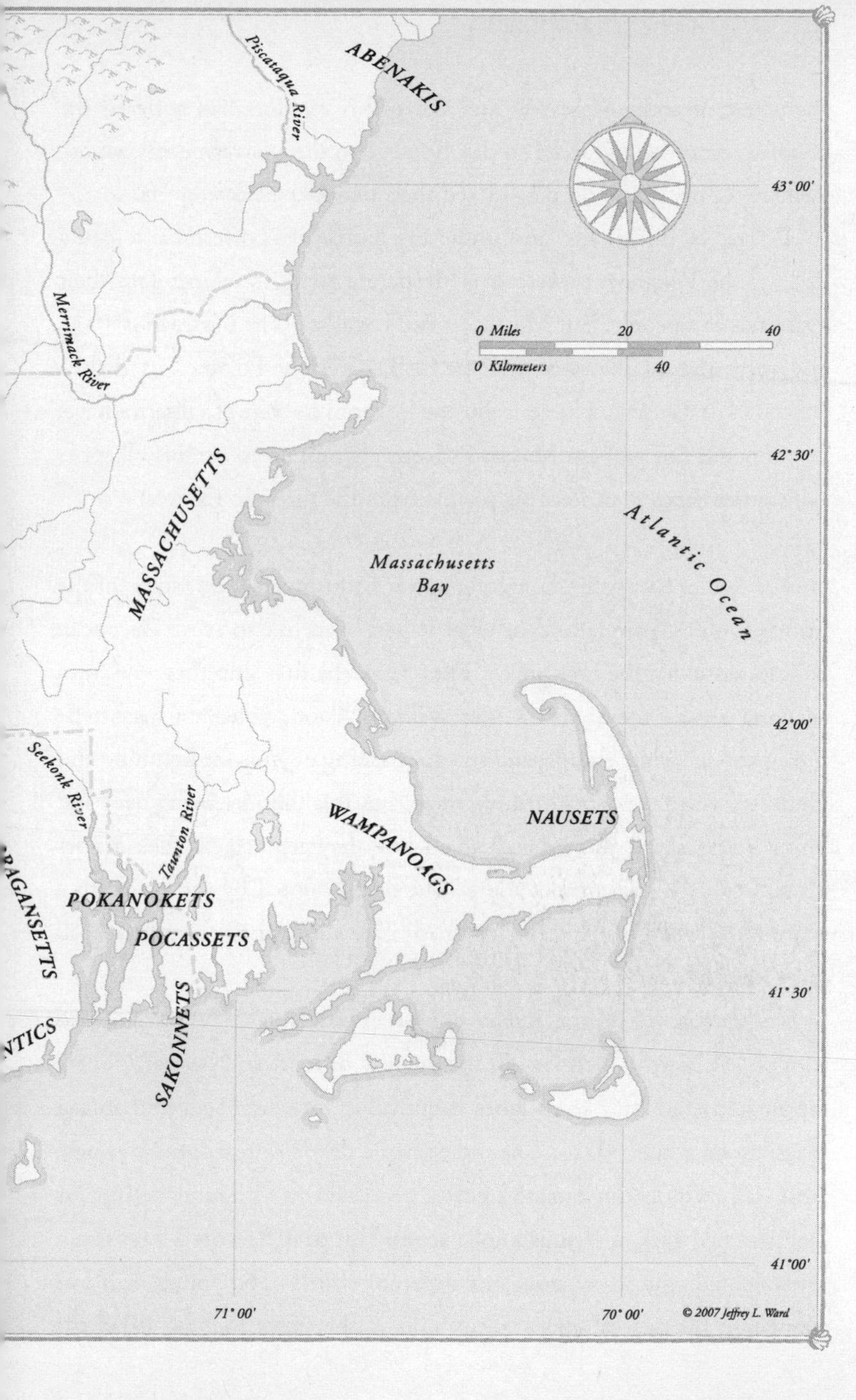
ABENAKIS
Piscataqua River
Merrimack River
MASSACHUSETTS
Massachusetts Bay
Atlantic Ocean
0 Miles
20
40
0 Kilometers
40
43° 00'
42° 30'
42°00'
41° 30'
41°00'
Seekonk River
Taunton River
WAMPANOAGS
NAUSETS
AGANSETTS
POKANOKETS
POCASSETS
SAKONNETS
NTICS
71° 00'
70° 00'
© 2007 Jeffrey L. Ward

men. Just recently, Massasoit and ten of his warriors had suffered the humiliation of being forced to pay homage to the Narragansetts, whose sachem, Canonicus, now considered the Pokanokets his subjects.

Wasted by disease and now under the thumb of a powerful and proud enemy, the Pokanokets were in a desperate struggle to maintain their existence as a people. But Massasoit had his allies. The Massachusetts to the north and the Nausets on Cape Cod shared the Pokanokets' dislike for the Narragansetts. Numerically, the Pokanokets were at a disadvantage, but this did not prevent Massasoit from attempting to use his alliances with other tribes to protect his people from the threat to the west.

◆ ◆ ◆ No one was sure how long ago it had occurred, but some of the Indians' oldest people told of what it had been like to see a European sailing vessel for the first time. "They took the first ship they saw for a walking island," the English settler William Wood wrote, "the mast to be a tree, the sail white clouds, and the discharging of guns for lightning and thunder, which did much trouble them, but this thunder being over and this moving-island steadied with an anchor, they manned out their canoes to go and pick strawberries there. But being saluted by the way with a [cannon's] broadside . . . , [they turned] back, not daring to approach till they were sent for."

As early as 1524, the Italian explorer Giovanni da Verrazano had stopped at Narragansett Bay in the vicinity of modern Newport. There he encountered "two kings more beautiful in form and stature than can possibly be described. . . . The oldest had a deer's skin around his body, artificially wrought in damask figures, his head was without covering, his hair was tied back in various knots; around his neck he wore a large chain ornamented with many stones of different colors. The young man was similar in his general appearance. This is the finest looking tribe, the handsomest in their costumes, that we have found in our voyage." Almost a century before the arrival of the *Mayflower*, Verrazano may have met Massasoit's great-grandfather.

By 1602, when the English explorer Bartholomew Gosnold visited the region, European codfishing vessels had become an increasingly familiar sight along the New England coast. After giving Cape Cod its name, Gosnold ventured to the Elizabeth Islands at the southwestern corner of the Cape, where he built a small fort on the island of Cuttyhunk. A few days after his arrival, fifty Indians in nine canoes arrived from the mainland for the purposes of trade. It was apparent to Gosnold that one of the Indians was looked to with great respect. This may have been Massasoit's father. It is possible that Massasoit himself, who would have been in his early teens, was also present.

Gosnold presented the sachem with a pair of knives and a straw hat, which he placed on his head. Then the Indians "all sat down in manner

◆ *A nineteenth-century photograph of the Gosnold Memorial, which was erected on the island of Cuttyhunk to commemorate Gosnold's landing on American soil.*

like greyhounds upon their heels" and began to trade. With the exception of mustard ("whereat they made a sour face"), the Indians appeared to enjoy all the strange foods the English had to offer. For their part, Gosnold and his men enjoyed the Indians' tobacco, a dried green powder that when smoked in carefully crafted clay pipes proved addictively pleasant.

Gosnold was at a loss to understand the Natives' language, but the Indians were immediately able to mimic the Englishmen's speech. At one point, a sailor sat smoking beside an Indian and said, "How now, sir, are you so saucy with my tobacco?" The Indian repeated the phrase word for word, "as if he had been a long scholar in the language."

But Gosnold's introduction to the area and its people turned as sour as his mustard. While out searching for food, two of his men were attacked by four Indians. No one was hurt (in part because one of the Englishmen cut the strings of the Natives' bows with his knife), but Gosnold decided to abandon his fort and sailed for England.

It was a pattern that would be repeated over and over again in the years ahead. Soon after Gosnold returned to England with word of his discovery, the explorer Martin Pring sailed for Cape Cod and built a fort of his own in the vicinity of modern Truro. After a summer of harvesting sassafras, Pring also began to wear out his welcome with the locals. When an Indian-lit fire almost destroyed his fort, Pring took the hint and sailed for home.

Beginning in 1605, the Frenchman Samuel Champlain explored the Cape and produced detailed maps of several harbors and inlets. In 1611, the year that the playwright William Shakespeare produced *The Tempest*, the English explorer Edward Harlow voyaged to the region. By the time he returned to London, he had captured close to half a dozen Indians and killed at least as many in several brutal battles. One of his Indian captives was quite tall, and Harlow helped repay his debts from the voyage by showing him on the city streets "as a wonder."

The Indian's name was Epenow, and he soon realized that there was nothing the English valued more than gold. He told his captors that back on Martha's Vineyard, an island just to the south of Cape Cod, there was a gold mine that only he could lead them to. An expedition was promptly mounted, and as soon as the English ship came within swimming distance of the island, Epenow jumped over the side and escaped.

Around this time, in 1614, Captain John Smith led a voyage of exploration to the region. There were several vessels in Smith's expedition, and one of the commanders, Thomas Hunt, decided to take as many Native captives as his ship could hold and sell them as slaves in Spain. Hunt's actions badly damaged Indian-English relations in New England for years to come.

The following year, a French ship wrecked on the north shore of Cape Cod, and the Indians decided to do to the French what the English had done to them. Indians from up and down the coast gathered together at the wreck site, and William Bradford later learned how they "never left dogging and waylaying [the French] till they took opportunities to kill all but three or four, which they kept as slaves, sending them up and down, to make sport with them from one sachem to another."

One of the Frenchmen was quite religious. He learned enough of the Natives' language to tell his captors that "God was angry with them for their wickedness, and would destroy them and give their country to another people." Scorning the prophecy, a sachem assembled his subjects around a nearby hill and, with the Frenchman beside him on the hilltop, demanded if "his God had so many people and [was] able to kill all those?" The Frenchman responded that he "surely would." In three years' time, everything the captive had predicted had come to pass.

◆ ◆ ◆ In the spring of 1619, the English explorer Thomas Dermer sailed south from Maine in a small open boat. Accompanying Dermer was a Native guide who'd been abducted by Thomas Hunt in 1614. The Indian's name was Tisquantum, or Squanto, and after five long years in Spain, England, and Newfoundland, he was sailing toward his home at

◆ *John Smith's map of New England, 1634.*

Patuxet, the site of modern Plymouth. In a letter written the following winter, Dermer described what they saw: "[We] passed along the coast where [we] found some ancient [Indian] plantations, not long since populous now utterly void; in other places a remnant remains, but not free of sickness. Their disease the plague, for we might perceive the sores of some that had escaped, who descried the spots of such as usually die. When [we] arrived at my savage's native country [we found] all dead." Squanto's reaction to the desolation of his homeland, where as many as two thousand people had once lived, can only be imagined. However, at some point after visiting Patuxet, he began to see the destruction of the plague as an opportunity.

Upon Epenow's return to Martha's Vineyard, the former captive had become a sachem, and it seems that Squanto had similar ambitions. Squanto took Dermer to Nemasket, a settlement about fifteen miles inland from Patuxet, where Squanto learned that not everyone in his village had died. Several of his family members were alive and well. He may already have begun to think about reestablishing a community in Patuxet that was independent of Pokanoket control. In the aftermath of the plague, Massasoit was obviously vulnerable, and as Bradford later said of the former Indian captive, "Squanto sought his own ends and played his own game." But first he had to see for himself the condition of Massasoit and the Pokanokets, so he convinced Dermer that they should push on to the sachem's village.

It took about a day to walk from Nemasket to Pokanoket. There they met what Dermer described as "two kings," who were undoubtedly Massasoit and his brother Quadequina, and fifty warriors. Massasoit was quite happy to see the Englishman and his Native guide. Dermer wrote that the sachem and his brother were "well satisfied with [what] my savage and I discoursed unto them [and] being desirous of novelty, gave me content in whatsoever I demanded." Massasoit still had one of the French captives in his possession and agreed to hand him over to Dermer. After locating yet another Frenchman and meeting Epenow on Martha's Vineyard, Dermer left Squanto with Native friends near Nemasket and headed south to spend the winter in Virginia.

When Thomas Dermer returned to the region the following summer, he discovered that the Pokanokets possessed a newfound and "inveterate malice to the English," and for good reason. That spring, an English ship had arrived at Narragansett Bay. The sailors invited a large number of Massasoit's people aboard the vessel, then proceeded to shoot them down in cold blood.

Almost everywhere Dermer went in the summer of 1620, he came under attack. He would certainly have been killed at Nemasket had not Squanto, who had spent the winter in the region, come to his rescue. But not even Squanto could save Dermer when he and his men arrived at Martha's Vineyard. Epenow and his warriors fell on Dermer's party, and only Dermer, who was badly wounded, and one other Englishman escaped, while Squanto was taken prisoner. Soon after reaching Virginia a few weeks later, Dermer was dead.

Epenow appears to have distrusted Squanto from the start. He understood that if the English should ever try to settle in this land, those such as Squanto and himself, who could speak the Englishmen's language, would possess a powerful and potentially dangerous advantage. They could claim to know what the English were saying, and no one would know whether or not they were telling the truth. For his part, Epenow had proven his loyalty to his people by attacking Dermer and his men. But Squanto's true motives were anyone's guess.

Six years ago, Squanto had been abducted by pale, hairy-faced men whose weapons killed with blasts of fire and smoke. He had been thrust inside a huge, birdlike vessel that had taken him across an endless ocean. He had found himself in one of the largest cities in Europe: a crowded, dirty, smelly place of narrow streets and tall wooden houses.

But most disturbing of all had been his return home. Almost everyone he had once known was dead and the village of Patuxet abandoned. Because of his years among the English, he was now looked to with suspicion. Perhaps there was anger growing inside of him. Perhaps it was ambition.

Massasoit shared Epenow's distrust of Squanto, and by the fall of 1620, Squanto had been moved from Martha's Vineyard to Pokanoket, where he remained a prisoner. When the *Mayflower* arrived at Provincetown Harbor in November, it was generally assumed by the Indians that the ship had been sent to avenge the attack on Dermer. In the weeks ahead, the Pilgrims would do little to change that assumption.

In the meantime, Squanto waited for his chance.

FOUR
Beaten with Their Own Rod

◆ ◆ ◆

THE *MAYFLOWER* HAD arrived at Provincetown Harbor on Saturday, November 11. Since the next day was a Sunday, the Pilgrims remained aboard ship, worshipping God under the direction of Elder Brewster. As Puritans, they believed that the entire Sabbath must be devoted to worship—both a morning and an afternoon meeting along with personal and family prayers throughout the day. Work and especially play on a Sunday were forbidden.

On Monday, the four battered pieces of the shallop were taken ashore in the smaller rowboat. As the carpenter and his assistants began to put the vessel back together, the passengers enjoyed their first day ashore. After more than two months at sea, there was a "great need" for washing, and the women found a small freshwater pond near the present site of Provincetown. For generations to come, Monday would be wash day in New England, a tradition that began with the women of the *Mayflower*.

At low tide, amid the barnacles and seaweed, they found plenty of blue mussels attached in clumps to the shoreside rocks. Passengers and sailors alike enjoyed the first fresh food any of them had tasted in a very long time, only to fall victim to vomiting and diarrhea from shellfish poisoning.

The harbor also contained thousands of ducks and geese—"the greatest store of fowl that ever we saw." But it was the whales that astounded them. "[E]very day we saw whales playing hard by us," they wrote. These were Atlantic right whales, huge creatures that feed on plankton. Jones and one of his mates, who had experience hunting whales in Greenland, claimed that if only they'd had some harpoons they might have taken between three thousand and four thousand pounds' worth of valuable whale oil.

For the Pilgrims, who were expected to provide the Adventurers with a regular supply of goods, it was extremely frustrating to be surrounded by all this potential wealth and yet have no way of capturing any of it. One day a whale, apparently enjoying the afternoon sun on her dark, blubbery back, lay on the water's surface within only a few yards of the *Mayflower*, "as if she had been dead." It was just too much of a temptation. As a small crowd looked on, two muskets were loaded, but when the first was fired, the barrel burst into pieces. Amazingly, no one was injured, and the whale, after issuing "a snuff," swam leisurely away.

The shallop was proving to be a problem. Instead of days, it was going to be weeks before the boat was completed. Some of the passengers began to insist that they should launch a land expedition. When the *Mayflower* first sailed into the harbor, the mouth of a river had been sighted several miles to the southeast. Some of them, probably headed by Captain Miles Standish, wanted to take a small party to investigate this potential settlement site.

The dangers of such a trip were considerable. So far they had seen no local inhabitants, but for all they knew, huge numbers of hostile Natives might be waiting just a few miles down the Cape. It was eventually decided, however, that the expedition was worth the risk. Standish's party consisted of sixteen men, including William Bradford, Stephen Hopkins, and Edward Tilley. Each man was equipped with a musket, sword, and corselet, a light form of body armor that included a metal breastplate.

On Wednesday, November 15, they were rowed ashore. Provincetown Harbor, as well as much of the bay side of the lower Cape, is characterized by wide tidal flats. Even a small boat runs aground many yards away from the beach, and during the fall of 1620 the passengers were forced to wade through the shallows to shore. With the temperature on the verge of freezing, it was a long, cold slog to the beach, especially weighted down with armor and weapons.

Standish soon had them marching single file along the shore. He was not a tall man—in the years ahead he won the nickname Captain Shrimp—but his courage was never questioned. Before leaving for America, the Pilgrims had contacted another potential candidate for the position of military leader: Captain John Smith. No one in England knew more about America than Smith. He had been at the founding of Jamestown in 1607; in 1614, he had led a voyage of exploration to what he named New England, creating the most detailed map of the region to date. (It was Smith's companion on that voyage, Thomas Hunt, who had abducted Squanto.) When the Pilgrims approached him in London, Smith wanted desperately to return to America, particularly to "the country of the Massachusetts," which he described as "the paradise of those parts." But the Pilgrims decided that they wanted no part of him. Smith bitterly related how they had insisted that his "books and maps were better cheap to teach them than myself."

A
DESCRIPTION
of *New England*:
OR
THE OBSERVATIONS, AND
discoueries, of Captain *Iohn Smith* (Admirall
of that Country) in the North of *America*, in the year
of our Lord 1614: *with the successe of sixe Ships,
that went the next yeare* 1615; *and the*
accidents befell him among the
French men of warre:

With the proofe of the present benefit this
Countrey affoords: whither this present yeare,
1616, *eight voluntary Ships are gone
to make further tryall*.

At LONDON
Printed by *Humfrey Lownes*, for *Robert Clerke*; and
are to be sould at his house called the Lodge,
in Chancery lane, ouer against Lin-
colnes Inne. 1616.

◆ *Title page of Captain John Smith's book,* A Description of New England 1616.

Smith's fatal flaw, as far as the Pilgrims were concerned, was that he knew too much. In the beginning of the settlement, they would have had no choice but to do as he said, and this could be dangerous. Smith possessed a strong personality, and a man of his worldly nature might come to dominate what they intended to be a mostly religious society. "[T]hey would not . . . have any knowledge by any but themselves," Smith wrote, "pretending only religion their governor and frugality their counsel, when indeed it was . . . because . . . they would have no superiors."

If the Pilgrims did possess Smith's map of New England, though, they failed to make good use of it. Rivers were considered essential to a settlement site, and Smith's map clearly indicated that the nearest major river was the Charles River, less than a day's sail to the northwest, at present-day Boston. The Pilgrims, however, insisted on exploring the entire bay side of Cape Cod, even though there was no evidence on Smith's map of a decent river along this more than fifty-mile stretch of coastline.

As Smith later wrote, much of the suffering that lay ahead for the Pilgrims could easily have been avoided if they had paid for his services or, at the very least, used his map. "[S]uch humorists [i.e., fanatics] will never believe . . . ," he wrote, "till they be beaten with their own rod."

◆ ◆ ◆ Standish and his men had marched just a mile or so down the beach when up ahead they saw half a dozen people and a dog walking toward them. They initially assumed it was Master Jones and some of the sailors, who they knew were already ashore with the *Mayflower*'s spaniel. But when the people started to run inland for the woods, they realized that these weren't sailors; they were the first Native people they had seen. One of the Indians paused to whistle for the dog, and the group disappeared into the trees.

They followed at a trot, hoping to make contact. But as soon as the Indians saw that they were being pursued, they made a run for it—setting out "with might and main" along the shore to the south. Standish and his party did their best to chase them, but it was slow going in the ankle-deep sand, and after several months aboard ship, they were in no shape for a sprint across a beach.

Even though they were quickly left behind, they followed the Indians' footprints. From the tracks, they could tell that the Indians ran up each hill and then paused to look back to see whether they were still being pursued. After what the Pilgrims judged to be ten miles of marching, they stopped for the night. With three men on guard at a time, they gathered around a large fire and tried to get some sleep.

The next morning Standish and his men once again set off in pursuit of the Indians. They followed the tracks past the head of a long tidal creek into a heavily wooded area, "which tore our armor in pieces." Finally, around ten in the morning, they emerged into a deep, grassy valley, where they saw their first American deer. But it was water they truly needed. The only liquid they had brought with them was a bottle of aqua vitae (a strong liquor), and they were now suffering from violent thirst. At last, at the foot of a small rise of land, they found a pool of freshwater—called today Pilgrim Spring. They claimed to have "drunk our first New England water with as much delight as ever we drunk drink in all our lives." From a group of lifelong beer and wine drinkers, this was high praise indeed.

Once they'd refreshed themselves, they marched to the shoreline, where they could see the *Mayflower* just four miles to the northwest across the arc of the bay. They made camp, and that night they built a large fire as part of a prearranged signal to let their friends and loved ones know that all was well.

As they continued south the next morning, they came across evidence that they were not the first Europeans to have visited this place. First they found some sawed planks and an old iron ship's kettle—perhaps from the French shipwreck of 1615. Then, near the river mouth that they'd seen from the *Mayflower,* they discovered the remains of what must have been Martin Pring's seventeen-year-old fort. But it was evidence of a Native sort that soon attracted their attention.

On a high shoreside hill, they found an area where the sand had recently been patted smooth. As three of them dug, the others gathered around in a defensive ring with their muskets ready. Not far down, they found a basket made of woven reeds filled with so much corn that two men could barely lift it. Nearby, they found a basket containing corn that was still on the cob, "some yellow and some red, and others mixed with blue." One of the more remarkable characteristics of Indian corn, or maize, is that, if kept dry, the kernels can be stored forever. In Mexico, storage pits containing perfectly preserved corn have been dug up that were at least a thousand years old.

The Pilgrims paused to discuss what they should do next. They had brought wheat, barley, and peas with them aboard the *Mayflower* for planting in the spring. Most European settlers in a similar situation would have had enough faith in their own, supposedly superior, technology that they would have had no use for a buried bag of Native seed.

But the Pilgrims were not the usual European immigrants. For one thing, they were desperate. Due to the sad state of their provisions, as well as the lateness of the season, they knew they were in a survival situation from the start. Hence, they were willing to try just about anything if it meant they might survive their first year. They decided they had no choice but to take the corn. The place where they found the buried seed is still called Corn Hill.

The decision to steal the corn was not without risks. They were, after all, taking something of obvious value from a people who had done their best, so far, to avoid them. The Pilgrims might have decided to wait until they had the chance to speak with the Indians before they took the corn, but the last thing they had was time. They told themselves that they would pay back the corn's owners as soon as they had the chance.

They poured as much corn as would fit into a kettle, which they hung from a tree branch, and with two men shouldering the burden, they started back to the *Mayflower.* They planned to retrieve the rest of the corn once the shallop had been completed. They also hoped to explore more of the two creeks. If some earlier European visitors had thought the location suitable for a settlement of some sort, perhaps it might serve their own needs.

By dusk it was raining. After a long, wet night spent within a quickly constructed barricade of tree trunks and branches, they continued on to the north only to become lost, once again, in the woods. Deep within a grove of trees, they came across a young sapling that had been bent down to a spot on the ground where a Native-made rope encircled some acorns. Stephen Hopkins explained that this was an Indian deer trap similar to the ones he'd seen in Virginia. As they stood examining the device, William Bradford, who was in the rear, stumbled upon the trap. The sapling jerked up, and Bradford was snagged by the leg. Instead of being annoyed, Bradford could only marvel at this "very pretty device, made with a rope of their own making, and having a noose as artificially made as any roper in England can make." Adding the noose to what soon became a collection of Native specimens and artifacts, they continued on to the harbor, where they found a welcoming party on shore headed by Master Jones and Governor Carver. "And thus," Bradford wrote, "we came both weary and welcome home."

◆ ◆ ◆ It took another few days for the carpenter to finish the shallop, and when it was done on Monday, November 27, yet another exploring mission was launched, this time under the direction of Christopher Jones instead of Standish. As the master of the *Mayflower*, Jones was not required to help the Pilgrims find a settlement site, but he obviously thought it in his best interests to see them on their way.

There were thirty-four of them, twenty-four passengers and ten sailors, aboard the open shallop. The wind was out of the northeast, and the shallop had a difficult time getting away from the point within which the

◆ *A drawing of John Smith's shallop, which was used to map Chesapeake Bay in 1608 and would have been very similar to the Pilgrims'.*

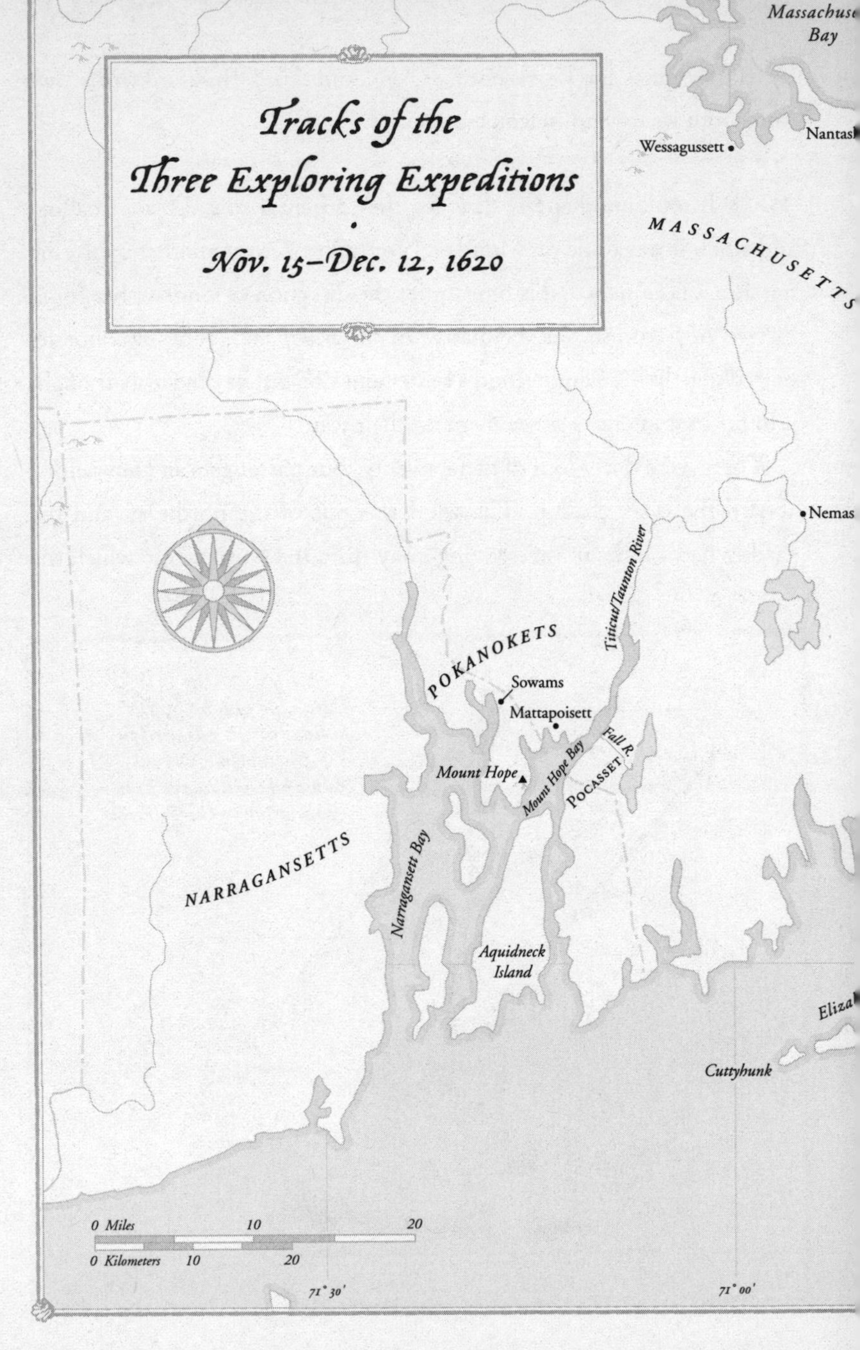

Tracks of the
Three Exploring Expeditions
Nov. 15–Dec. 12, 1620
Massachuse
Bay
Nantas
Wessagussett
MASSACHUSETTS
Nemas
Titicut/Taunton River
POKANOKETS
Sowams
Mattapoisett
Fall R.
Mount Hope
Mount Hope Bay
POCASSET
NARRAGANSETTS
Narragansett Bay
Aquidneck
Island
Eliza
Cuttyhunk
0 Miles
10
20
0 Kilometers
10
20
71° 30′
71° 00′

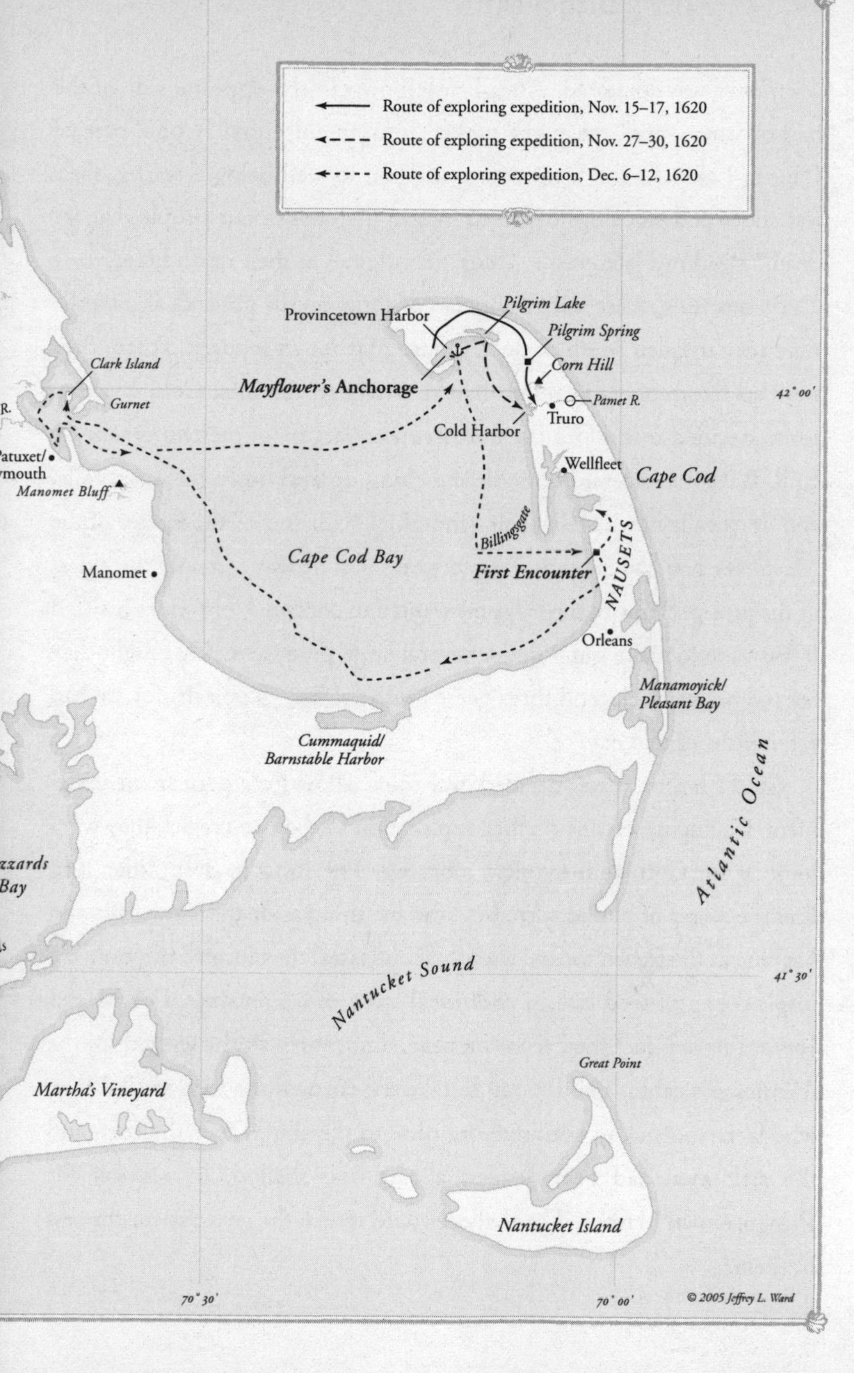
Route of exploring expedition, Nov. 15–17, 1620
Route of exploring expedition, Nov. 27–30, 1620
Route of exploring expedition, Dec. 6–12, 1620
Provincetown Harbor
Pilgrim Lake
Pilgrim Spring
Corn Hill
Clark Island
Gurnet
Mayflower's Anchorage
Pamet R.
Truro
42° 00′
Cold Harbor
Patuxet/
ymouth
Manomet Bluff
Wellfleet
Cape Cod
Billingsgate
NAUSETS
Cape Cod Bay
Manomet
First Encounter
Orleans
Manamoyick/
Pleasant Bay
Cummaquid/
Barnstable Harbor
Atlantic Ocean
zzards
Bay
Nantucket Sound
41° 30′
Great Point
Martha's Vineyard
Nantucket Island
70° 30′
70° 00′
© 2005 Jeffrey L. Ward

Mayflower was anchored. After being blown to the opposite side of the harbor, they spent the night tucked into an inlet that is now part of Pilgrim Lake. As the temperatures dipped to well below freezing, their wet shoes and stockings began to freeze. "[S]ome of our people that are dead," Bradford later wrote, "took the original of their death here."

By morning, there were six inches of snow on the ground, and by the time they'd sailed south back to Pamet Harbor in modern Truro, they were so frostbitten and numb that they named the inlet Cold Harbor. Jones decided to explore the northern and largest of the two creeks by land. But after several hours of "marching up and down the steep hills, and deep valleys, which lay half a foot thick with snow," the master of the *Mayflower* had had enough. At fifty years old, he was certainly the eldest of the group. Some of the Pilgrims wanted to continue, but Jones insisted it was time to make camp under several large pine trees. That night they feasted on six ducks and three geese "with soldiers' stomachs for we had eaten little all that day."

Cold Harbor, it was decided, was too shallow for a permanent settlement. Giving up on any further exploration of the two creeks, they went looking for Corn Hill the next morning. The snow made it difficult to find the stores of buried corn, but after brushing aside the snowdrifts and hacking at the frozen topsoil with their cutlasses, they located not only the original bag of seed but an additional store of ten bushels. For Master Jones, this was just the excuse he needed to return to the warmth of the *Mayflower*'s cabin. He decided to take the corn, along with several men who were too sick to continue on, back to the ship. Once the corn and the sick men had been loaded aboard the shallop, he set sail for Provincetown Harbor. The shallop would return the next day for the rest of them.

Standish was once again in charge. The next morning, he led the eighteen remaining men on a search for Indians. But after several hours of tramping through the woods and snow, they had found nothing. The Native Americans moved with the seasons—inland in the winter, near the water in the summer—which meant that the Pilgrims, who were staying, for the most part, near the shore, were unlikely to meet many Indians during their explorations of Cape Cod.

On their way back to the harbor, Standish and his men found "a place like a grave, but it was much bigger and longer than any we had yet seen." There were boards positioned over the grave, suggesting that someone of importance had been buried here. They "resolved to dig it up."

They found several additional boards and a mat of woven grass. One of the boards was "finely carved and painted, with three tines . . . on the top, like a crown." This may have been a carving of Poseidon's trident, suggesting that the board originally came from a ship—most probably the French ship that had wrecked on this coast in 1615. Farther down, they found a new mat wrapped around two bundles, one large and one small.

They opened the larger bundle first. The contents were covered with a fine, sweet-smelling reddish powder. Along with some bones, they found the skull of a man with "fine yellow hair still on it, and some of the flesh unconsumed." With the skull was a sailor's canvas bag containing a knife and sewing needle. Then they turned to the smaller bundle. Inside were the skull and bones of a small child, along with a tiny wooden bow "and some other odd knacks."

Was this a castaway from the French ship and his Indian son? Had this particular sailor been embraced by the local Indians and died among them as a person "of some special note"? Or had the Indians killed and buried the sailor "in triumph over him"?

The Pilgrims had left Holland so that they could live like Englishmen again. But here was evidence that there were others in America who must be taken into account. Otherwise, they might share the fate of this yellow-haired sailor, whose bones and possessions had been left to rot in the sand.

◆ ◆ ◆ Later that day, just a short distance from Cold Harbor, Standish and his men found some Indian houses whose occupants had clearly left in a great hurry. The description of what they found, recorded in a brief book about their first year in America cowritten by William Bradford and Edward Winslow, is so detailed that it remains one of the best first-person accounts of an Indian wigwam, or wetu, that we have:

> The houses were made with long young sapling trees, bended and both ends stuck into the ground; they were made round, like unto an arbor, and covered down to the ground with thick and well wrought mats, and the door was not over a yard high, made of a mat to open; the chimney was a wide open hole in the top, for which they had a mat to cover it close when they pleased; one might stand and go upright in them, in the midst of them were four little trunches [i.e., Y-shaped stakes] knocked into the ground and small sticks laid over, on which they hung their pots . . . ; round about the fire they lay on mats, which are their beds. The houses were double matted, for as they were matted without, so were they within, with newer & fairer mats.

Among the Indians' clay pots, wooden bowls, and reed baskets was an iron bucket from Europe that was missing a handle. There were several deer heads, one of which was still quite fresh, as well as a piece of broiled herring. As they had done with the graves of the blond-haired sailor

◆ *A modern-day re-creation of a Wampanoag wetu.*

and Indian child, the Pilgrims decided to take "some of the best things" with them.

Looting houses, graves, and storage pits was hardly the way to win the trust of the local inhabitants. To help pay for the damage they'd already done, they decided to leave behind some beads and other tokens for the Indians "in sign of peace." But it was getting dark. The shallop had returned, and they planned to spend the night back aboard the *Mayflower.* They had to get going, and in their haste to depart, they neglected to leave the beads and other trade goods. It would have been a small gesture to be sure, but it would have marked their only act of friendship since their arrival in the New World.

◆ ◆ ◆ The explorers learned of some good news once back aboard the *Mayflower.* A son named Peregrine had been born to Susanna and

William White. But a death was soon to follow the baby's birth. Edward Thompson, the Whites' servant, died on Monday, December 4.

Since Truro's Pamet Harbor was not going to serve their needs, they needed to find another settlement site. The pilot, Robert Coppin, had a rather hazy memory of a "good harbor" with a "great navigable river" about twenty-five miles across Cape Cod Bay. The reference to a large river suggests that Coppin was thinking of the Charles River and the future site of Boston. After much discussion, it was decided to pick up where they had left off and follow the shoreline of the Cape south, then west, and eventually north. Under no circumstances were they to venture beyond the harbor described by Coppin, which he called Thievish Harbor, since an Indian had stolen one of his company's harpoons when he was there several years earlier. For the Pilgrims, who had so far stolen a good deal of corn and Native artifacts, Thievish Harbor might be just the place to settle.

The shallop set out from the *Mayflower* once more on Wednesday, December 6. The *Mayflower*'s two pilots, Robert Coppin and John Clark, had replaced Master Jones and were accompanied by the master gunner and three sailors. The Pilgrims were represented by Bradford, Carver, Standish, Winslow, John Tilley and his brother Edward, John Howland, Richard Warren, Stephen Hopkins, and Hopkins's servant, Edward Doty—less than half the number of the previous expedition. Illness and freezing temperatures—it was now in the low twenties, if not colder—had already taken a considerable toll.

Almost as soon as they set sail, the salt spray froze on their coats—"as if they had been glazed," Bradford wrote. They sailed south into Wellfleet Bay, about fifteen miles beyond Truro. On the shore they saw a dozen or so Indians working around a large dark object that they later discovered was a pilot whale, a small, black whale around twenty feet long. The

Indians were cutting the whale's blubber into long strips when they saw the shallop approaching and fled.

Once ashore, the Pilgrims built themselves a barricade and a large fire, and as night descended, they noticed the smoke from another fire about four miles away. The next day was spent looking for a possible settlement site, with some of them taking to the shallop while others remained on land. Once again, they found plenty of graves and abandoned wigwams, but no people and no suitable places to anchor a large ship. They decided to sail for Thievish Harbor the following day.

Toward nightfall, the shore party met with those in the shallop at a tidal creek known today as Herring River. As they had done the previous night, they built themselves a circular barricade of tree trunks and branches, with a small opening where they stationed several guards. Around midnight, the silence was broken by "a great hideous cry." The watchmen shouted out, "Arm! Arm!" Several muskets were fired, and all was silent once again. One of the sailors said he'd heard wolves make a similar noise in Newfoundland. This seemed to comfort them, and they went back to sleep.

About 5 A.M. they began to rouse themselves. Most of them were armed with matchlocks—muskets equipped with long-burning wicks that were used to light the gunpowder. They were not the most reliable weapons, particularly in the wet and cold, since it was difficult to keep the powder dry. Several men decided to fire off their guns, just to make sure they were still working.

After prayer, they began to prepare themselves for breakfast and the long journey ahead. In the predawn twilight, some of the men carried their weapons and armor down to the shallop. Laying them beside the boat, they returned to the camp for breakfast. It was then they heard another "great and strange cry."

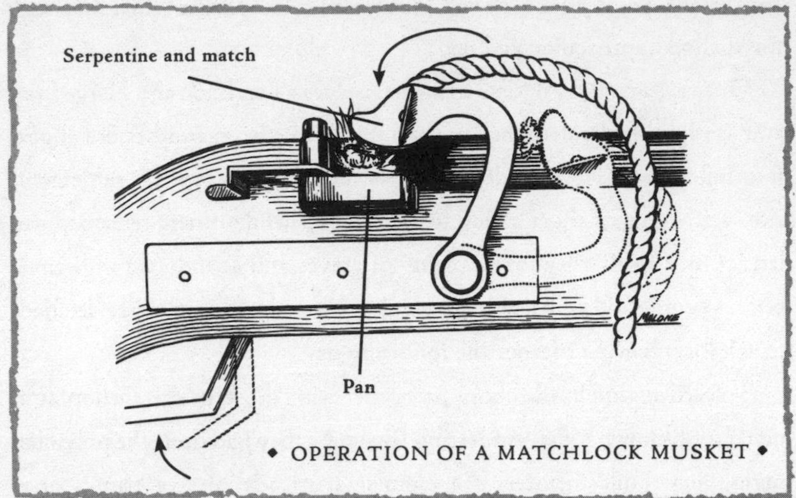

◆ OPERATION OF A MATCHLOCK MUSKET ◆

One of the men burst out of the trees and came running for the barricade, screaming, "They are men—Indians, Indians!" Suddenly the air was filled with arrows. Every man reached for his gun. They dipped their matches into the embers of the fire, and with their matches lit, began to blast away. But Standish ordered them "not to shoot, till we could take aim." He didn't know how many Indians were out there in the woods, and they might need every shot.

In the meantime, those who had left their muskets beside the shallop sprinted back to get them. The Indians soon had them trapped behind the boat. Standish and those guarding the entrance to the barricade called out to make sure they were unhurt. "Well, well, everyone," they shouted. "Be of good courage!" Three of them at the boat fired their muskets, but the others were without a way to light their matches. One of the men in the barricade picked up a burning log from the fire and ran with it to the shallop, an act of bravery that, according to Bradford, "did not a little discourage our enemies." For their part, the Indians' war cries were a particularly potent psychological weapon that the Pilgrims would never forget, later transcribing them as "Woath! Woach! Ha! Ha! Hach! Woach!"

They estimated that there were at least thirty Indians, "although some thought that they were many more yet in the dark of the morning." As the French explorer Samuel Champlain had discovered fourteen years earlier on the south coast of Cape Cod, the Indians' bows and arrows were fearsome weapons. Made from a five-and-a-half-foot piece of solid hickory, maple, ash, or witch hazel, a Native bow was so powerful that one of Champlain's men was skewered by an arrow that had already passed through his dog—making a gruesome shish kebab of the French sailor and his pet.

The feathered arrows were over a yard long, and each warrior kept as many as fifty of them in a quiver made from dried reeds. With his quiver slung over his left shoulder and with the hair on the right side of his head cut short so as not to interfere with the bowstring, a Native warrior was capable of firing arrows much faster than a musket-equipped Englishman could fire bullets. Indeed, it was possible for a skilled bowman to have as many as five arrows in the air at once, and the Pilgrims were forced to take shelter as best they could.

There was one Indian in particular, "a lusty man and no whit less valiant, who was thought to be their captain." He stood behind a tree within "half a musket shot" of the barricade, peppering them with arrows as the Pilgrims did their best to blast him to bits. The Native leader dodged three different gunshots but, seeing one of the Englishman taking "full aim at him," wisely decided to retreat. As fragments of bark and wood flew around him, he let out "an extraordinary shriek" and disappeared with his men into the woods.

Some of the Pilgrims, led no doubt by Standish, followed for about a quarter of a mile, then stopped to shoot off their muskets. "This we did," Bradford wrote, "that they might see we were not afraid of them nor discouraged." Before they departed in the shallop, they collected a total of eighteen arrows, "some . . . headed with brass, others with harts' horn, and others with eagles' claws," for eventual shipment back to England. None of the men had suffered even a scratch. "Thus it pleased God," Bradford wrote, "to vanquish our enemies and give us deliverance."

Despite Bradford's claims, what became known as the First Encounter could hardly be considered a victory. The Pilgrims could not blast, fight, and kill their way to a permanent settlement in New England. After the First Encounter, it was clear that friends were going to be difficult to find here on Cape Cod.

It was on to Thievish Harbor.

◆ ◆ ◆ With the wind out of the southeast, they sailed along the southern edge of Cape Cod Bay. Then the weather got worse. The wind picked up, and with the temperature hovering around freezing, sleet combined with the salt spray of the bay to drench the passengers to the bone. The wind continued to build, and as night came on, the boat became unmanageable in the large waves. All seemed lost, when the pilot, Robert Coppin, cried out, "Be of good cheer, I see the harbor!" By now it was blowing a gale, and in the freezing rain, the visibility was terrible. But Coppin saw something that convinced him they were about to enter Thievish Harbor.

They were bashing through the rising seas when their mast splintered into three pieces. Once they'd gathered up the broken mast and sail and stowed them away, they took up the oars and started to row. The tide, at least, was with them. But it quickly became clear that instead of the entrance to a harbor, they were steering for a wave-pummeled beach where the huge breakers might destroy their boat and kill them all. Coppin cried out, "Lord be merciful unto us, for my eyes never saw this place before!"

Just when all seemed lost, the sailor at the steering oar cried out some much-needed words of encouragement, and with the waves bursting against the shallop's side, they tried to row their way out of danger. "So he bid them be of good cheer," Bradford wrote, "and row lustily, for there was a fair sound before them, and he doubted not but they should find one place or other where they might ride in safety."

The shallop had nearly run into a shallow cove at the end of a thin, sandy peninsula called the Gurnet. Once they rowed the shallop around the tip of the Gurnet, they found themselves in the shelter of what they later discovered was an island.

In the deepening darkness of the windy night, they discussed what they should do next. Some insisted that they remain aboard the shallop in case of Indian attack. But most of them were more fearful of freezing to death, so they went ashore and built a large fire. When at midnight the wind shifted to the northwest and the temperature dropped till "it froze hard," all were glad that they had decided to come ashore.

The next day, a Saturday, proved to be "a fair, sunshining day." They now realized that they were on a heavily wooded island and, for the time being, safe from Indian attack. John Clark, one of the *Mayflower*'s pilots, had been the first to set foot on the island, and from that day forward it was known as Clark's Island.

They were on the western edge of a large, wonderfully sheltered bay. Even though they had "so many motives for haste," they decided to spend the day on the island, "where they might dry their stuff, fix their pieces, and rest themselves." The shallop needed a mast, and they undoubtedly cut down as straight and sturdy a tree as they could find and fashioned it into a new spar. The following day was a Sunday, and as Bradford recorded, "on the Sabbath day we rested."

They spent Monday exploring the harbor that was to become their new home. They tested the water's depth and found it deep enough for ships the size of the *Mayflower.* They went on land, but nowhere in either *Of Plymouth Plantation* or *Mourt's Relation,* the book Bradford and Winslow wrote after their first year in America, is there any mention of a Pilgrim stepping on a rock.

Like Cape Cod to the southeast, the shore of Plymouth Bay is nondescript and sandy. But at the foot of a high hill, just to the north of a brook, was a rock that must have been impossible to miss. More than twice as big as the mangled chunk of stone that is called Plymouth Rock today, this two-hundred-ton granite boulder stood above the low shoreline. But did the Pilgrims use it as a landing place?

• *A photograph from the nineteenth century that shows the sandy and rocky coast where the Pilgrims first arrived.*

At half tide and above, a small boat could have sailed right up alongside the rock. For these explorers, who were suffering from chills and coughs after several weeks of wading up and down the frigid tidal flats of Cape Cod, using the rock as a landing point must have been difficult to resist. But if they did use it as their first stepping-stone onto the banks of Plymouth Harbor, Bradford never made note of the historic event. That would be left to later generations of mythmakers.

They marched across the shores of Plymouth "and found divers cornfields and little running brooks, a place (as they supposed) fit for situation." Best of all, despite the signs of farming, they found no evidence of any recent Indian settlements. The next day they boarded the shallop and sailed for the *Mayflower* with the good news.

It had been a long month of exploration. Later, looking back on their trek along the shore of Cape Cod, Bradford could not help but see their journey in biblical terms. New World Israelites, they had, with God's help, finally found their Canaan. But back then, in the late afternoon of Tuesday, December 12, as the shallop approached the *Mayflower*, Bradford and his companions had little reason to believe they had found the Promised Land.

Much of Plymouth Harbor was so shallow that a ship the size of the *Mayflower*, which was twelve feet deep, had to anchor more than a mile from shore. The harbor was also without a navigable river extending into the land's interior. It was true that there were no Native settlements nearby, but that didn't mean they wouldn't be attacked. The Indians in the region had already surprised them once; it would probably happen again. Worst of all, they were approaching what Bradford called "the heart of winter," and many of them were sick—indeed, some were on the verge of death.

And then that evening, when they returned to the *Mayflower* after a long day's sail across the bay, William Bradford received what would have been, for many men, the final blow. He learned that five days before, Dorothy May Bradford, his wife of seven years and the mother of his three-year-old son, John, had slipped over the side of the *Mayflower* and drowned.

◆ ◆ ◆ Bradford never wrote about the circumstances of his wife's death. Much later in the century, the Puritan historian Cotton Mather recorded that Dorothy Bradford had accidentally fallen overboard and "was drowned in the harbor." That she fell from an anchored ship has caused some to wonder whether she committed suicide.

Dorothy certainly had reasons to despair: She had not seen her son in more than four months; her husband had left the day before on his third dangerous trip away from her in as many weeks. On the same day the shallop had departed, seven-year-old Jasper More, one of the four abandoned children placed on the *Mayflower*, died in the care of the Brewster family. Two other More children would die in the months ahead. For Dorothy, whose own young son was on the other side of the Atlantic, the deaths of these and the other children may have been especially difficult to bear.

We think of the Pilgrims as tough adventurers strengthened by religious faith, but they were also human beings in the midst of what was, and continues to be, one of the most difficult emotional challenges a person can face: immigration and exile. Less than a year later, another group of English settlers arrived at Provincetown Harbor and were so overwhelmed by this "naked and barren place" that they convinced themselves that the Pilgrims must all be dead. In fear of being abandoned by the ship's captain, the panicked settlers began to strip the sails from the masts "lest the ship should get away and leave them." If Dorothy experienced just a portion of the terror and sense of abandonment that gripped these settlers, she may have felt that suicide was her only choice.

Even if his wife's death had been unintentional, Bradford firmly believed that God controlled what happened on earth; every event *meant* something. John Howland had been rescued in the midst of a storm at sea, but Dorothy, his "dearest consort," had drowned in the calm waters of Provincetown Harbor.

The only clue Bradford left us about his feelings can be found in a poem he wrote toward the end of his life.

Faint not, poor soul, in God still trust,
Fear not the things thou suffer must;
For, whom he loves he doth chastise,
And then all tears wipes from their eyes.

FIVE
The Heart of Winter

◆ ◆ ◆

THE *MAYFLOWER* LEFT Provincetown Harbor on Friday, December 15. Headwinds from the northwest prevented the ship from entering Plymouth Harbor until the following day. Both Plymouth Harbor and Duxbury Bay to the north are contained within two crescents of sand: the Gurnet, an extension of Duxbury Beach, to the north and Long Beach to the south. The *Mayflower* anchored just within Goose Point at the end of Long Beach, a mile and a half from Plymouth Rock.

Not until Wednesday, December 20, after three more days of exploration, did they decide where to begin building a permanent settlement. Some voted for Clark's Island, their camp during the shallop's first night in the harbor, as the safest spot in case of Indian attack. Others thought a river almost directly across from the island was better. Unfortunately, Jones River, which they named for the *Mayflower*'s master, was not deep enough to handle a vessel of more than 30 tons (the *Mayflower* was 180 tons), and the settlement site would have been difficult to defend against the Indians. That left the area near the Rock.

The future site of Plymouth Plantation had several advantages. Rising up from shore was a 165-foot hill that provided a spectacular view of the surrounding coastline. On a clear day, it was even possible to see the tip of Cape Cod, almost thirty miles away. A cannon-equipped fort on this hill would provide all the security they could ever hope for.

The presence of the Rock as a landing place was yet another plus. Even more important was the "very sweet brook" that flowed beside it, carving out a channel that allowed small vessels to sail not only to the

Rock but up what they called Town Brook. Just inside the brook's entrance was a wide salt marsh where, Bradford wrote, "we may harbor our shallops and boats exceedingly well." There were also several fresh-water springs along the high banks of the brook that bubbled with "as good water as can be drunk"—an increasingly important consideration since they had so little beer left.

The biggest advantage of the area was that it had already been cleared by the Indians. And yet nowhere could they find evidence of any recent Native settlements. The Pilgrims saw this as a miraculous gift from God. But if a miracle had indeed occurred at Plymouth, it had taken the form of a holocaust almost beyond human imagining.

Just three years before, even as the Pilgrims had begun preparations to settle in America, there had been between one thousand and two thousand people living along these shores. As a map drawn by Samuel Champlain in 1605 shows, the banks of the harbor had been dotted with wigwams, each with smoke rising from the hole in its roof and with fields of corn, beans, and squash growing nearby. Dugout canoes made from hollowed-out pine trees skimmed across the waters, which in summer were full of bluefish and striped bass. The lobsters were so numerous that the Indians plucked them from the shallows of the harbor.

Then, from 1616 to 1619, disease brought this centuries-old community to an end. No witnesses recorded what happened along the shores of Plymouth, but in the following decade the plagues returned, and Roger Williams, the future founder of Rhode Island, told how entire villages became emptied of people. "I have seen a poor house left alone in the wild woods," Williams wrote, "all being fled, the living not able to bury the dead. So terrible is the apprehension of an infectious disease, that not only persons, but the houses and the whole town, take flight."

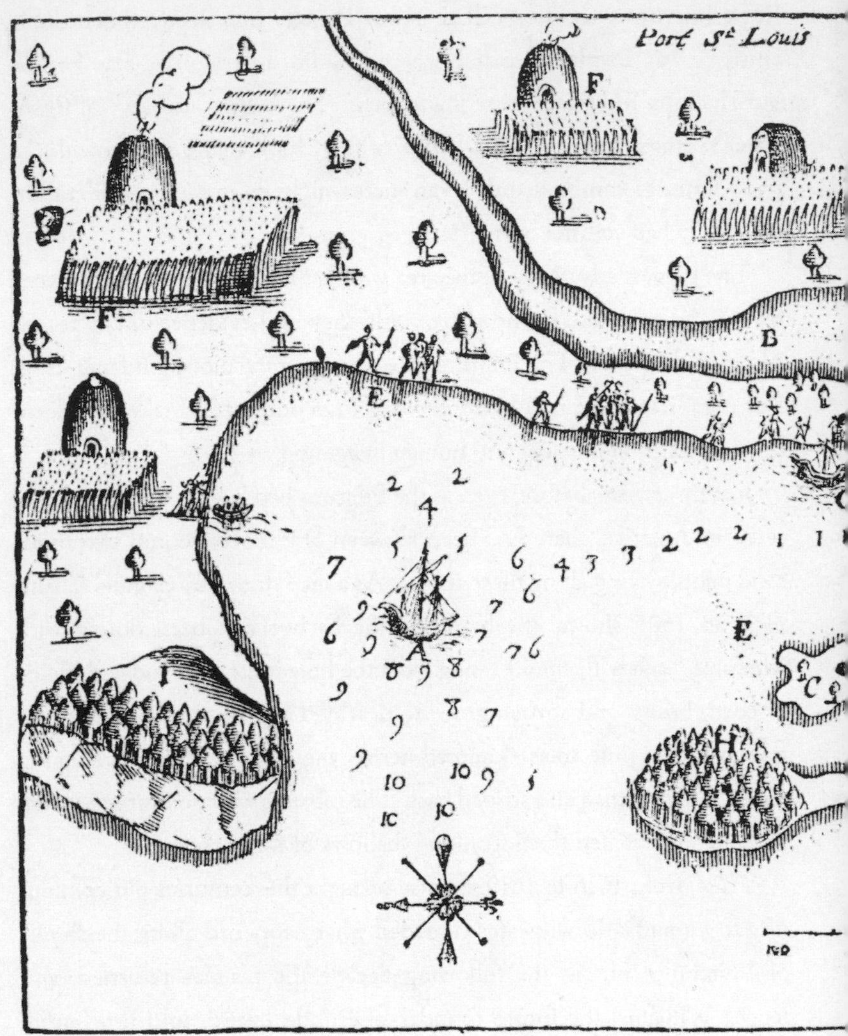

No Native dwellings remained in Plymouth in the winter of 1620, but gruesome evidence of the sickness was scattered all around the area. "[T]heir skulls and bones were found in many places lying still above the ground," Bradford wrote. "A very sad spectacle to behold."

◆ *Samuel Champlain's map of Plymouth Harbor.*

It was here, on the bone-whitened hills of Plymouth, that the Pilgrims hoped to begin a new life.

◆ ◆ ◆ They decided to build their houses on what is called today Cole's Hill, overlooking the salt marsh. Situated between the shore and the much higher hill, soon to be known as Fort Hill, Cole's Hill was flat enough for a small settlement and was easily accessible from the brook. That night twenty people remained on shore. They planned to begin building houses the next morning.

But Thursday, December 21, proved so stormy that the *Mayflower* was forced to set an additional anchor. The people on shore were without food, so despite the winds, the shallop set out from the *Mayflower* "with much ado with provisions." The terrible weather lasted throughout the following day, making it impossible to begin work on the houses.

In the meantime, the *Mayflower* had become a grim hospital ship. In addition to colds, coughs, and fevers, scurvy tormented the passengers.

James Chilton had died even before the *Mayflower* arrived in Plymouth Harbor. That Thursday, Richard Britteridge passed away, followed two days later by Christopher Martin's stepson, Solomon Prower. On Friday morning, Mary Allerton gave birth to a stillborn son.

Not until Saturday, December 23, were they able to transport a work party from the *Mayflower* to shore. With their axes and saws, they felled trees and carried the timber to the building site. The fact that Monday, December 25, was Christmas Day meant little to the Pilgrims, who believed that religious celebrations of this sort were an insult to the true word of Christ. Of more importance to them, December 25 was the day they erected the frame of their first house. "[N]o man rested that day," Bradford wrote. But toward sunset, the familiar cries of Indians were heard in the surrounding forest. The Pilgrims took up their muskets and stared tensely into the darkness as the cries echoed briefly and died away.

The Pilgrims' intense spiritual lives did not prevent them from living with the constant fear that Satan and his minions were *out there*, working against them. It was a fear that must have been difficult to contain as they stared into the gloom of the American night. After waiting a few more tense minutes, they decided to send the shallop back to the *Mayflower*, leaving the usual number of twenty ashore. That night they were drenched by yet another rainstorm.

◆ ◆ ◆ It took them two more weeks to complete the first building, a twenty-foot-square "common house." Known as an earthfast house, the Pilgrims' first structure probably had walls of cut tree trunks interwoven with branches and twigs that were cemented together with clay. This "wattle-and-daub" construction was typical of farmers' cottages in rural England, as was the building's thatched roof, which was made of cattails and reeds from the nearby marsh. The house's tiny windows were made of parchment. The chimney—if, in fact, the house did have a chimney instead of a simple hole in the roof—would have been made of four boards that funneled up the smoke from an open fire on the dirt floor. It was a dark and smoky space, but for the first time, the Pilgrims had a real roof over their heads.

On the morning of Thursday, December 28, they turned their attention to the high hill, where they began to construct a wooden platform on which to mount the various cannons they had brought with them aboard the *Mayflower.* This was also the day they started to plan the organization of the settlement. First they needed to decide how many houses to build. It was determined that "all single men that had no wives to join them" should find a family to live with, which brought the total number of houses down to nineteen. From the beginning, it was decided that "every man should build his own house, thinking by that course, men would make more haste than working in common."

Miles Standish appears to have had a hand in determining the layout of the town. The most easily defended settlement pattern consisted of a street with parallel alleys and a cross street. The Pilgrims created a similar design that included two rows of houses "for safety." For the time being, Plymouth was without a church and town green, features that came to typify a New England town.

In the weeks ahead, the death toll required them to change their plans. Instead of nineteen, only seven houses were built the first year, plus another four buildings for common use, including a small fortlike structure called a rendezvous. The houses were built along a street that ran from Fort Hill down to the sea. Known today as Leyden Street, it was crossed by a "highway" running from north to south down to Town Brook. Around this intersection, the town of Plymouth slowly came into being, even as death reduced the newcomers to half their original number.

◆ ◆ ◆ Thursday, January 11, was "a fair day." Given the uncertainty of the weather, they knew they must make as much progress as possible on the houses—especially since, it was still assumed, the *Mayflower* would soon be returning to England.

The frantic pace of the last two months was beginning to take its toll

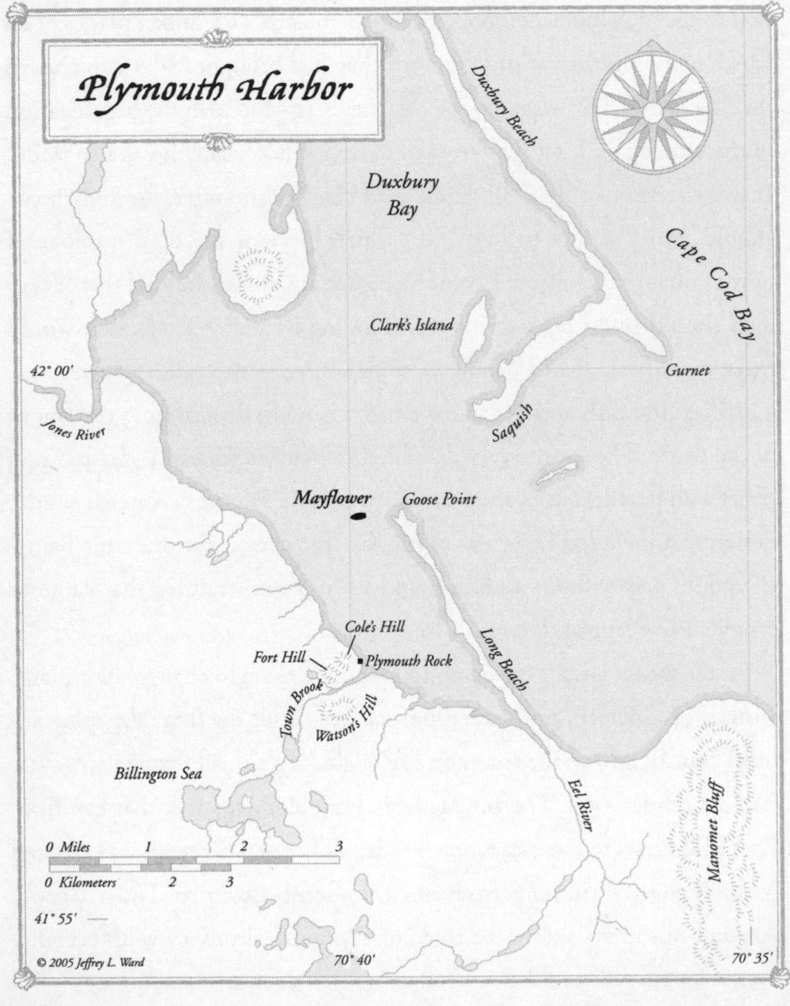

on William Bradford. He had suffered through a month of exposure to the freezing cold on the exploratory missions, and the stiffness in his ankles made it difficult to walk. But there was more troubling him than physical discomfort. Dorothy's passing had opened the floodgates: Death was everywhere.

That day, as Bradford worked beside the others, he was "vehemently taken with a grief and pain" that pierced him to his hipbone. He collapsed and was carried to the common house. At first it was feared Bradford might not last the night. But "in time through God's mercy," he began to improve, even as illness continued to spread among them.

The common house soon became as "full of beds as they could lie one by another." Like the Native Americans before them, the Pilgrims were struggling to survive on a hillside where death had become a way of life. In the days ahead, so many fell ill that there were barely half a dozen people left to tend the sick. Progress on the houses came to a standstill as the healthy ones became full-time nurses—preparing meals, tending fires, washing the "loathsome clothes," and emptying chamber pots. Bradford later singled out William Brewster and Miles Standish as incredible sources of strength:

> And yet the Lord so upheld these persons as in this general calamity they were not at all infected either with sickness or lameness. And what I have said of these I may say of many others who died in this general visitation, and others yet living; that whilst they had health, yea or any strength continuing, they were not wanting to any that had need of them. And I doubt not that their recompense is with the Lord.

◆ *William Bradford's silver drinking cup, made in England in 1634.*

At one point, Bradford requested a small container of beer from the *Mayflower*, hoping that it might help in his recovery. With little left for the return voyage to England, the sailors responded that if Bradford "were their own father he should have none." Soon after, disease began to ravage the crew of the *Mayflower*, including many of their officers and "lustiest men." Early on, the boatswain, "a proud young man," according to Bradford, who would often "curse and scoff at the passengers," grew ill. Despite his treatment of them, several of the Pilgrims attended to the young officer. In his final hours, the boatswain experienced a kind of deathbed conversion, crying out, "Oh, you, I now see, show your love like Christians indeed one to another, but we let one another die like dogs." Master Jones also appears to have undergone a change of heart. Soon after his own men began to fall ill, he let it be known that beer was now available to the Pilgrims, "though he drunk water homeward bound."

◆ ◆ ◆ On Friday, January 12, John Goodman and Peter Brown were cutting thatch for their roofs about a mile and a half from the settlement. They had with them the two dogs, a small spaniel and a huge mastiff. English mastiffs were frequently used in bearbaitings—a savage sport popular in London in which a dog and a bear fought each other to the death. Mastiffs were also favored by English noblemen, who used them to catch poachers. The Pilgrims' mastiff appears to have been more of a guard dog brought to protect them against wild beasts and Indians.

That afternoon, Goodman and Brown paused from their labors for a midday snack, then took the two dogs for a short walk in the woods. Near the banks of a pond they saw a large deer, and the dogs took off in pursuit. By the time Goodman and Brown had caught up with the dogs, they were all thoroughly lost.

It began to rain, and by nightfall it was snowing. They had hoped to find an Indian wigwam for shelter but were forced, in Bradford's words, "to make the earth their bed, and the element their covering." Then they heard what they took to be "two lions roaring exceedingly for a long time together." These may have been eastern cougars, also known as mountain lions, a species that once ranged throughout most of North and South America. The cry of a cougar has been compared to the scream of a woman being murdered, and Goodman and Brown were now thoroughly terrified. They decided that if a lion should come after them, they would scramble into the limbs of a tree and leave the mastiff to do her best to defend them.

All that night they paced back and forth at the foot of a tree, trying to keep warm in the freezing darkness. They still had the sickles they had used to cut thatch, and with each wail of the cougars, they gripped the handles a little tighter. The mastiff wanted desperately to chase whatever was out there in the woods, so they took turns holding back the dog by her collar. At daybreak, they once again set out in search of the settlement.

After passing several streams and ponds, Goodman and Brown came upon a huge piece of open land that had recently been burned by the Indians. For centuries, the Indians had been burning the landscape on a seasonal basis, a form of land management that created surprisingly open forests, where a person might easily walk or even ride a horse amid the trees. Come summer, this five-mile-wide section of blackened ground would resemble, to a remarkable degree, the wide and rolling fields of their native England.

Not until the afternoon did Goodman and Brown find a hill that gave them a view of the harbor. Now that they were able to orient themselves, they were soon on their way back home. When they arrived that night, they were, according to Bradford, "ready to faint with travail and want of victuals, and almost famished with cold." Goodman's frostbitten feet were so swollen that they had to cut away his shoes.

◆ ◆ ◆ The final weeks of January were spent transporting goods from the *Mayflower* to shore. On Sunday, February 4, yet another storm lashed Plymouth Harbor. The rain was so fierce that it washed the clay daubing from the sides of the houses, while the *Mayflower*, which was floating much higher in the water than usual after the removal of so much freight, wobbled dangerously in the wind.

Tensions among the Pilgrims were high. With two, sometimes three people dying a day, there might not be a plantation left by the arrival of spring. Almost everyone had lost a loved one. Christopher Martin, the *Mayflower*'s governor, had died in early January, soon to be followed by his wife, Mary. Three other families—the Rigsdales, Tinkers, and Turners—were entirely wiped out, with more to follow. Thirteen-year-old Mary Chilton, whose father had died back in Provincetown Harbor, became an orphan when her mother passed away that winter. Other orphans included seventeen-year-old Joseph Rogers, twelve-year-old Samuel Fuller, eighteen-year-old John Crackston, seventeen-year-old Priscilla Mullins, and thirteen-year-old Elizabeth

Tilley (who also lost her aunt and uncle, Edward and Ann). By the middle of March, there were four widowers: William Bradford, Miles Standish, Francis Eaton, and Isaac Allerton; Allerton was left with three surviving children between the ages of four and eight. With the death of her husband, William, Susanna White, mother to the newborn Peregrine and five-year-old Resolved, became the plantation's only surviving widow. By the spring, 52 of the 102 who had originally arrived at Provincetown were dead.

◆ *The wicker cradle reputed to have been brought to America by William and Susanna White.*

And yet, amid all this tragedy, there were miraculous exceptions. The families of William Brewster, Francis Cook, Stephen Hopkins, and John Billington were completely untouched by disease. The Strangers Billington and Hopkins had a total of six living children among them, accounting for more than a fifth of the young people in the entire plantation. The future of Plymouth was beginning to look less like a Separatist community of saints than a mix of both groups.

Even more worrisome than the emotional and physical strain of all this death was the growing fear of Indian attack. The Pilgrims knew that the Native inhabitants were watching them, but so far the Indians had refused to come forward. It was quite possible that they were simply waiting the Pilgrims out until there were not enough left to put up a fight. It became necessary, therefore, to make the best show of strength they could.

Whenever the alarm was sounded, the sick were pulled from their beds and propped up against trees with muskets in their hands. They would do little good in case of an actual attack, but at least they were out there to be counted. The Pilgrims also tried to conceal the fact that so many of them had died by secretly burying the dead at night. They did such a good job of hiding their loved ones' remains that it was not until more than a hundred years later, when a violent rainstorm washed away the topsoil and revealed some human bones, that the location of these hastily dug graves was finally identified.

◆ ◆ ◆ On Friday, February 16, one of the Pilgrims was hidden in the reeds of a salt creek about a mile and a half from the plantation, hunting ducks. That afternoon, the duck hunter found himself closer to an Indian than any of them had so far come.

He was lying amid the cattails when a group of twelve Indians marched past him on the way to the settlement. In the woods behind him, he heard "the noise of many more." Once the Indians had safely passed, he sprang to his feet and ran for the plantation to sound the alarm. Miles Standish and Francis Cook were working in the woods when they heard the signal. They dropped their tools, ran down the hill, and armed themselves, but once again, the Indians never came. Later that day, when Standish and Cook returned to get their tools, they discovered that they'd disappeared. That night, they saw "a great fire" near where the duck hunter had first spotted the Indians.

The next day, a meeting was called "for the establishing of military orders amongst ourselves." Not surprisingly, Miles Standish was officially named their captain. In the midst of the meeting, someone realized that two Indians were standing on the top of what became known as Watson's Hill on the other side of Town Brook, about a quarter mile to the south. The meeting immediately ended, and the men hurried to get their muskets. When the Pilgrims reassembled under the direction of their newly designated captain, the Indians were still standing on the hill.

The two groups stared at each other across the valley of Town Brook. The Indians gestured for them to approach. The Pilgrims, however, made it clear that they wanted the Indians to come to them. Finally, Standish and Stephen Hopkins, with only one musket between them, began to make their way across the brook. Before they started up the hill, they laid the musket down on the ground "in sign of peace." But "the savages," Bradford wrote, "would not tarry their coming." They ran off to the shouts of "a great many more" hidden on the other side of the hill. The Pilgrims feared an assault might be imminent, "but no more came in fight."

Once Standish and Hopkins returned home, they decided it was time to mount "our great ordnances" on the hill. On Wednesday of the follow-

◆ *Although the architectural details in this drawing are inaccurate (for example, the first houses had no chimneys), this nineteenth-century depiction of the Pilgrim settlement gives a good impression of Plymouth's topography and landscape.*

ing week, Christopher Jones supervised the transportation of the "great guns" from the *Mayflower*—close to half a dozen iron cannons that ranged between four and eight feet in length and weighed as much as half a ton. With the cannons in place, each capable of hurling iron balls as big as three and a half inches in diameter as far as 1,700 yards, what was once a ramshackle collection of houses was on its way to becoming a well-defended fortress.

Jones and the sailors had brought along a freshly killed goose, crane, and mallard, and once the day's work was completed, they all sat down to a feast and were, in Bradford's words, "kindly and friendly together." Jones had originally intended to return to England as soon as the Pilgrims found a settlement site. But once disease began to ravage his crew, he realized that he must remain in Plymouth Harbor "till he saw his men begin to recover."

In early March, there were several days of unseasonably warm weather, and "birds sang in the woods most pleasantly." At precisely one o'clock on March 3, they heard their first rumble of American thunder. "It was strong and great claps," they wrote, "but short." They later realized that even though temperatures had been bitterly cold during their earlier explorations along Cape Cod, the winter had been, for the most part, unusually mild—a lucky break that undoubtedly prevented even more of them from dying.

On Friday, March 16, they had yet another meeting about military matters. And as had happened the last time they had gathered for such a purpose, they were interrupted by the Indians. But this time there was only one of them atop Watson's Hill, and unlike the previous two Indians, this man appeared to be without hesitation or fear. He began to walk toward them "very boldly." The alarm was sounded, and still the

Indian continued walking down Watson's Hill and across the brook. Once he'd climbed the path to Cole's Hill, he came past the row of houses toward the rendezvous, where the women and children had been assembled in case of attack. It was clear that if no one stopped him, the Indian was going to walk right into the entrance of the rendezvous. Finally, some of the men stepped into the Indian's path and indicated that he was not to go in. Apparently enjoying the fuss he had created, the Indian "saluted" them and with great enthusiasm spoke the now famous words, "Welcome, Englishmen!"

SIX
In a Dark and Dismal Swamp

◆ ◆ ◆

THEY COULD NOT help but stare. He was so different from themselves. For one thing, he towered over them, "a tall straight man." His hair was black, short in front and long in back, and his face was hairless. Interestingly, the Pilgrims made no mention of his skin color in their writings.

What impressed them most was that he was "stark naked," with just a fringed strap of leather around his waist. When a cold gust of wind kicked up, one of the Pilgrims was moved to throw his coat over the Indian's bare shoulders.

He was armed with a bow and just two arrows, "the one headed, the other unheaded." The Pilgrims do not seem to have attached any special significance to them, but the arrows may have represented the alternatives of war and peace. In any event, they offered him something to eat. He immediately requested beer.

With their supplies running short, they offered him some "strong water"—perhaps the aqua vitae they'd drunk during their first days on Cape Cod—as well as some biscuits, butter, cheese, pudding, and a slice of roasted duck, "all of which he liked well."

He introduced himself as Samoset—at least that was how the Pilgrims heard it—but he may actually have been telling them his English name, Somerset. He was not, he explained in broken English, from this part of New England. He was a sachem from Pemaquid Point in Maine, near Monhegan Island, a region frequented by English fishermen. It was from these fishermen, many of whom he named, that he'd learned to speak English. Despite occasional trouble understanding him, the Pilgrims

◆ *A nineteenth-century engraving of the Pilgrims meeting Samoset. While the Pilgrim and Native American dress here is based on later stereotypes, this image does show the cultural differences between the two groups.*

hung on Samoset's every word as he told them about their new home.

He explained that the harbor's name was Patuxet, and that just about every person who had once lived there had "died of an extraordinary plague." The supreme leader of the region was named Massasoit, who lived in a place called Pokanoket about forty miles to the southwest. Samoset said that the Nausets controlled the part of Cape Cod where the Pilgrims had stolen the corn. The Nausets were "ill affected toward the English" after Hunt had abducted twenty or so of their men back in 1614. He also said that there was another Indian back in Pokanoket named Squanto, who spoke even better English than he did.

With darkness approaching, the Pilgrims were ready for their guest to leave. As a practical matter, they had nowhere for him to sleep; in addition, they were not yet sure whether they could trust him. But Samoset made it clear he wanted to spend the night. Perhaps because they assumed he'd fear abduction and quickly leave, they offered to take him out to the *Mayflower*. Samoset cheerfully called their bluff and climbed into the shallop. Claiming that high winds and low tides prevented them from leaving shore, the Pilgrims finally allowed him to spend the night with Stephen Hopkins and his family. Samoset left the next morning, promising to return in a few days with some of Massasoit's men.

◆ ◆ ◆ All that winter, Massasoit had watched and waited. From the Nausets he had learned of the Pilgrims' journey along the bay side of Cape Cod and their eventual arrival at Patuxet. His own warriors had kept him updated as to the progress of their various building projects, and despite the Pilgrims' secret burials, he undoubtedly knew that many of the English had died over the winter.

For as long as any Indians could remember, European fishermen and explorers had been visiting New England, but these people were different. First of all, there were women and children—probably the first European women and children the Indians had ever seen. They were also behaving unusually. Instead of attempting to trade with the Indians, they kept to themselves and seemed much more interested in building a settlement. These English people were here to stay.

Massasoit was unsure what to do next. A little over a year before, the sailors aboard an English ship had killed a large number of his people for no reason. As a consequence, Massasoit had felt compelled to attack the explorer Thomas Dermer when he arrived the following summer with Squanto at his side, and most of Dermer's men had been killed in fights on Cape Cod and Martha's Vineyard. Squanto had been taken prisoner on the Vineyard, but now he was with Massasoit in Pokanoket. Squanto

◆ *Early-twentieth-century painting of Massasoit.*

had told him of his years in Europe, and once the *Mayflower* appeared at Provincetown Harbor and made its way to Plymouth, he had offered his services as an interpreter. But Massasoit was not yet sure whose side Squanto was on.

Over the winter, Massasoit gathered together the region's powwows, or shamans, for a three-day meeting "in a dark and dismal swamp." Swamps were where the Indians went in time of war. They provided a natural shelter for the sick and old; they were also highly spiritual places, where unseen spirits mixed with the hoots of owls.

Massasoit's first impulse was to curse the English. Bradford later learned that the powwows had first attempted to "execrate them with their conjurations." Powwows communicated with the spirit world in an extremely physical manner, through what the English described as "horrible outcries, hollow bleatings, painful wrestlings, and smiting their own bodies." Massasoit's powwows were probably not the first and certainly not the last Native Americans to turn their magic on the English. To the north, at the mouth of the Merrimack River, lived Passaconaway, a sachem who was also a powwow—an unusual combination that gave him extraordinary powers. It was said he could "make the water burn, the rocks move, the trees dance, metamorphise himself into a flaming man."

But not even Passaconaway was able to injure the English. In 1660, he admitted to his people, "I was as much an enemy to the English at their first coming into these parts, as anyone whatsoever, and did try all ways and means possible to have destroyed them, at least to have prevented them sitting down here, but I could in no way effect it; . . . therefore I advise you never to contend with the English, nor make war with them." At some point, Massasoit's powwows appear to have made a similar recommendation.

The powwows were not the only ones who discussed what to do with the Pilgrims. There was also Squanto. Ever since the appearance of the *Mayflower,* the former captive had begun to work his own kind of magic on Massasoit, insisting that the worst thing he could do was to attack the Pilgrims. Not only did they have muskets and cannons, they possessed the seventeenth-century equivalent of a weapon of mass destruction: the plague. At some point, Squanto began to insist that the Pilgrims had the ability to unleash disease on their enemies. If Massasoit became an ally to the Pilgrims, he would suddenly be in a position to free the Pokanokets from the Narragansetts. "[E]nemies that were [now] too strong for him," Squanto promised, "would be constrained to bow to him."

Reluctantly, Massasoit decided that he must "make friendship" with the English. To do so, he needed an interpreter, and Squanto—the only one fluent in both English and Massachusett, the language of the Pokanoket—assumed that he was the man for the job. Though he'd been swayed by Squanto's advice, Massasoit didn't want to place his faith in the former captive, whom he regarded as a trickster with selfish motives. So he first sent Samoset, a visiting sachem, to the Pilgrim settlement.

But now it was time for Massasoit to visit the English himself. He had to turn to Squanto.

◆ ◆ ◆ On March 22, five days after his initial visit, Samoset returned to Plymouth with four other Indians, Squanto among them. Squanto spoke about places that now seemed like a distant dream to the Pilgrims—besides spending time in Spain and Newfoundland, Squanto had lived in the Corn Hill section of London. The Indians had brought a few furs to trade, along with some fresh herring. But the real purpose of their visit was to inform the Pilgrims that Massasoit and his brother Quadequina were nearby. About an hour later, the sachem appeared on Watson's Hill with a large entourage of warriors.

The Pilgrims described him as "a very lusty [or strong] man, in his best years, an able body, grave of countenance, and spare of speech." Massasoit stood on the hill, his face painted dark red, his entire head glistening with bear grease. Draped around his neck were a wide necklace made of white shell beads and a long knife hanging from a string. His men's faces were also painted, "some black, some red, some yellow, and some white, some with crosses, and other antic works." Some of

◆ *Nineteenth-century engraving of the first peace treaty between Governor Carver and Massasoit.*

them had furs draped over their shoulders; others were naked. But every one of them possessed a stout bow and a quiver of arrows. These were unmistakably warriors: "all strong, tall, all men in appearance." Moreover, there were sixty of them.

For the Pilgrims, who could not have gathered more than twenty adult males and whose own military leader was not even five and a half feet tall, it must have been a most intimidating display of physical strength and power. Squanto ventured over to Watson's Hill and returned with the message that the Pilgrims should send someone to speak to Massasoit. Edward Winslow's wife, Elizabeth, was so sick that she would be dead in just two days, but he agreed to act as Governor Carver's messenger. Clad in armor and with a sword at his side, he went with Squanto to greet the sachem.

First he presented Massasoit and his brother with a pair of knives, some copper chains, some alcohol, and a few biscuits, "which were all willingly accepted." Then he delivered a brief speech. King James of

England saluted the sachem "with words of love and peace," Winslow proclaimed, and looked to him as a friend and ally. He also said that Governor Carver wished to speak and trade with him and hoped to establish a formal peace. Winslow was under the impression that Squanto "did not well express it," but Massasoit seemed pleased. The sachem ate the biscuits and drank the liquor, then asked if Winslow was willing to sell his sword and armor. The Pilgrim messenger politely declined. It was decided that Winslow would remain with Quadequina as a hostage while Massasoit went with twenty of his men, minus their bows, to meet the governor.

Captain Standish and half a dozen men armed with muskets met Massasoit at the brook. They exchanged greetings, and after seven of the warriors were designated as hostages, Standish accompanied Massasoit to a house, still under construction, where a green rug and several cushions had been spread out on the dirt floor. On cue, a drummer and trumpeter began to play as Governor Carver and a small parade of musketeers made their way to the house.

Upon his arrival, Carver kissed Massasoit's hand; the sachem did the same to Carver's, and the two leaders sat down on the green rug. It was now time for Massasoit to share in yet another ceremonial drink of liquor. Carver took a swig of aqua vitae and passed the cup to Massasoit, who took a large gulp and broke into a sweat. As the meeting continued, during which the two groups worked out a six-point agreement, Massasoit was observed to tremble "for fear."

Instead of Carver and the Pilgrims, it may have been Massasoit's interpreter who caused the sachem to shake. The Pilgrims later learned that Squanto claimed they kept the plague in barrels buried beneath their storehouse. The barrels actually contained gunpowder, but the Pilgrims undoubtedly guarded the storehouse, which made Squanto's claims believable. If the interpreter told Massasoit of the deadly contents of the barrels during the meeting on March 22, it is little wonder Massasoit was seen to tremble.

Bradford and Winslow recorded the agreement with the Pokanoket sachem as follows:

1. That neither he nor any of his should injure or do hurt to any of our people.
2. And if any of his did hurt to any of ours, he should send the offender, that we might punish him.
3. That if any of our tools were taken away when our people were at work, he should cause them to be restored, and if ours did any harm to any of his, we would do the like to him.
4. If any did unjustly war against him, we would aid him; if any did war against us, he should aid us.
5. He should send to his neighbor confederates, to certify them of this, that they might not wrong us, but might be likewise comprised in the conditions of peace.
6. That when their men came to us, they should leave their bows and arrows behind them, as we should do our pieces when we came to them.

Once the agreement had been completed, Massasoit was escorted from the settlement, and his brother was given a similar reception. Quadequina quickly noticed something that his higher-ranking brother had not chosen to comment on. Even though the Indians had been required to lay down their bows, the Pilgrims continued to carry their muskets—a clear violation of the treaty they had just signed with Massasoit. Quadequina "made signs of dislike, that [the guns] should be carried away." The English could not help but admit that the young Indian had a point, and the muskets were put aside.

Squanto and Samoset spent the night with the Pilgrims while Massasoit and his men, who had brought along their wives and children, slept in the woods, just a half mile away. Massasoit promised to return in a little more than a week to plant corn on the southern side of Town Brook. Squanto, it was agreed, would remain with the English. As a final gesture of friendship, the Pilgrims sent the sachem and his people a large kettle of English peas, "which pleased them well, and so they went their way."

After almost five months of uncertainty and fear, the Pilgrims had finally established diplomatic relations with the Native leader who, as far as they could tell, ruled this portion of New England. But as they were soon to find out, Massasoit's power was not as widespread as they would have liked. The Pokanokets had decided to align themselves with the English, but many of Massasoit's allies had yet to be convinced that the Pilgrims were good for New England.

The next day, Squanto left to fish for eels. At that time of year, the eels lay sleeping in the mud, and after wading out into the cold water of a nearby tidal creek, he used his feet to "trod them out." By the end of the day, he returned with so many eels that he could barely lift them all with one hand. That night the Pilgrims ate the eels happily, praising them as "fat and sweet," and Squanto was on his way to becoming the one person in New England they could not do without.

◆◆◆Two weeks later, on April 5, the *Mayflower*, her empty hold filled with stones from the Plymouth Harbor shore to replace the weight of the unloaded cargo, set sail for England. Like the Pilgrims, the crew had been cut down by disease. Jones had lost his boatswain, his gunner, three quartermasters, the cook, and more than a dozen sailors. He had also lost a cooper, but not to illness. John Alden had decided to stay in Plymouth.

The *Mayflower* made excellent time on her voyage back across the Atlantic. The same winds that had battered her the previous fall now pushed her along, and she arrived at her home port of Rotherhithe just down the Thames River from London, on May 6, 1621—less than half the time it had taken her to sail to America. Master Jones learned that his wife, Josian, had given birth to a son named John. Soon enough, Jones and the *Mayflower* were on their next voyage, this time to France for a cargo of salt.

Perhaps still suffering the effects of that awful winter in Plymouth, Jones died on March 5, 1622, after his return from France. For the next two years, the *Mayflower* lay idle, not far from her captain's grave on the banks of the Thames. By 1624, just four years after her historic voyage to America, the ship had become a rotting hulk. That year, she was found to be worth just £128 (roughly $24,000 today), less than a sixth of her value back in 1609. Her subsequent fate is unknown, but she was probably broken up for scrap, the final casualty of a voyage that had cost her master everything he could give.

◆ ◆ ◆ Soon after the *Mayflower* departed for England, the shallow waters of Town Brook became alive with fish. Two species of herring—alewives and bluebacks—returned to the fresh waters where they had been born in order to reproduce.

Squanto explained that these fish were essential to planting a successful corn crop. Given the poor quality of the land surrounding Plymouth, it was necessary to fertilize the soil with dead herring. Although Native women were the ones who did the farming (with the sole exception of planting tobacco, which was considered men's work), Squanto knew enough of their techniques to give the Pilgrims a crash course in Indian agriculture.

The seed the Pilgrims had stolen on the Cape is known today as northern flint corn, with kernels of several colors, and was called *weachimineash* by the Indians. Using mattocks—hoes with stone heads and wooden handles—the Indians gathered mounds of earth about a yard wide, where several fish were included with the seeds of corn. Once the corn had sprouted, beans and squash were added to the mounds. The vines from the beans attached to the growing cornstalks, creating a blanket of shade that protected the plants' roots against the hot summer sun while also

◆ *Corn that was called* **weachimineash** *by the Wampanoags, or northern flint corn today.*

keeping out weeds. Thanks to Squanto, the Pilgrims' stolen corn thrived, while their own barley and peas suffered in the soil of the New World.

In April, while laboring in the fields on an unusually hot day, Governor Carver began to complain about a pain in his head. He returned to his house to lie down and quickly lapsed into a coma. A few days later, he was dead.

After a winter of so many secret burials, the Pilgrims laid their governor to rest with as much pomp and circumstance as they could muster—"with some volleys of shot by all that bore arms." Carver's brokenhearted wife followed her husband to the grave five weeks later. Carver's one surviving male servant, John Howland, was left without a master; in addition to becoming a free man, Howland may have inherited at least a portion of Carver's estate. The humble servant who had been pulled from the ocean a few short months ago was on his way to becoming one of Plymouth's foremost citizens.

Carver's passing could not have come at a worse time. Just as the settlement was recovering from the horrors of the first winter, it had lost the man on whose judgment it had come to depend. The Pilgrims had hoped to load the *Mayflower* with goods for her return trip, but that had been impossible. With half the settlers dead and only a pile of stones in the ship's hold and a few Native artifacts to show for the thousands of pounds the Adventurers had spent, Weston and the other merchants might begin to doubt the profitability of the settlement and withdraw further financial support.

The new treaty with Massasoit had greatly reduced the threat of Indian attack, but there was still dissent inside the settlement. The tension of that terrible winter had led to angry words among many, most notably Miles Standish and John Billington. In June, Stephen Hopkins's servants Edward Doty and Edward Leister injured each other in a duel and were sentenced to have their heads and feet tied together. There was a desperate and immediate need for strong and steady leadership.

William Bradford was the natural choice. Even though he was still sick, Bradford agreed to take on the greatest challenge of his life. In addition to Isaac Allerton, who served as his assistant, he had William Brewster, Edward Winslow, and Miles Standish to look to for advice. But as governor, he inevitably came to know the loneliness of being Plymouth's ultimate decision maker. More than ever before, Bradford, who had left his son in Holland and lost his wife in Provincetown Harbor, was alone.

SEVEN
Thanksgiving

◆ ◆ ◆

A FEW WEEKS after William Bradford's election to governor, Edward Winslow and Susanna White showed the rest of the settlement that it was indeed possible to start anew. Susanna had lost her husband, William, on February 21; Edward had lost his wife, Elizabeth, on March 24. Just a month and a half later, on May 12, Edward and Susanna became the first couple in Plymouth to marry. Six weeks may seem too short a time to grieve, but in the seventeenth century, it was quite normal for a widow or widower to remarry within three months of his or her spouse's death.

In accordance with "the laudable custom of the Low Countries," Edward and Susanna were married in a civil ceremony. Bradford, who presided over the union, explained that "nowhere . . . in the Gospel" did it say a minister should be involved in a wedding. In the decades to come, marriages in Plymouth continued to be secular affairs, one of the few traditions they kept from their time in Holland.

◆ ◆ ◆ By the beginning of July, Bradford decided that they should visit "their new friend Massasoit." They had not, as of yet, had an opportunity to explore the interior of the surrounding countryside, and it was time they made their presence known beyond Plymouth and Cape Cod. They also needed to address an unexpected problem. Ever since establishing diplomatic relations with Massasoit in March, the Pilgrims had hosted a continual stream of Indian visitors, particularly from the village of Nemasket just fifteen miles to the west. If they continued to entertain and feed all these guests, they would not have enough food to survive the next winter.

They proposed a clever solution: They would present Massasoit with a copper chain; if the sachem had a messenger or friend he wanted the Pilgrims to entertain, he would give the person the chain, and the Pilgrims would happily provide him with food. All others, however, would be turned away.

On July 2, Edward Winslow and Stephen Hopkins left Plymouth at around 9 A.M., with Squanto as their guide. Besides some gifts for Massasoit (the copper chain and a red cotton horseman's coat), they carried their muskets and a cooked partridge for food. They might have a horseman's coat, but they did not, as of yet, have any horses. Like the Indians, they had to walk the forty or so miles to Pokanoket.

They soon came upon a dozen men, women, and children who were returning to Nemasket after gathering lobsters in Plymouth Harbor—one of the seasonal rituals that kept the Indians constantly on the move. As they talked with their new companions, the Englishmen learned that to walk across the land in southern New England was to travel in time. All along this narrow, hard-packed trail were circular foot-deep holes in the ground that had been dug where "any remarkable act" had occurred. It was each person's responsibility to maintain the holes and to tell fellow travelers what had once happened at that particular place so that "many things of great antiquity are fresh in memory." Winslow and Hopkins began to see that they were crossing a mythic land, where a sense of community extended far into the distant past. "So that as a man travelleth . . . ," Winslow wrote, "his journey will be the less tedious, by reason of the many historical discourses [that] will be related unto him."

They also began to appreciate why these memory holes were more important than ever before to the Native inhabitants of the region.

Everywhere they went, they were stunned by the emptiness of the place. "Thousands of men have lived there," Winslow wrote, "which died in a great plague not long since: and pity it was and is to see, so many goodly fields, and so well seated, without men to dress and manure the same." With so many dead, the Pokanokets' connection to the past was hanging by a thread—a connection that the memory holes and their stories helped to maintain.

At Nemasket, they enjoyed a meal of corn bread, herring roe, and boiled acorns. Squanto suggested that they push on another few miles before nightfall to give themselves enough time to reach Pokanoket the next day. Soon after leaving Nemasket, the path joined a narrow, twisting river called the Titicut, which was used as a kind of Native American highway. Whether by dugout canoe or by foot, the Indians followed the river between Pokanoket and Plymouth, and in the years ahead, the Titicut, which the English eventually renamed the Taunton River, led the Pilgrims to several new settlement sites above Narragansett Bay.

But the Titicut was much more than a transportation system; it also

◆ *A present-day photograph of the Taunton River where it meets Mount Hope Bay*

provided the Indians with a seasonal source of herring and other fish. Around sunset, Winslow and Hopkins reached a spot on the river where the Indians were catching striped bass, and that night they "lodged in the open fields."

Six Indians decided to continue on with them the next morning. They followed the riverbank for about half a dozen miles until they came to a shallow area, where they were told to take off their pants and wade across the river. They were midstream, with their possessions in their arms, when two Indians appeared on the opposite bank.

In the aftermath of the plague, the Narragansetts had started to raid Pokanoket territory, and the two Pokanoket Indians probably feared that Winslow and Hopkins' group was the enemy. Winslow judged one of the Indians to be at least sixty years old, but despite their age, both men displayed great "valor and courage" as they ran "very swiftly and low in the grass to meet us at the bank" with their arrows drawn. On realizing that they knew the Native people with Winslow and Hopkins, the old warriors "welcomed us with such food as they had." Winslow later learned that these were the last two survivors of a once thriving village.

As the sun reached its height, the traveling became quite hot, and the Indians cheerfully offered to carry guns and extra clothing for the settlers. They came upon other Indians along the way, but all proved friendly, and before the day was over, they reached Massasoit's village, known as Sowams. In the years to come, as the Pilgrims began to purchase land from the Pokanoket sachem, they spoke of Sowams as "the garden of the patent"—a fertile sweep of land with two rivers providing easy access to Narragansett Bay. As anyone could plainly see, Massasoit was positioned at a place that made Plymouth seem, by comparison, a hilly wasteland.

The sachem invited them into his wigwam, where the Pilgrims presented him with the copper chain and horseman's coat. Winslow reported that once the sachem had "put the coat on his back and the chain about his neck, he was not a little proud to behold himself, and his men also to see their king so bravely attired."

The sachem gathered his people around him and began to deliver a long and exuberant speech. "Was not he Massasoit commander of the country about him?" he proclaimed. He spoke of the many villages that paid him tribute with corn, furs, or other gifts, and of how those villages would all trade with the Pilgrims. With the naming of each place, his men responded with a refrain about Massasoit's power over the village and how the village would be at peace with the English and provide them with furs. This went on until thirty or more settlements had been named. "[S]o that as it was delightful," Winslow wrote, "it was tedious unto us."

By this time, Winslow and Hopkins were desperate for something to eat. It had been more than a day since they'd had a decent meal, but the entire village of Sowams appeared to be without any food. Massasoit had only recently returned to the village after a long time away, and his people had not yet been able to hunt for any fish or birds. By arriving unannounced, Winslow and Hopkins had unintentionally placed Massasoit in a difficult and potentially embarrassing situation. He was happy to see them, but he had no food to offer.

Once he'd completed his speech, Massasoit lit his pipe and encouraged all of them to smoke as he "fell to discoursing of England." He said he was now "King James his man," and so the French were no longer welcome in Narragansett Bay. When he learned that the English king had been a widower for more than a year, Massasoit expressed wonder that James had chosen to live "without a wife."

It was getting late, and it was now clear to the Pilgrims that there was nothing for them to eat. So they asked to go to bed. Much to their surprise, the sachem insisted that they share the wigwam's sleeping platform with himself and his wife, "they at the one end and we at the other." What's more, two of Massasoit's warriors crowded onto the platform with them.

That night, neither Winslow nor Hopkins slept a wink. Not only were they starving, they were kept awake by the Indians' habit of singing themselves to sleep. They also discovered that the dirt floor of the wigwam was alive with lice and fleas, while mosquitoes buzzed around their ears.

The next day, several minor sachems made their way to Sowams to see the two Englishmen. The increasingly crowded village took on a carnival atmosphere as the sachems and their men entertained themselves with various games of chance in which painted stones and stiff reeds were used, much like dice and cards, to gamble for an opponent's furs and knives. Winslow and Hopkins challenged some of them to a shooting contest. Although the Indians declined, they requested that the English demonstrate the accuracy of their muskets. One of them fired a round of small shot at a target, and the Natives were amazed "to see the mark so full of holes." Early that afternoon, Massasoit returned with two large striped bass. The fish were quickly boiled, but since there were more than forty mouths to feed, the bass did not go far. Small as it was, it was the first meal Winslow and Hopkins had eaten in two nights and a day.

Their second night at Sowams proved to be as sleepless as the first. Even before sunrise, the two Englishmen decided that they best be on their way, "we much fearing," Winslow wrote, "that if we should stay any longer, we should not be able to recover home for want of strength."

Massasoit was "both grieved and ashamed that he could no better entertain" the Pilgrims, but that did not prevent the visit from ending on a most positive note. Squanto, it was decided, would remain at Pokanoket so that he could go from village to village to establish trading relations for the Pilgrims, who had brought necklaces, beads, and other goods to exchange with the Indians for furs and corn. It may also have been that Massasoit wanted the chance to speak with the interpreter alone. Until Squanto returned to Plymouth, another Indian named Tokamahamon would serve as the Englishmen's guide.

Two days later, on the night of Saturday, July 7, after a solid day of rain, Winslow and Hopkins arrived back at Plymouth. They were wet, weary, and famished, but they had succeeded in strengthening their settlement's ties with Massasoit and the Indians to the west. It would be left to a boy—and a Billington at that—to do the same for the Indians to the east.

◆ ◆ ◆ Back in January, fourteen-year-old Francis Billington had climbed into a tree near the top of Fort Hill. Looking inland to the west, he claimed he saw "a great sea." Like his father, the Billington boy had already developed a reputation as a troublemaker. When the *Mayflower* had still been at anchor in Provincetown Harbor, he had fired off a musket in his family's cabin that had nearly blown up a barrel of gunpowder, which would have destroyed the ship and everyone aboard. Given the boy's history, no one seemed to take his claim about a large inland sea very seriously. Eventually, however, someone agreed to accompany the teenager on a trip into the woods. About two miles in, they came upon a huge lake that was "full of fish and fowl." Even William Bradford, who had no great love of the Billington family, had to admit that the lake would be "an excellent help to us in time," particularly since it was the source of Town Brook. To this day, the lake, which is close to five miles around, is known as the Billington Sea.

In late March, Francis's father, John, had berated Miles Standish and narrowly escaped public punishment. Toward the end of July, Francis's older brother John Jr. got into some trouble of his own. Not long after

◆ *Nineteenth-century photograph along the border of the Billington Sea.*

the return of Winslow and Hopkins, the sixteen-year-old lost his way in the woods somewhere south of the settlement. For five days, he wandered, living on nuts, roots, and anything else he could find until he stumbled on the Indian village of Manomet, some twenty miles from Plymouth. Instead of returning the boy to the English, the Manomet sachem, Canacum, passed him to the Nausets of Cape Cod—the very people who had attacked the Pilgrims during the First Encounter back in December. The Nausets, led by sachem Aspinet, were also the ones whose corn pits and graves the Pilgrims had disturbed. With the boy in their possession, the Nausets were able to send an unmistakable message to the English: "You stole something of ours; well, now we have something of yours."

Eventually word came back from Massasoit that Billington was alive and well and living with the Nausets. The Pilgrims had no choice but to return to the scene of their earlier crime.

Bradford ordered a party of ten men—more than half the adult males in the settlement—to set out in the shallop with both Squanto, who had recently returned from his trading mission in the region, and Tokamahamon as guides. Not long after departing from Plymouth in the shallop, they were hit by a tremendous thunderstorm that forced them to stop at Cummaquid, a shallow harbor near the base of Cape Cod.

At dawn the next morning, they found themselves stuck in the tidal flats. They could see several Indians collecting lobsters, and Squanto and Tokamahamon went to speak with them. The Pilgrims were soon introduced to the Indians' sachem, Iyanough. Still in his twenties, he impressed them as "very personable, courteous, and fair conditioned."

At Cummaquid, they discovered that all was not forgotten on Cape Cod when it came to past English injustices in the region. An ancient woman, whom they judged to be a hundred years old, made a point of seeking out the Pilgrims "because she never saw English." As soon as she set eyes on them, she burst into tears, "weeping and crying excessively." They learned that three of her sons had been captured seven years before by Thomas Hunt, and she still mourned their loss. "We told them we were sorry that any Englishman should give them that offense," Winslow wrote, "that Hunt was a bad man, and that all the English that heard of it condemned him for the same."

Iyanough and several others offered to accompany them to Nauset, about twenty miles to the east. Unlike the winter before, when the shores of Cape Cod had been empty of people, the Pilgrims found Indians almost everywhere they looked. They brought the shallop to within wading distance of shore at First Encounter Beach, where they'd been attacked about six months before by the Nausets. They were soon approached by a huge number of Indians. Given their history in this place, the Pilgrims ordered the crowd to back away from the boat. They could only hope that their alliance with Massasoit kept them safe. With their muskets ready, they insisted that only two Indians approach at a time. One of the first to come forward was the man whose corn they had stolen. The Pilgrims arranged to have him visit their settlement, where they promised to pay him back for his loss.

It was growing dark by the time Aspinet arrived with more than a hundred Nauset men, many of whom must have participated in the First Encounter back in December. Half the warriors remained on shore with their bows and arrows while the others waded out to the boat unarmed. One of Aspinet's men carried John Billington Jr. in his arms. Looking none the worse for his time in captivity, the teenager wore a string of shell beads around his neck. The Pilgrims presented Aspinet with a knife, and peace was declared between the two peoples. From the Pilgrims' perspective, it was a great relief to have finally righted the wrongs they'd committed during their first weeks in America.

But Aspinet had some disturbing news. The Narragansetts were said to have killed several of Massasoit's men and taken Massasoit himself captive. "This struck some fear in us," Winslow wrote. If the Narragansetts should decide to attack their settlement, it would be a catastrophe: There were only about half a dozen men back at Plymouth. They needed to return as quickly as possible, for if Massasoit had indeed been captured, they were, according to the terms of the treaty, at war with the most powerful tribe in the region.

◆ ◆ ◆ Massasoit had indeed been taken, temporarily it turned out, by the Narragansetts. But the Pilgrims soon learned that the greatest threat was not from the Narragansetts but from the Pokanokets' supposed allies. For those who had opposed Massasoit's treaty with the Pilgrims, this was just the opportunity they had been looking for. One sachem in particular—Corbitant from the village of Mattapoisett just to the east of

Massasoit's headquarters at Sowams—was attempting to use the sachem's troubles to break the Pokanoket-English alliance. Corbitant had arrived at the nearby village of Nemasket and was now attempting to "draw the hearts of Massasoit's subjects from him." Bradford decided to send Squanto and Tokamahamon to Nemasket to find out what Corbitant was up to.

The next day, one of Massasoit's men, a warrior named Hobbamock who spoke some English, arrived at Plymouth, gasping for breath and covered in sweat. He'd just run the fifteen miles from Nemasket, and he had terrible news. Squanto, he feared, was dead. When Hobbamock had last seen the interpreter, one of Corbitant's warriors had been holding a knife to his chest. If Squanto was dead, Corbitant told the Indians at Nemasket, "the English had lost their tongue." Bradford immediately called a meeting of his advisers.

The Pilgrims were men of God, but this did not mean they were against using force. This was their chance to show the Indians the consequences of challenging the English—either directly or indirectly through one of their allies.

They decided to hit Corbitant quickly and to hit him hard. Standish volunteered to lead ten men on a mission to Nemasket. If Squanto had in fact been killed, they were to seize Corbitant. And since he'd been disloyal to Massasoit, Corbitant was to suffer the same gruesome fate of all notorious traitors back in England: Standish was to cut off his head and bring it back to Plymouth for public display.

They left the next morning, Tuesday, August 14, with Hobbamock as their guide. Hobbamock was a pniese—a warrior of special abilities and stamina (it was said a pniese could not be killed in battle) who was responsible for collecting tribute from other tribes for his sachem. From the start, Standish and Hobbamock had much in common, and the two warriors quickly developed a close relationship.

Soon after they left Plymouth, it began to rain. About three miles from Nemasket, they ventured off the trail and waited for dark. In the summer rain, Standish told his men about his plan. Hobbamock was to lead them to Corbitant's wigwam around midnight. Once Standish had positioned them around the dwelling, he and Hobbamock would charge inside and take Corbitant. The men were instructed to shoot any Indians who attempted to escape. For those with no previous military experience, it sounded terrifying, and Standish did his best to give his men some confidence. Soon "all men [were] encouraging one another to the utmost of their power."

After a last, quick meal, it was time for the assault. In the starless dark, Hobbamock directed them to the wigwam. The dwelling was probably larger than most, with a considerable number of men, women, and children inside, sleeping on the low platforms built along the interior walls. By this late hour, the central fire had dwindled to a few glowing embers. The drum of rain on the wigwam's reed mats masked the sounds of the Pilgrims taking their positions.

Standish burst in, shouting Corbitant's name. It was very dark inside, and with Hobbamock acting as his interpreter, the Pilgrim captain demanded to know where the sachem was. But the people inside the wigwam were too terrified to speak. Some leaped off their sleeping platforms and tried to force their way through the walls of the wigwam. Soon the guards outside were shooting off their muskets as the people inside screamed and wept. Several women clung to Hobbamock, calling him friend. What had been intended as a bold strike against the enemy was threatening to become a chaotic mess.

Gradually they learned that Corbitant had been at Nemasket, but no one was sure where he was now. They also learned that Squanto was still alive. Hobbamock pulled himself up through the wigwam's smoke hole and, balancing himself on the roof, called out for the interpreter. Tokamahamon, it turned out, was also alive and well.

The next morning, they discovered that Corbitant and his men had fled, probably for their home at Mattapoisett. Standish delivered the message to the residents of Nemasket that "although Corbitant had now escaped us, yet there was no place should secure him and his from us if he continued his threatening us." A man and a woman had been wounded that night, and the Pilgrims offered to bring them back to Plymouth for medical attention. The following day the Pilgrims' self-taught surgeon, Samuel Fuller, tended to the Indians' injuries, and they were free to return home.

Over the next few weeks, Bradford learned of the reaction to Standish's midnight raid. Just as his military officer had predicted, the show of force—no matter how confused—had won the Pilgrims some new respect. Several sachems sent their "gratulations" to Governor Bradford. Epenow, the Martha's Vineyard sachem who had attacked Thomas Dermer, made overtures of friendship. Even Corbitant let it be known that he now wanted to make peace. By this time, Massasoit was back in Sowams, and with the Pilgrims having proven themselves to be loyal supporters, "a much firmer peace" existed throughout the region.

On September 13, nine sachems—including Corbitant, Epenow, Massasoit's brother Quadequina, and Canacum, the sachem who had sent John Billington Jr. to the Nausets—journeyed to Plymouth to sign a new treaty. About this time, Bradford determined that an expedition should be sent north to the land of the Massachusetts. Squanto had warned them that the Massachusetts, who lived in the vicinity of modern Boston, "had often threatened us." It was time to make peace with them as well.

They soon discovered where they *should* have settled. As they sailed their shallop across the huge bay that is modern Boston Harbor, they were filled with envy. Instead of the shallow water of Plymouth Harbor, here was a place where ships of any size could venture right up to land. Instead of little Town Brook, there were three navigable rivers that came together at an easily defensible neck of high ground known as Shawmet.

This was a place where an English settlement might grow into a major

port, with rivers providing access to the fur-rich interior of New England. But the thought of relocating themselves after so much loss and sacrifice was too much for the Pilgrims to bear. They decided to stay put. It would be left to others to transform this place into the "city on a hill" called Boston. The Pilgrims' ambitions were more modest. They were quite content with a village by a brook. The important thing was their spiritual life, and for that to flourish as it once had in Leiden, they needed their minister, John Robinson, and the rest of the congregation to join them in the New World.

◆ ◆ ◆ We do not know the exact date of the celebration we now call the First Thanksgiving, but it was probably in late September or early October, soon after their corn, squash, beans, barley, and peas had been harvested. It was also a time during which Plymouth Harbor played host to a tremendous number of migrating birds, particularly ducks and geese, and Bradford ordered four men to go out "fowling." It took only a few hours for Plymouth's hunters

◆ *An early-twentieth-century depiction of the First Thanksgiving. Note how the myths of the Pilgrims have taken hold: in addition to the inaccuracies of dress, it was the Indians who fed the Pilgrims by providing five freshly killed deer.*

• *A cooking pot that may have come to America with Miles and Rose Standish.*

to kill enough ducks and geese to feed the settlement for a week. Now that they had "gathered the fruit of our labors," Bradford declared it time to "rejoice together . . . after a more special manner."

The term Thanksgiving was not used by the Pilgrims themselves. Instead of a spiritual ceremony, the gathering had more in common with a traditional English harvest festival—a secular celebration that dated back to the Middle Ages in which villagers ate, drank, and played games.

Despite what many people think today, the Pilgrims did not spend the day sitting around a long table draped with a white linen cloth, clasping each other's hands in prayer as a few curious Indians looked on. Instead of an English affair, the First Thanksgiving soon became an overwhelmingly Native celebration when Massasoit and a hundred Pokanokets (more than twice the entire English population of Plymouth) arrived at the settlement and provided five freshly killed deer. Even if all the Pilgrims' furniture was brought out into the sunshine, most of the celebrants stood, squatted, or sat on the ground as they gathered around outdoor fires, where the deer and birds turned on wooden spits and where pottages—stews into which varieties of meats and vegetables were thrown—cooked invitingly.

In addition to ducks and deer, there was, according to Bradford, a "good store of wild turkeys" in the fall of 1621. Turkeys were not new to the Pilgrims. When the conquistadors arrived in Mexico in the sixteenth century, they discovered that the Indians of Central America possessed turkeys as well as gold. The birds were brought to Spain as early as the

1520s, and by the 1540s they had reached England. By 1575, the Central American turkey had become common at English Christmases. The wild turkeys of New England were bigger and much faster than the birds the Pilgrims had known in Europe and were often pursued in winter when they could be tracked in the snow.

The Pilgrims may have also added fish to their meal of birds and deer. In fall, there were plenty of striped bass, bluefish, and cod. Perhaps most important to the Pilgrims was that with a recently harvested barley crop, it was now possible to brew beer. Alas, the Pilgrims were without pumpkin pies or cranberry sauce. There were also no forks, which did not appear at Plymouth until the last decades of the seventeenth century. The Pilgrims ate with their fingers and their knives.

Neither Bradford nor Winslow mention it, but the First Thanksgiving coincided with what was, for the Pilgrims, a new and startling phenomenon: the turning of the green leaves of summer to the yellows, reds, and purples of a New England autumn. In Britain, the cloudy fall days and warm nights cause the autumn colors to be rather dull. In New England, on the other hand, the sunny fall days and cool but not freezing nights unleash brilliant colors within the tree leaves, with oaks turning red, brown, and russet; hickories golden brown; birches yellow; red maples scarlet; sugar maples orange; and black maples glowing yellow. It was a display that must have contributed to the enthusiasm with which the Pilgrims later wrote of the festivities that fall.

◆ ◆ ◆ The First Thanksgiving marked the conclusion of a remarkable year. Eleven months earlier the Pilgrims had arrived at the tip of Cape Cod, fearful and uninformed. They had spent the next month angering every Native American they happened to come across. By all rights, none of the Pilgrims should have survived the first winter. Like the French sailors before them, they all might have been either killed or taken captive by the Indians.

That it had worked out differently was a testament not only to the Pilgrims' grit, resolve, and faith, but to their ability to take advantage of some extraordinary good fortune. Massasoit's decision to offer them assistance had saved the Pilgrims' lives, but there had already been several instances in which they could have squandered the opportunity the sachem had given them. Placing their faith in God, the Pilgrims might have insisted on isolating themselves. But by becoming an active part of the diplomatic process in southern New England—by sending Winslow and Hopkins to Sowams, by paying back the Nausets for the corn, and most important, by making clear their loyalty to Massasoit at the "hurly-burly" in Nemasket—they had taken charge of their own destiny in the region.

In 1620, New England was far from paradise. Indeed, the New World was, in many ways, much like the Old—a place where the fertility of the soil was a concern, a place where disease and war were constant threats. There were profound differences between the Pilgrims and Pokanokets to be sure—especially when it came to technology, culture, and spiritual beliefs—but in these early years, when an alliance appeared to be good for both of them, the two peoples had more in common than is generally thought today. For the Pilgrims, some of whom had slept in a wigwam and all of whom had enjoyed eating and drinking with the Indians during that First Thanksgiving, these were not barbarians (even if some of their habits, such as their refusal to wear clothes, struck them as "savage"); these were human beings, much like themselves—"very trust[worth]y, quick of apprehension, ripe witted, just," according to Edward Winslow.

For his part, Massasoit had managed one of the great comebacks of all time. Once in danger of being forced to pay tribute to the Narragansetts, he had found a way to give the Pokanokets, who were now just a fraction of the Narragansetts in terms of population, a kind of equality with the rival tribe. Massasoit had come to the Pilgrims' rescue when, as his son would remember fifty-four years later, the English were "as a little child." He could only hope that the Pilgrims would continue to honor their debt to the Pokanokets long after the English settlement had grown into maturity.

PART II
Community

EIGHT
The Wall

◆ ◆ ◆

IN MID-NOVEMBER, Bradford received word from the Indians on Cape Cod that a ship had appeared at Provincetown Harbor. It had been just eight months since the departure of the *Mayflower*, and the Pilgrims were not yet expecting a supply ship from the Adventurers in London. It was immediately feared that the ship was from England's mortal enemy, France.

For more than a week, the ship stayed at the tip of Cape Cod. Then, at the end of November, a lookout atop Fort Hill saw it turn toward Plymouth Harbor. Many of the men were out working in the surrounding countryside and had to be called back immediately. A cannon was fired, and the tiny settlement was filled with excitement as men rushed in from all directions while Standish assembled them into a fighting force. Soon, in the words of Edward Winslow, "every man, yea, boy that could handle a gun were ready, with full resolution, that if [the ship] were an enemy, we would stand in our just defense."

To their amazement and delight, it proved to be an English ship: the *Fortune*, about a third the size of the *Mayflower*, sent by the Adventurers with thirty-seven passengers aboard. In an instant, the size of the colony had almost doubled.

Everyone aboard the *Fortune* was in good health, and almost immediately after coming ashore, Martha Ford gave birth to a son, John. But all was not well. Most of the new passengers were single men who must have been upset at the lack of young women among the Pilgrims. With the arrival of the *Fortune*, there was now a total of sixty-six men in the colony and just sixteen women. For every eligible female, there were six eligible men, and for young girls such as fifteen-year-old Elizabeth Tilley, nineteen-year-old Priscilla Mullins, and fourteen-year-old Mary Chilton (all of them orphans), the mounting pressure to marry must have been intense. Plus, there was no place to put all the passengers. Bradford had no choice but to divide them up among the preexisting seven houses and four public buildings.

But the biggest problem created by the arrival of the *Fortune* had to do with food. Weston had failed to provide the passengers aboard the *Fortune* with any provisions for the settlement. Instead of strengthening their situation, the addition of thirty-seven more mouths to feed at the beginning of winter put them in a difficult position. Bradford figured out that even if they cut their daily rations in half, their current store of corn would last only another six months. After a year of relentless toil and hardship, they faced yet another winter without enough food. "[B]ut they bore it patiently," Bradford wrote, "under hope of [future] supply."

Happily, there were some familiar faces aboard the *Fortune*. The Brewsters welcomed their eldest son, Jonathan, a thirty-seven-year-old ribbon weaver, whom they hadn't seen in almost a year and a half. Others from Leiden included Philip de la Noye, whose French surname was eventually changed to Delano and whose descendants would include future U.S. president Franklin Delano Roosevelt. The newly remarried Edward Winslow greeted his twenty-four-year-old brother, John. There was also Thomas Prence, the twenty-one-year-old son of a Gloucestershire carriage maker, who soon became one of the leading members of the settlement.

The most notable new arrival was Robert Cushman, whose chest pains aboard the *Speedwell* during the summer of 1620 had convinced him to remain in England. Cushman was the one who had negotiated the agreement with Thomas Weston that stated how the Pilgrims would pay the Adventurers—the agreement that Bradford and the others had refused to honor in Southampton. It was now time, Cushman told them, to sign the controversial agreement. Cushman also presented the Pilgrims with a new patent from the Council for New England making it legal for them to live in Plymouth, rather than by the Hudson River.

Unfortunately, from Cushman's perspective, Weston had also written a letter to the now deceased Governor Carver, which scolded the Pilgrims for not having loaded the *Mayflower* with goods for her return to England. "I know your weakness was the cause of it," Weston wrote, "and I believe more weakness of judgment than weakness of hands."

Bradford was naturally outraged by Weston's accusation. Bradford acknowledged that the Adventurers had, so far, nothing to show for their investment, but their losses were only financial. Governor Carver had worked himself to death that spring, and "the loss of his and many other industrious men's lives cannot be valued at any price."

Despite his criticisms, Weston claimed to be one of the few financial backers the Pilgrims could still count on. "I promise you," he wrote, "I will never quit the business, though all the other Adventurers should." Only after Cushman assured them that Weston was a man to be trusted did Bradford and the others reluctantly sign the agreement.

Over the next two weeks, they loaded the *Fortune* with beaver skins, sassafras, and clapboards made of split oak (much smaller than modern clapboards, they were used for making barrels instead of siding for houses). Valued at around £500 (roughly $100,000 today), the cargo came close to cutting their debt in half. Certainly this would help restore the Adventurers' confidence in the settlement.

On December 13, 1621, after a stay of just two weeks, the *Fortune* was on her way back to London. Cushman returned with her, leaving his fourteen-year-old son, Thomas, in Bradford's care. In addition to Bradford's letter to Weston, Cushman was given a manuscript account of the Pilgrims' first thirteen months in America that was published the following year and is known today as *Mourt's* [an apparent mispelling of the editor George Morton's last name] *Relation*. Written by Bradford and Edward Winslow, the small book ends with Winslow's upbeat account of the First Thanksgiving and the abundance of the New World. But, just days after the *Fortune*'s departure, the Pilgrims had reason to question Winslow's happy view of life in Plymouth.

◆ ◆ ◆ The Pilgrims soon began to realize that their alliance with the Pokanokets had created serious problems with the far more powerful Narragansetts. The previous summer, William Bradford had exchanged what he felt were positive and hopeful messages with the Narragansett sachem, Canonicus. Since then, however, Canonicus had grown increasingly jealous of the Pokanoket-Plymouth alliance. The Narragansetts, it was rumored, were preparing to attack the English settlement.

Toward the end of November, a Narragansett messenger arrived at Plymouth looking for Squanto. He had a mysterious object from Canonicus in his hands. When he learned that the interpreter was away, he "seemed rather to be glad than sorry" and hurriedly handed over what the Pilgrims soon realized was a bundle of arrows wrapped in the skin of a rattlesnake.

When Squanto returned to Plymouth, he told them that the arrows were "no better than a challenge." Bradford responded by pouring gunpowder and bullets into the snakeskin and sending it back to Canonicus. This appeared to have the desired effect. "[I]t was no small terror to the savage king," Winslow reported, "insomuch as he would not once touch the powder and shot, or suffer it to stay in his house or country." The powder-stuffed snakeskin was passed like a hot potato from village to village until it finally made its way back to Plymouth.

Despite this response, the Pilgrims were deeply troubled by the Narragansett threat. Their little village was, they realized, wide open to attack. Their cannons might pose a threat to a ship attempting to enter Plymouth Harbor but were of little use in stopping Native warriors, especially if they attacked at night.

Bradford, doubtless at Standish's urging, decided to build an eight-foot-high wall of wood around the entire settlement. If they were to include the cannon platform atop Fort Hill and their dozen or so houses on Cole's Hill below it, the wall had to be at least 2,700 feet—more than a half mile—in length. Hundreds, if not thousands, of trees needed to be cut down, their trunks stripped of branches and chopped or sawed to the proper length, then set deep into the ground. The tree trunks of the fort had to be set so tightly together that a man could not possibly fit through the gaps between them. In addition, Standish insisted that they construct three protruding gates, known as flankers, that would also serve as defensive shooting platforms in case of attack.

By any measure, it was a huge task, but for a workforce of fewer than fifty men living on starvation rations, it was almost impossible. The vast majority of the new arrivals were Strangers, and even though they tended to be young and strong, they were less likely to help the Pilgrim separatists with such an awesome labor.

The differences between the Strangers and the Pilgrims quickly came to a head on December 25. For the Pilgrims, Christmas was a day just like any other; for most of the Strangers from the *Fortune*, on the other hand, it was a religious holiday, and they informed Bradford that it was "against their consciences" to work on Christmas. Bradford reluctantly gave them the day off and led the rest of the men out for the usual day's work.

But when they returned at noon, they found the once quiet streets of Plymouth in a state of joyous bedlam. The Strangers were playing games, including stool ball, a cricketlike game popular in the west of England. This was typical of how most Englishmen spent Christmas, but this was not the way the members of a pious Puritan community were to conduct themselves. Bradford proceeded to take away the players' balls and bats. It was not fair, he insisted, that some played while others worked. If they wanted to spend Christmas praying quietly at home, that was fine by him; "but there should be no gaming or reveling in the streets."

Writing about this confrontation years later, Bradford claimed it was "rather of mirth than of weight." And yet, for a young governor who had to face not only the challenges presented by a hostile Native nation but a growing divide among his own people, it was a crucial incident. It was now clear that no matter how it was done in England, Plymouth played by its own, God-ordained rules, and everyone—Separatist or Anglican—was expected to obey.

For many of the new arrivals, it was all quite astonishing. Bradford had declared it illegal to follow the customs of their mother country. But, for now they had more important things to worry about than whether or not it was right to play stool ball on Christmas Day. The Narragansetts were threatening, and they had a wall to build.

◆ ◆ ◆ It took them a little more than a month to build the wall. The chopping and sawing was backbreaking, time-consuming work made all the more difficult by their equipment. Narrow and poorly balanced, an English ax wobbled with each stroke, and without oxen to help them drag the tree trunks in from the forest, they were forced to lug the ten- to twelve-foot lengths of timber by hand. They dug a two- to three-foot-deep trench, first using picks to break through the frozen topsoil and then, in all likelihood, a large hoelike tool to dig a trench that was deep and wide enough to accommodate the ends of the logs. Adding to their difficulties was the lack of food. Some of the workers grew so faint with hunger that they were seen to stagger on their way back to the settlement at the end of the day.

Nevertheless, by March, it was complete: a massive, sap-dripping, bark-peeling wall between them and the surrounding forest. A new sense of order and control had been placed upon the wilderness. Plymouth was now a defined settlement. By building the wall, the Pilgrims had made it clear that they intended to remain there for a very long time.

Miles Standish developed a military plan to go with the new fortress. The men were divided into four companies, each with its own commander, and were assigned positions and duties to perform in the event of an attack. There was also a plan in case a fire should break out. Most of the men would work to put out the flames, but a group was assigned to stand on guard in case the Indians attempted to use the fire as a diversion. Standish drilled the men regularly and set up plans to enact if he should be away from the settlement during an attack. They were now ready to reestablish contact with the rest of the world.

• • • They had long since planned to visit the Massachusetts to the north to trade for furs. But as they prepared the shallop to depart, Hobbamock, the Pokanoket pniese who had led the midnight raid on Nemasket the summer before and who had been living with the Pilgrims throughout the winter, asked to speak with Bradford and Standish. Hobbamock had heard that the Massachusetts had become allies with the Narragansetts and were planning to attack Standish and the trading party. With Standish eliminated, the Narragansetts would then attack the settlement. Even more disturbing, Hobbamock insisted that Squanto was in on the plot. According to Hobbamock, all that winter, while the Pilgrims had been building their wall, Squanto had been meeting secretly with Indians throughout the region.

Without letting Squanto know of Hobbamock's claims, Standish and Bradford met with several members of the community to discuss what to do next. As they all knew, they could not simply "mew up ourselves in our new-enclosed town." They were running out of food. If they were to trade for more corn, they needed to leave their own settlement. They decided Standish would depart immediately for his trading mission with the Massachusetts and show no signs of knowing about a possible Massachusett-Narragansett alliance.

Left unresolved was how to treat Hobbamock's accusations concerning Squanto. As had become obvious to all of them, the two Indians were very jealous of each other. It was quite possible that Hobbamock had lied about Squanto's involvement in the conspiracy, if indeed a conspiracy existed at all. Bradford and Squanto had developed a strong relationship over the last year, while Standish and Hobbamock had also become close. Rather than confront Squanto, it was decided to use the rivalry between the two Indians to their advantage.

In April, Standish and ten men, accompanied by both Squanto and Hobbamock, departed in the shallop for Massachusetts. A few hours later, an Indian who was a member of Squanto's family appeared outside

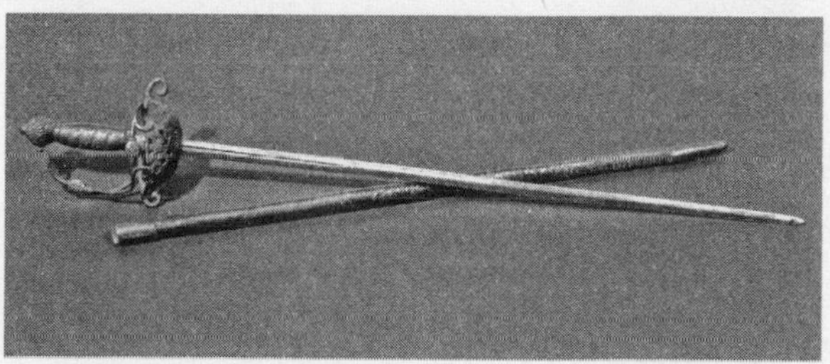

◆ *A German-made rapier attributed to Miles Standish.*

the gates of town. His face was bloody, and he had apparently been running for a long time. He kept looking behind him as if those who had been chasing him might appear at any moment. He shouted out that he had come from Nemasket and he had frightening news. The Narragansetts had teamed up with the Pokanokets for an assault on Plymouth. Being a member of Squanto's family, he had spoken in the Pilgrims' defense and had, as a consequence, received a blow to the head. The enemy might be on their doorstep at any moment.

It was a strange, alarming, and confusing performance. It was difficult to believe that Massasoit had joined with the Narragansetts against them. The timing also seemed suspicious. The Indian had arrived just after Standish and company had left for Massachusetts. Without their military leader to protect them, the Pilgrims were especially vulnerable. Indeed, the Indian's sudden appearance seemed calculated to provoke a quick and possibly disastrous response on the Pilgrims' part.

Given Hobbamock's recent claims about Squanto, there was ample reason to suspect that he was behind all this. But why was Squanto attempting to get them to attack Massasoit? Bradford immediately ordered that the cannons be fired as a warning signal. It was probably too late to call Standish back, but it was important that anyone working in the countryside return to the safety of town.

As it turned out, Standish *was* in earshot of the signal. Upon hearing the signal, he and his men immediately turned back for town—something Squanto, who was in fact the one behind this drama, had never anticipated.

Back at the settlement, Hobbamock angrily insisted that the claims of Squanto's relatives were all lies. Being a pniese, he was certain he would have been consulted by Massasoit if the sachem had been planning some kind of attack. Bradford "should do well," Hobbamock insisted, "to continue his affections" toward Massasoit. So as not to create any unnecessary suspicion, it was decided to send Hobbamock's wife to Pokanoket, where she could determine whether there was any truth to the claims of Squanto's relative.

As Hobbamock had predicted, all was peace at Pokanoket. Hobbamock's wife revealed the reason behind her visit to Massasoit, who was outraged to learn that Squanto had attempted to turn the Pilgrims against him.

Over the next few weeks, it became increasingly clear that Squanto had been working long and hard to overthrow Massasoit. All winter he had been spreading false rumors to villages throughout the region. The Pilgrims, he claimed, possessed the plague, and they were about to unleash it. However, if a village sent him sufficient tribute, Squanto told them that he could prevent the Pilgrims from spreading disease. Gradually, more and more Indians began to look to Squanto rather than Massasoit for protection. Squanto had hoped the false alarm raised by his family member might cause the Pilgrims to attack Massasoit and so Squanto would emerge as New England's most important Native leader.

It was a bold, risky, and outrageous plan. By playing the English against the Pokanokets, he was trying to revive his family's fortunes. For Squanto, it had all been about honor, "which he loved as his life," Winslow wrote, "and preferred before his peace." In just a year, Squanto had gone from being Massasoit's prisoner to being one of his chief rivals. But his ambitions, it now seemed, had gotten the better of him.

Under the terms of the treaty drawn up the previous year, Bradford was required to turn Squanto over to Massasoit for punishment. But Bradford could not bear the thought of being without his interpreter.

His attachment to Squanto appears to have gone well beyond the need for an Indian who could speak both languages. Squanto had become part of the Plymouth community about the same time that Bradford had become governor, and Bradford was willing to risk the anger of the supreme sachem of the Pokanokets if it meant keeping Squanto as his interpreter.

In May, Massasoit appeared at Plymouth and was "much offended and enraged" against Squanto. He said that the traitor must die. Bradford attempted to calm down the sachem, but not long after he returned to Pokanoket, Massasoit sent a messenger insisting that Squanto be put to death immediately. While acknowledging that Squanto deserved to die, Bradford stubbornly insisted that his interpreter was vital to the plantation and therefore could not be executed. Within a day of leaving for Pokanoket, Massasoit's messenger was back again, this time with several warriors. They had brought their sachem's knife and had been instructed to return to Pokanoket with Squanto's head and hands. They even offered to pay off the governor with some furs.

Bradford refused the payment, but did agree to send for Squanto. The interpreter bravely appeared before Bradford and the Pokanokets, and insisted that none of this was his fault. It was Hobbamock who was "the author and worker of his overthrow." In the end, though, Squanto knew he had no choice but to accept whatever the governor thought was right.

Bradford seemed ready to turn him over to Massasoit's men when a boat appeared off the Gurnet. The Governor said he would not surrender Squanto until he could determine who was on the boat. If it was French, they might be on the verge of attack.

But Massasoit's men refused to wait. "[B]eing mad with rage," Winslow reported, "and impatient at delay, they departed in great heat." Squanto had lived to see another day.

• • • The boat was a shallop from an English ship hired by Thomas Weston, the London Adventurer. Weston had pledged his undying loyalty to the Pilgrim cause in an earlier letter, but in the months ahead, Bradford learned that all those promises were "but wind." Not only had Weston abandoned them, he was now their competitor. Weston had secured a patent for his own settlement and had the nerve to expect the Pilgrims to host his sixty or so settlers as their leaders searched for a settlement site. He communicated this information in a series of "tedious and impertinent" letters that Bradford hid from everyone but his most trusted friends.

Even though Weston had betrayed them, Bradford felt that he still should offer the men the requested hospitality. The settlement had been on half rations before the addition of all these men; now it was on the edge of starvation.

As if this wasn't bad enough, Bradford learned that the *Fortune*, the ship they had loaded with clapboards in the fall, had been captured by the French just before the ship arrived in England. They had lost everything. The voyage that was to have cut their debt in half had put them even deeper in the hole. "I pray you be not discouraged," wrote Robert Cushman, the Pilgrim who had negotiated the original agreement with the Adventurers, "but gather up yourself, to go through these difficulties cheerfully and with courage in that place wherein God hath set you, until the day of refreshing come."

Then they received a different sort of letter. To the northeast, off the coast of modern Maine, the codfishing season was in full swing. Between three hundred and four hundred vessels were gathered off that rocky coast, and a master of one of the ships had written the Pilgrims with some disturbing news from Jamestown, Virginia. That spring, the Indians had killed 347 English colonists—more than four times the total population of Plymouth. "Happy is he," the codfisherman wrote, "whom other men's harms doth make to beware."

At this point, the Pilgrims' relations with the Indians were at a new low. Thanks to Squanto's betrayal and Bradford's reluctance to punish his interpreter, they could no longer count on the support of their former allies the Pokanokets. Recognizing that the English were newly vulnerable, the Massachusetts and Narragansetts were said to be planning an assault on Plymouth.

Bradford decided that the wall was not enough. If they should become the victims of a Jamestown-like attack, they needed a heavily reinforced structure that was large enough for all of them. They needed a fort. If it were built atop the hill overlooking the town, it might very well save their lives. Even though food supplies were still low, the Pilgrims launched into the work. It was hoped that the mere presence of this strong, well-defended structure would be enough to discourage future Indian attacks.

But as the work progressed, many of the settlers began to lose their enthusiasm for the project. Given the uncertainty of the Indian threat, they found it hard to spend so much time and effort on another defensive measure—especially given their lack of food. What amazed Edward Winslow during the summer and fall of 1622 was how "reasonable men [will be led] to reason against their own safety."

If they were to have any hope of completing the fort, they needed more food. Even though they lived on the edge of one of the world's great fishing grounds, the Pilgrims had no skills or equipment to catch fish, so Winslow headed out in the shallop on an emergency mission to visit the fishermen of Maine, where he succeeded in securing some desperately needed food.

◆ *A nineteenth-century drawing of how the fort might have looked.*

◆ ◆ ◆ By fall, the fort was nearing completion, and Weston's men had left Plymouth to settle at Wessagussett, about twenty-two miles to the north. Taking their cue from the Pilgrims, the men at Wessagussett immediately began building a fort of their own. It was then decided the two settlements should band together in search of provisions and take Wessagussett's thirty-ton vessel, the *Swan*, on a trading voyage to the south of Cape Cod.

Miles Standish was to lead the expedition, but in November, the normally healthy captain was struck by a bad fever. So William Bradford decided to go instead, with Squanto as his guide and interpreter. Since May, Squanto had done his best to win back the confidence of both Bradford and Massasoit. Winslow claimed that by the time the *Swan* departed from Plymouth, Squanto had secured a "peace" with the

Pokanoket sachem. It is difficult to imagine how Squanto could have regained Massasoit's trust, but Squanto, at least, believed that all was once again right. It was now safe for him to leave Plymouth.

In order to sail to the south of Cape Cod, they had to get through the same shoals that had almost wrecked the *Mayflower* two years before. Once again, they were quickly surrounded by breaking waves. The *Swan*'s master "saw no hope of passage." They headed for shore where Squanto said they might spend the night. Using the shallop to scout ahead of them, they followed a narrow and crooked channel and soon had the *Swan* safely anchored in the harbor of modern Chatham, known then as Manamoyick.

That evening Bradford and Squanto went ashore to speak with the local Indians. Only after the Manamoyicks had hidden away most of their goods and provisions were they willing to entertain the two in their wigwams. It took some convincing, but eventually they agreed to trade. Over the next few days, with Squanto's help, Bradford secured some corn and beans.

Just before they were about to leave for a second attempt at crossing the breakers, Squanto suddenly fell ill. Bradford described it as an "Indian fever, bleeding much at the nose (which the Indians take for a symptom of death)." Within a few days, Squanto—the Indian whom Bradford valued so highly that he had put the entire plantation at risk rather than see him killed—was dead.

Bradford claimed Squanto asked him "to pray for him that he might go to the Englishmen's God in Heaven; and bequeathed sundry of his things to sundry of his English friends as remembrances of his love." For Bradford, it was yet another terrible loss. With Dorothy, Governor Carver, and now Squanto dead, he once again had to regroup and find a way to continue on.

Bradford assumed that his trusted interpreter had died of natural causes. But he may have been the victim of a plot masterminded by Massasoit. Although difficult to document, there were several suspected poisonings of high-ranking Indians in New England during the seventeenth century. That Squanto, who had survived the infectious streets of London, should suddenly die from disease on Cape Cod is highly unlikely. Massasoit may have finally gotten his revenge on Squanto.

Without Squanto to guide them, the Pilgrims now turned to Hobbamock as their guide—a warrior loyal to both Massasoit and Miles Standish. But it remained to be seen whether Massasoit still held Squanto's betrayal against the Pilgrims. A year ago, there had been trust and friendship between Plymouth and the Pokanokets. Now there was uncertainty and lingering bitterness. In the months ahead, a brutal darkness would fall across New England.

NINE
At Death's Door

◆ ◆ ◆

Plymouth by the winter of 1623 was a place of exceptional discipline, a community where shared religious beliefs and family ties had united the Leideners from the start, and where two years of strong leadership on the part of William Bradford had convinced even the Strangers that it was in their best interests to work together. Some twenty miles to the north, at Wessagussett, an entirely different community had come into being.

Wessagussett was more like early Jamestown—a group of unattached men with relatively little in common. In the beginning, they worked together to build a fort. But once that was completed, they were unprepared to face the hard New England winter. Suffering from a deadly combination of hunger and despair, the colonists seemed unable to adapt to the demands of the New World.

Wessagussett was also right beside a settlement of Massachusett Indians. Not only was the threat of attack greater, but there was also a powerful form of temptation. The Indians possessed corn that they were saving for the spring.

In February, John Sanders, the settlement's leader, wrote to Governor Bradford, asking if it was right to steal some of the Indians' corn, especially if they promised to reimburse them once they'd grown their own corn in the summer. This was, of course, almost exactly what the Pilgrims had done two years before, but Bradford urged them to leave the corn alone, "for it might so exasperate the Indians . . . [that] all of us might smart for it."

About this time, Miles Standish traveled to Manomet, just fifteen miles to the south of Plymouth, to pick up some of the corn Bradford had bought during his trading voyage with Squanto. Standish was being entertained by sachem Canacum when two Massachusett Indians arrived with word from sachem Obtakiest at Wessagussett.

One of the Indians was a warrior of immense pride named Wituwamat, who bragged of having once killed several French sailors. Wituwamat possessed an ornately carved knife that he had taken from one of his victims. Soon after his arrival, he presented the knife to Canacum and began "a long speech in an audacious manner." Without the assistance of an interpreter, Standish was not sure what Wituwamat was saying, but he did know that once the Indian had completed his speech, he—not Standish—became Canacum's favored guest and Wituwamat's "entertainment much exceeded the captain's."

Standish was not the sort to overlook a social slight. He objected angrily to his rude treatment by Canacum and scolded the two Massachusett Indians for not paying him the proper respect. In an attempt to pacify the captain, Canacum insisted that Standish invite his three English companions, who were then loading the shallop with corn, to join them beside the fire. But Standish stormed out of the wigwam and spent the night with his men in a temporary shelter they had built beside the shallop.

Standish's anger appears to have blinded him to the fact that something far more important than a social slight had occurred at Manomet. Only in hindsight did Standish see the interchange between Wituwamat and Canacum as the first sign that the Indians in the region were plotting against the Pilgrims. For, as it turned out, Standish and Wituwamat were destined to meet again.

◆ ◆ ◆ While Standish was at Manomet, an Indian messenger arrived at Plymouth with the news that Massasoit was gravely ill. Bradford decided he must send someone—not only to attend to Massasoit, but to make contact with the crew of a Dutch vessel that the messenger claimed had been driven ashore, almost to the door of the sachem's wigwam. Since Winslow had already visited Massasoit and could speak Dutch, he was chosen for the expedition to Pokanoket.

Winslow was accompanied by Hobbamock and John Hamden, a gentleman from London who was spending the winter with the Pilgrims. About midway in their forty-mile journey, they received word from some Indians that Massasoit was dead. "This news struck us blank," Winslow wrote. The Indians also said that the Dutch had already left Pokanoket.

Hobbamock was the most profoundly affected by the news of the sachem's passing, and he insisted that they return immediately to Plymouth. But Winslow was not so sure. If Massasoit was really dead, then Corbitant, who lived just to the east of Pokanoket, would in all likelihood become the most powerful sachem in the region. Even though he was, in Winslow's words, "a most hollowhearted friend toward us," it might be in their best interests to stop at Corbitant's village and pay their respects. Given that less than a year ago both Winslow and Hobbamock had been part of an expedition sent to kill Corbitant, this was an extremely dangerous plan. But after some consideration, all of them thought it worth the risk.

As they made their way to Corbitant's village, Hobbamock could not contain his sorrow over the loss of Massasoit. "My loving sachem, my loving sachem!" he cried. "Many have I known, but never any like thee." He said that with Massasoit's death he feared Plymouth "had not a faithful friend left among the Indians." He then proceeded to deliver a remarkable eulogy:

> [H]e was no liar, he was not bloody and cruel . . .; in anger and passion he was soon reclaimed; easy to be reconciled towards such as had offended him; [he] ruled by reason in such measure as he would not scorn the advice of mean men; and . . . he governed his men better with few strokes, than others did with many; truly loving where he loved.

Corbitant, they soon discovered, was not at home. He was still at Pokanoket, his wife said; she wasn't sure whether or not Massasoit was still alive. Winslow hired a runner to go to Pokanoket to get the latest news. Just a half hour before sunset, the messenger returned with word that the sachem "was not yet dead, though there was no hope we should find him living." Winslow decided to set out immediately for Pokanoket.

◆ ◆ ◆ It was still dark when they arrived at Massasoit's village. His wigwam was so jammed with people that they had difficulty making their way to the sachem's side. Several powwows hovered over him, "making such a hellish noise, as it distempered us that were well," Winslow wrote. Massasoit's arms, legs, and thighs were being massaged by half a dozen women, who rubbed his skin "to keep heat in him." Winslow asked that Massasoit be told that "his friends, the English, were come to see him."

The sachem was unable to see, but he could still hear. He weakly asked which one of the English was present. The Indians said Winslow's name as "Winsnow," and Massasoit responded, "Keen Winsnow?" or "Are you Winslow?" The Pilgrim answered "ahhee," or "yes." Massasoit's response: "Matta neen wonckanet namen, Winsnow!" or "O Winslow, I shall never see thee again."

Winslow explained that Governor Bradford had wished he could be there, but important business had required him to remain at Plymouth.

Instead, Winslow had come with some medicine and food "most likely to do [the sachem] good in this his extremity." Massasoit had eaten nothing in a very long time, and Winslow attempted to feed him some fruit preserves from the tip of a knife. Once the sweetened fruit had dissolved in Massasoit's mouth, he swallowed—for the first time in two days.

Winslow began to examine the interior of the sachem's mouth. It was "exceedingly furred," and his tongue was so swollen that it was little wonder he had been unable to eat anything. After scraping the "corruption" from his mouth and tongue, Winslow fed him more of the preserves.

Massasoit may have been suffering from typhus, probably brought to the village by the recently departed Dutch traders. Typhus thrived in the crowded conditions typical of an Indian village or, for that matter, an English one. According to a modern description of typhus, symptoms include "fever and chills, vomiting, constipation or diarrhea, muscle ache and delirium or stupor. The tongue is first coated with a white fur, which then turns brown. The body develops small red eruptions which may bleed." In severe cases, the death rate can reach 70 percent.

Within a half hour of receiving his first taste of Winslow's fruit preserves, Massasoit had improved to the extent that his sight had begun to return. Winslow had brought several bottles of medicine, but they had broken along the way. He asked Massasoit if he could send a messenger to get some more from the surgeon back in Plymouth, as well as a couple of chickens, so that he might cook up a broth. This was readily agreed to, and by 2 A.M. a runner was on his way with a letter from Winslow.

The next day, Massasoit was well enough to ask Winslow to shoot a duck and make an English pottage similar to what he had eaten at Plymouth. Fearing that his stomach was not yet ready for meat, Winslow insisted that he first try a pottage of greens and herbs. After much hunting about, Winslow and John Hamden were able to find only a few strawberry leaves and a sassafras root. They boiled the two together, and after straining the results through Winslow's handkerchief and combining it with some roasted corn, they fed the mixture to Massasoit. He drank at least a pint of the broth and soon had his first bowel movement in five days.

Before fading off to sleep, the sachem asked Winslow to wash out the mouths of all the others who were sick in the village, "saying they were good folk." Reluctantly Winslow went about the work of scraping the mouths of all who desired it, a duty he admitted to finding "much offensive to me, not being accustomed with such poisonous savors." This was a form of diplomacy that went far beyond the usual exchange of greetings and gifts.

That afternoon Winslow shot a duck and prepared to feed Massasoit the promised pottage. By this time, the sachem had improved remarkably. "Never did I see a man so low . . . recover in that measure in so short a time," Winslow wrote. The duck's meat was quite fatty, and Winslow said it was important to skim the grease from the top of the broth, but Massasoit was now so hungry he insisted on making "a gross meal of it"—gobbling down the duck, fat and all. An hour later, he was vomiting so violently that he began to bleed from the nose.

For the next four hours the blood poured down, and Winslow began to fear that this might be the end. But eventually the bleeding stopped, and the sachem slept for close to eight hours. When he awoke, he was feeling so much better that he asked that the two chickens, which had just arrived from Plymouth, be kept as breeding stock rather than cooked for his benefit.

All the while, Indians from as many as a hundred miles away continued to arrive at Pokanoket. Before Winslow's appearance, many of those in attendance had commented on the absence of the English and suggested that they cared little about Massasoit's welfare. With this remarkable recovery, everything had changed. "Now I see the English are my friends and love me," Massasoit announced to the crowd; "and whilst I live, I will never forget this kindness they have showed me."

Before their departure, Massasoit took Hobbamock aside and had some words with the trusted pniese. Not until the following day, after they had spent the night with Corbitant, who now declared himself to be one of the Pilgrims' strongest allies, did Hobbamock reveal the subject of his conversation with Massasoit.

Plymouth, the sachem claimed, was in great danger because of Weston's men at Wessagussett, who had upset the Massachusetts so much that the Indians had decided to wipe out the settlement. But to attack Wessagussett would surely anger the Pilgrims, who would take revenge for the deaths of their countrymen. The only solution, the Massachusetts had determined, was to launch raids on both English settlements.

But the Massachusetts had just forty warriors; if they were to attack Wessagussett and Plymouth simultaneously, they needed help. Massasoit claimed that they had gotten the support of half a dozen villages on Cape Cod, as well as the Indians at Manomet and Martha's Vineyard. An attack was imminent, Massasoit insisted, and the only option the Pilgrims had was "to kill the men of Massachusetts, who were the authors of this intended mischief." If the Pilgrims waited until after the Indians had attacked Wessagussett, it would be too late.

It was alarming to learn that they were, in Winslow's words, "at the pit's brim, and yet feared nor knew not that we were in danger." After more than two years of threatened violence, it now appeared that the Pilgrims might have no choice but to go to war.

◆ ◆ ◆ As Winslow, Hobbamock, and John Hamden hurried back to Plymouth to tell Governor Bradford of the plot, Phineas Pratt, one of the leaders of the sorry settlement of Wessagussett, was beginning to think it was time to flee to Plymouth.

Their sufferings had become unendurable. They had nothing to eat, and the Indians were terrifying them. The warriors, led by a pniese named Pecksuot, gathered outside the wall of the Wessagussett fort. "Machit pesconk!" they shouted, which Pratt translated as "naughty guns." An attack seemed at hand, so the English increased the number of men on watch. But without food, the guards began to die at their posts. One bitterly cold night, Pratt reported for guard duty. "I [saw] one man dead before me," he remembered, "and another [man dead] at my right hand and another at my left for want of food."

Word had reached the settlement that the Massachusetts planned to attack both Wessagussett and Plymouth. Sachem Obtakiest was waiting for the snow to melt so that his warriors' footprints could not be tracked when they left one settlement for the other. "[T]heir plot was to kill all the English people in one day," Pratt wrote. He decided to leave as soon as possible for Plymouth. "[I]f [the] Plymouth men know not of this treacherous plot," he told his companions, "they and we are all dead men."

With a small pack draped across his back, Pratt walked out of the fort as casually as he could manage with a hoe in his hand. He began to dig at the edge of a large swamp, pretending to search for groundnuts. He looked to his right and to his left and, seeing no Indians, disappeared into the swamp.

He ran till about three o'clock in the afternoon, camped for the night, and by three the next day, he had reached the site of what would become the village of Duxbury, just to the north of Plymouth. As he ran across the Jones River, haunted by the fear that the Indians were about to catch up to him, he said to himself, "[N]ow am I a deer chased [by] wolves." He found a well-worn path and was running down a hill when up ahead he saw an Englishman walking toward him. It was John Hamden, who had recently returned from Pokanoket with Edward Winslow. Suddenly overcome by exhaustion, Pratt collapsed onto the trunk of a fallen tree. "Mr. Hamden," he called out, "I am glad to see you alive."

◆ ◆ ◆ Hamden explained that Massasoit too had told them of the plot against Plymouth and Wessagussett and that Governor Bradford had recently convened a public meeting to discuss how the plantation should proceed. It was irritating to the Pilgrims to know that they had been put into this mess not by anything *they* had done but by the irresponsible actions of Weston's men. The one bit of good news was that thanks to Winslow's efforts at Pokanoket, Massasoit was once again on their side. There was little doubt what the sachem expected of them: They were to launch a preemptive strike against the Massachusetts.

The fact remained, however, that so far no Indians had even threatened Plymouth. If they were to start an attack, it would be based on rumors—and they all knew from experience how misleading the rumors could be. Then again, with a sachem as trustworthy and powerful as Massasoit telling them to act, what more justification did they need? Yes, they decided, their future safety depended on a swift and daring assault.

William Bradford decided that Standish should make an example of "that bloody and bold villain" Wituwamat and bring back his head to Plymouth, "that he might be a warning and terror to all of that disposition." Standish had been itching to settle a score with Wituwamat ever since the Massachusett warrior had snubbed him at Manomet. The

Of plimoth plantation.

And first of ye occasion, and Indusments ther unto; the which that I may truly unfould, I must begine at ye very roote & rise of ye same. The which I shall endeuor to manefest in a plaine stile; with singuler regard unto ye simple trueth in all things, at least as near as my slender Judgmente can attaine the same.

1. Chapter

It is well knowne unto ye godly, and judicious; how ever since ye first breaking out of ye lighte of ye gospell, in our Honourable Nation of England (which was ye first of nations, whom ye Lord adorned ther with, after ye grosse darknes of popery which had covered, & overspred ye Christian worled) what warrs, & opposisions ever since satan hath raised, maintained, and continued against the saincts, from time, to time, in one sorte, or other. Some times by bloody death & cruell torments; other whiles Imprisonments, banishments, & other hard usages; As being loath his kingdom should goe downe, the trueth prevaile; and ye Churches of God reverte to their anciente puritie; and recover, their primative order, libertie, & bewtie. But when he could not prevaile by these means, against the maine trueths of ye gospell; but that they began to take rooting in many places; being watered with ye bloud of ye martires, and blessed from heaven with a gracious encrease. He then begane to take him to his anciente strategemes, used of old against the first Christians. That when by ye bloody, & barbarous persecutions of ye Heathen Emperours, he could not stoppe, & subuerte the course of ye Gospell; but that it speedily overspred, with a wounderfull celeritie, the then best known parts of ye world. He then begane to sow errours, heresies, and wounderfull dissentions amongst ye professours them selves (working upon their pride, & ambition, with other corrupte passions, Incidente to all mortall men; yea to ye saints them selves in some measure) by which wofull effects followed; as not only bitter contentions, & hartburnings, schismes, with other horrible confusions. But Satan tooke occasion & advantage therby to foyst in a number of vile ceremoneys, with many unprofitable Cannons, & decrees which have since been as snares, to many poore, & peacable souls, even to this day. So as in ye anciente times, the persecuti-

• *Opening page of William Bradford's* Of Plymouth Plantation, *his account of the Plymouth settlement, including the attack on Wessagussett.*

captain put together a force that included Hobbamock and just seven Englishmen—any more and the Massachusetts might suspect what the English were planning. They would sail for Wessagussett pretending to be on a trading mission. Instead of launching a full-scale attack, they would, after secretly warning Weston's men, "take [the Indians] in such traps as they lay for others."

They were scheduled to leave the same day Pratt staggered out of the forest. Standish postponed their departure so that he could get as much information as possible from the young man. The Pilgrims found Pratt's story "good encouragement to proceed in our intendments," and with the help of a fair wind, Standish and his men left the next day for Wessagussett.

◆ ◆ ◆ Before landing, they stopped at the *Swan*, which was anchored just offshore from Wessagussett. The little vessel was deserted, but after Standish's men fired off a musket, the ship's master and several other men from Wessagussett walked down to the water's edge. They had been gathering groundnuts and seemed surprisingly unworried, given what the Pilgrims had been led to believe. Standish asked why they had left the ship without anyone on guard. "[L]ike men senseless of their own misery," they replied that they had no fear of the Indians. In fact, many of them had hired themselves out as servants to the Indians and were living with the Massachusetts in their wigwams.

If this was indeed the case, then why was Standish preparing to launch an attack? Had Pratt simply told the Pilgrims what they wanted to hear?

Standish was not about to allow anything—not even evidence that all was peace at Wessagussett—to stop his plan. He explained that he was going to kill as many Indians as he could, then the settlers could either return with him to Plymouth or take the *Swan* up to Maine, where they could look to English fishermen for help. Standish had even brought along some corn for them to eat during their voyage.

It was their hunger, not their fear of the Indians, that was the main concern of Weston's men. So they quickly embraced Standish's plan, since it meant they would soon have something to eat. Swearing all to secrecy, the captain told them to tell any Englishmen living outside the settlement to return as soon as possible to the safety of the fort. Unfortunately, it had started to rain, so several of the English chose to remain in the warmth of the Indians' wigwams.

In the meantime, a warrior approached the fort under the pretense of trading furs with Standish. The fiery captain tried to appear welcoming and calm, but it was clear to the Indian that Standish was up to no good. Once back among his friends, he reported that "he saw by his eyes that [the captain] was angry in his heart."

This prompted the Massachusett pniese Pecksuot to approach Hobbamock. He told the Pokanoket warrior that he knew exactly what Standish was up to and that he and Wituwamat were unafraid of him. "[L]et him begin when he dare," he told Hobbamock; "he shall not take us unawares."

Later that day, both Pecksuot and Wituwamat brashly walked up to Standish. Pecksuot was a tall man, and he made a point of looking down on the Pilgrim military officer. "You are a great captain," he said, "yet you are but a little man. Though I be no sachem, yet I am of great strength and courage."

For his part, Wituwamat continued to sharpen the same knife he had made such a show of when he last saw Standish several weeks before at Manomet. On the knife's handle was the carved outline of a woman's face. "I have another at home," he told Standish, "wherewith I have killed both French and English, and that has a man's face on it; by and by these two must marry."

"These things the captain observed," Winslow wrote, "yet bore with patience for the present."

◆ ◆ ◆ The next day, Standish invited both Wituwamat and Pecksuot into one of the settlement's houses for a meal. In addition to corn, he had brought along some pork. The two Massachusett pnieses were suspicious of the Plymouth captain, but that did not prevent them from accepting Standish's invitation. Wituwamat and Pecksuot were accompanied by Wituwamat's brother and a friend, along with several women. Besides Standish, there were three other Pilgrims and Hobbamock in the room.

Once they had all sat down and begun to eat, the captain signaled for the door to be shut. He turned to Pecksuot and grabbed the knife from the string around the pniese's neck. Before the Indian had a chance to respond, Standish had begun stabbing him with his own weapon. The point was needle sharp, and Pecksuot's chest was soon riddled with blood-spurting wounds. As Standish and Pecksuot struggled, the other Pilgrims assaulted Wituwamat and his companion. "[I]t is incredible," Winslow wrote, "how many wounds these two pnieses received before they died, not making any fearful noise, but catching at their weapons and striving to the last."

All the while, Hobbamock stood by and watched. Soon the three Indians were dead, and Wituwamat's teenage brother had been taken captive. A smile broke out across Hobbamock's face, and he said, "Yesterday, Pecksuot, bragging of his own strength and stature, said though you were a great captain, yet you were but a little man. Today I see you are big enough to lay him on the ground."

◆ *Detail from John Seller's 1675 map of New England.*

But the killing had just begun. Wituwamat's brother was quickly hanged. There was another company of Pilgrims elsewhere in the settlement, and Standish sent word to them to kill any Indians who happened to be with them. As a result, two more were put to death. In the meantime, Standish and his cohorts found another Indian in the settlement and killed him too.

With Hobbamock and some of Weston's men in tow, Standish headed out in search of more Indians. They soon came across sachem Obtakiest and a group of Massachusett warriors. The Indians quickly scattered along the edge of a nearby forest, each man hiding behind a tree. Arrows were soon whizzing through the brisk afternoon air, most of them aimed at Standish and Hobbamock. Hobbamock was a pniese and was therefore supposedly invulnerable. Throwing off his coat, he began to chase after the Indians behind the trees. Most of them fled so quickly that none of the English could keep up with them.

There was a powwow who stood his ground and aimed an arrow at Standish. The captain and another Englishman fired simultaneously at the powwow, and the bullets broke his arm. With that, the remaining Indians, which included sachem Obtakiest, ran for the shelter of a nearby swamp, where they paused to yell curses at the Plymouth captain. Standish challenged the sachem to fight him man-to-man, but after a final exchange of insults, Obtakiest and the others disappeared into the swamp.

Several women had been captured back at the settlement during the scuffle with Pecksuot and Wituwamat. Now that the killing spree had finally come to an end, Standish decided to release the women, even though he knew there were at least three of Weston's men still living with the Indians. If he had kept these women as hostages, Standish could easily have bargained for the Englishmen's lives. But killing Native warriors, not saving lives, appears to have been the captain's goal at Wessagussett, and he released the female hostages. All three Englishmen were later executed.

Now that the violence had come to an end, the majority of the Wessagussett survivors decided to sail to Maine. The Pilgrims waited until the *Swan* had cleared Massachusetts Bay, then turned their shallop south for Plymouth, with the head of Wituwamat wrapped in a piece of white linen.

◆ ◆ ◆ Standish arrived at Plymouth to a hero's welcome. After being "received with joy," the captain and his men marched up to the newly completed fort, where Wituwamat's head was planted on a pole on the fort's roof. This was a common practice back in England, where the heads of executed traitors were mounted above the entrance to London Bridge. As it turned out, the fort contained its first prisoner: an Indian who had been sent to catch Phineas Pratt.

The Indian was released from his chains and brought out for examination. After looking "piteously on the head" of Wituwamat, the captive confessed everything. The plot had not originally been sachem Obtakiest's idea. There were five—Wituwamat, Pecksuot, and three powwows, including the one Standish had injured at Wessagussett—who had convinced their sachem to launch an attack against the Pilgrims. Bradford released the prisoner on the condition that he carry a message to Obtakiest: If the sachem dared to continue in "the like courses," Bradford vowed, "he would never suffer him or his to rest in peace, till he had utterly consumed them."

It took many days for the Pilgrims to receive an answer. Finally a Massachusett woman appeared at Plymouth with Obtakiest's response. She explained that her sachem was eager to make peace with the Pilgrims, but none of his men were willing to approach the settlement. Ever since the massacre at Wessagussett, Obtakiest had kept on the move, fearful that Standish might return and "take further vengeance on him."

The Massachusetts were not the only Indians in the region to have escaped into the wilderness. All throughout Cape Cod—from Manomet to Nauset to Pamet—the Native inhabitants had fled in panic, convinced that Standish and his thugs were about to descend on their villages and kill every Indian in sight. "[T]his sudden and unexpected execution . . . ," Edward Winslow wrote, "hath so terrified and amazed them, as in like manner they forsook their houses, running to and fro like men distracted, living in swamps and other desert places, and so brought manifold diseases amongst themselves, whereof very many are dead."

Huddled in swamps and on remote islands, afraid to go back to their villages, Indians throughout the region began to die at a startling rate.

"[C]ertainly it is strange to hear how many of late have, and still daily die amongst them," Winslow wrote. Just about every notable sachem on the Cape died in the months ahead, including Canacum at Manomet, and Aspinet at Nauset. Among the Massachusetts, the Pilgrims had earned a new name: *wotawquenange*, which one English settler later translated as meaning "cutthroats."

◆ ◆ ◆ The Pilgrims knew that there were those back in England who would criticize them for launching an unprovoked attack on sachem Obtakiest and the Massachusetts. In the months ahead, Edward Winslow wrote a book called *Good Newes from New England.* As the title suggests, Winslow's account puts the Wessagussett raid in the best possible light. The Pilgrims, Winslow points out, had been operating in a climate of intense fear since learning about the massacres in Virginia the previous spring. When Massasoit revealed the plot against them, there was little else they could have been expected to do.

There was one man, however, who refused to forgive the Pilgrims for "the killing of those poor Indians." When he heard about the incident back in Leiden, Pastor John Robinson sent Governor Bradford a letter. "Oh, how happy a thing had it been," he wrote, "if you had converted some before you had killed any! Besides, where blood is once begun to be shed, it is seldom staunched of a long time after." The real problem, as far as Robinson saw it, was Bradford's willingness to trust Standish, a man the minister had come to know when he was in Leiden. The captain lacked "that tenderness of the life of man (made after God's image) which is meet."

Robinson concluded his letter to Bradford with words that proved ominously prophetic, given the ultimate course of New England's history: "It is . . . a thing more glorious, in men's eyes, than pleasing in God's or convenient for Christians, to be a terror to poor barbarous people. And indeed I am afraid lest, by these occasions, others should be drawn to affect a kind of ruffling course in the world."

• • • That summer the supply ship *Anne* arrived with sixty passengers, including the widow Alice Southworth. The Southworths and Bradfords had known each other in Leiden, and just a few weeks after the *Anne*'s arrival, William Bradford and Alice were married on August 14, 1623.

The festivities that followed were much more than the celebration of a marriage. A new order had come to New England. Massasoit attended the wedding ceremony, with a black wolf skin draped over his shoulder. Also attending were about 120 of his warriors, about twice as many men as he had been able to gather a little more than a year ago. They danced "with such a noise," one witness reported, "that you would wonder."

As Indians on Cape Cod to the east and in Massachusetts to the north continued to be gripped by fear and confusion, a supreme confidence had come to the Pokanokets. Massasoit was now firmly in control, and it had been Standish's assault at Wessagussett that had made it possible.

Prior to Wessagussett, Aspinet, sachem of the Nausets, had commanded more warriors than Massasoit. But now Aspinet was dead, and his people had scattered in panic. Over the next few years, Massasoit emerged as the leader of the Indian nation we now refer to as the Wampanoag. It was exactly the scenario Squanto had envisioned for himself the year before. But it was Massasoit who pulled it off. Just a few words, delivered from what had almost been his deathbed, had unleashed a chain of events that had completely changed the region. Serving as a grim reminder of the power of the Pokanoket-Pilgrim alliance was the skull of Wituwamat, still planted on a pole above the fort roof.

It was only appropriate that a new flag be raised for Massasoit's benefit. Instead of the English flag, the Pilgrims raised a blood-soaked piece of linen. It was the same cloth that had once covered Wituwamat's head, and it now flew bravely above the fort: a reddish brown smear against the blue summer sky.

TEN
A New England

◆ ◆ ◆

AS PASTOR ROBINSON had suggested, the Pilgrims had lost more than a little of their collective soul at the battle of Wessagussett. But so had the Pokanokets. By siding with the English, Massasoit had allied himself with a culture and technology on which his own people increasingly came to depend. Whether it was iron hoes and kettles, blankets, liquor, or guns, the English had what the Pokanokets wanted. There would be some good years ahead as the Pilgrims eagerly traded with them for furs. But as the beavers and other fur-bearing animals grew scarce, the only thing the Indians had to sell to the English was their land.

It had begun innocently enough in 1621, when Massasoit had given Patuxet to the Pilgrims as a gift. Back then it had been difficult to imagine a time when land would be anything but an endless resource. From the start, Plymouth authorities insisted that all Native land purchases must have prior court approval. By controlling the buying and selling of Indian land, the colony hoped to avoid possible confusion in the future while protecting the Natives from people who might cheat them out of their property.

Today, the sums paid for Massasoit's lands seem tiny. However, given the high cost of clearing Native land and the high value the Indians attached to English goods, the prices are almost justifiable. Certainly, the Pilgrims *felt* they were paying a fair price, and their descendants later insisted that they "did not possess one foot of land in this colony but what was fairly obtained by honest purchase of the Indian proprietors." What these later Pilgrim generations failed to recognize, however, was that the

Indians had a very different relationship with the land. Instead of giving up their property to the English through a land sale, they assumed they were simply granting the English the right to share the land with them. When it became clear what the Pilgrims were up to, the Indians had already lost much of their land.

◆ ◆ ◆ The fall of 1623 marked the end of Plymouth's food shortages. For the last two planting seasons, the Pilgrims had all grown crops together—the approach first used at Jamestown and other English settlements. But in April, Bradford had decided that each household should be assigned its own plot of land, with the understanding that each family kept whatever it grew. The change in attitude was dramatic. Families were now willing to work much harder than they had ever worked before. In previous years, the men had tended the fields while the women tended the children at home. "The women now went willingly into the field," Bradford wrote, "and took their little ones with them to set corn."

In 1625, William Bradford received the stunning news that the congregation's minister, John Robinson, had died in Leiden. A profound sense of sadness settled over the Plymouth church. Elder William Brewster kept on as their spiritual leader, but the Plymouth congregation would always feel as if something was missing.

◆ *A chest reputed to have been brought aboard the* Mayflower *by William Brewster.*

About the same time as Robinson's passing, a new settlement was started just to the north of Wessagussett. One of the settlement's founders was a jolly, down-on-his-luck lawyer from London named Thomas Morton, who arrived with a handful of servants. Morton named the new settlement Merrymount.

As the name of his settlement might suggest, Morton represented everything the Pilgrims had come to America to escape. In addition to being, in Bradford's words, of "more craft than honesty," Morton was an Anglican for whom a Sunday was best spent, not in prayer, but in hunting with his falcon or, better yet, sharing a drink with the local Indians. Instead of building a wall around Merrymount, Morton erected an eighty-foot-high maypole that he and his men danced around with their Native neighbors, making a mockery of the solemn religiousness of the Plymouth settlement. What was worse, Morton's friendship with the Indians quickly made him the favored trading partner in the region. He even dared to give them guns, since this helped the Indians provide more furs. It was because of this that Bradford decided to send Standish on yet another raid to the north—not to kill any Indians but to seize this "Lord of Misrule," who was eventually sent back to England.

In 1626, Holland purchased Manhattan from the Indians and established the colony of New Netherland. Since many of the Pilgrims knew the language, it was perhaps inevitable that Plymouth developed a strong relationship with the Dutch colony. The Dutch trading agent Isaack de Rasiere visited Plymouth in 1627, and his description of the English community on a typical Sunday provides fascinating evidence of just how strong Standish's influence continued to be, despite Pastor Robinson's warnings about the military leader.

> They assembled by beat of drum, each with his musket or firelock, in front of the captain's door; they have their cloaks on, and place themselves in order, three abreast, and are led by a sergeant without beat of drum. Behind comes the Governor, in a long robe; beside him on the right hand, comes the preacher with his cloak on, and on the left hand, the captain with his side-arms and cloak on, and with a small cane in his hand; and so they march in good order, and each sets his arms down near him. Thus they are constantly on their guard night and day.

Seven years after the *Mayflower* had sailed, Plymouth Plantation was still an armed fortress where each man worshipped with a gun at his side.

◆ ◆ ◆ By 1626, the Adventurers in London had disbanded. William Bradford and seven others—Winslow, Brewster, Standish, Alden, Howland, Allerton, and Thomas Prence, who had come over on the *Fortune* in 1621—agreed to take on the colony's debt with the understanding that they would be given total control over the fur trade. The following year, Isaack de Rasiere introduced the Pilgrims to wampum.

Wampum consisted of strings of beads made either from white periwinkle shells or the purple portion of quahog shells, with the purple beads being worth approximately twice as much as the white beads. To be accepted, wampum had to meet strict guidelines, and both the Indians and the English became expert in identifying whether or not the beads had been properly cut, shaped, polished, drilled, and strung. Wampum quickly became used as money in New England and revolutionized trade with the Indians. But despite some remarkable profits in the fur trade, Bradford and his fellow investors still struggled to pay off the colony's debt. Even though Winslow claimed that Plymouth was a place where "religion and profit jump together," the colony was unable to achieve any sort of financial success.

◆ ◆ ◆ In 1630, a fleet of seventeen ships arrived off the New England coast. Until that point, Plymouth had been the only significant English settlement in the region. In a matter of months, approximately a thousand Puritan English men, women, and children—more than three times the entire population of Plymouth—had been delivered to the Boston area. In the years ahead, the Puritan colony of Massachusetts Bay grew to include modern New Hampshire and Maine, while other Puritan settlers headed south to Connecticut.

Adding to the mix was the Massachusetts exile Roger Williams, who in 1636 founded what became the religiously tolerant colony of Rhode Island, a home for Baptists, Quakers, and other non-Puritans. New England had become exactly what its name suggested, a *new* England composed of separate colonies.

Over the course of the next decade, as King Charles made life more and more difficult for Puritans in England, an estimated twenty-one thousand Puritan immigrants flooded across the Atlantic to New England. Minimal from the beginning, the religious distinction between the "Pilgrims" and "Puritans" quickly became meaningless. Instead, the terms "Puritan" and "Pilgrim" came to signify two different groups of settlers—Pilgrims referred to those who arrived in Plymouth between 1620 and 1630, and Puritans were those who came to Massachusetts Bay and Connecticut after 1629.

In the beginning, the Massachussetts Bay settlement to the north

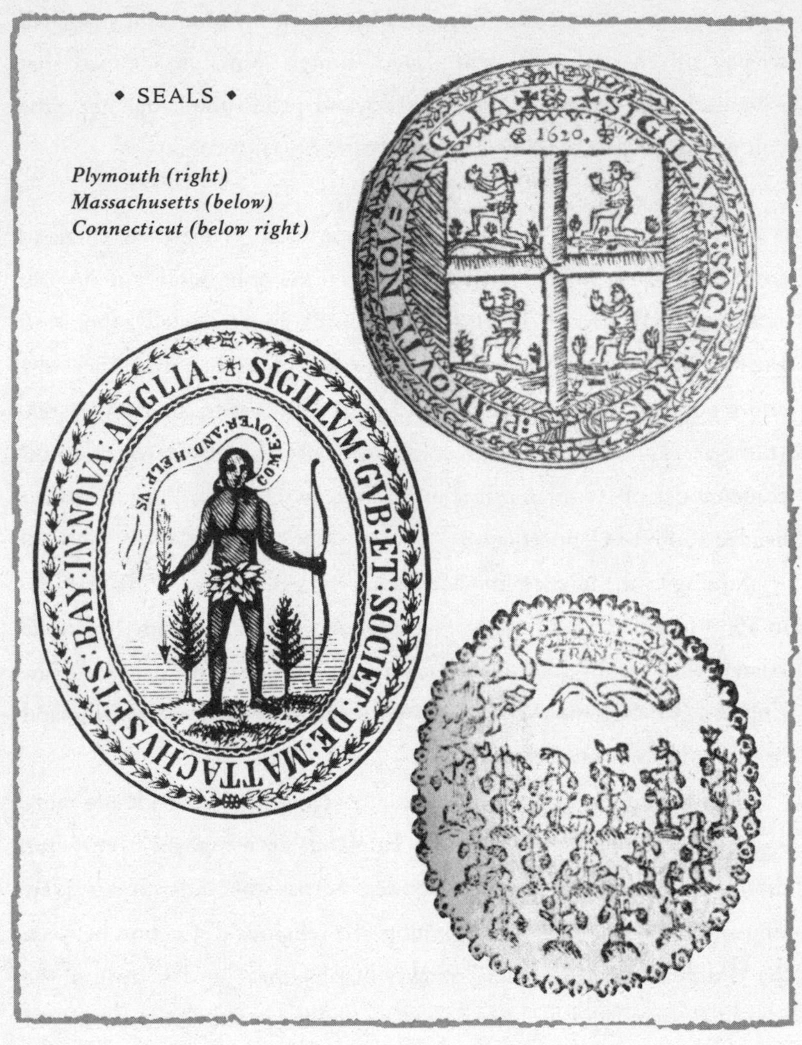

◆ SEALS ◆

Plymouth (right)
Massachusetts (below)
Connecticut (below right)

provided much-needed financial help for the Pilgrims. What the new arrivals wanted more than anything else were cattle and hogs, which the Pilgrims now had. Over the course of the next decade, Plymouth experienced an economic boom fueled, in large part, by the rising price of livestock. By the 1630s, the Pilgrims had established a series of trading posts that extended all the way from the Connecticut River to Castine, Maine. But inevitably, the leaders of Massachusetts Bay wanted to get in on this profitable trade, and as Massachusetts moved into the region with outposts of its own, tensions rose between the Pilgrims and Puritans.

It was only a matter of time before Massachusetts Bay's economic ambitions brought the Puritans into conflict with the region's other occupants, the Native Americans. In the lower portion of the Connecticut River valley lived the Pequots, a tribe whose economic power more than equaled that of the Puritans. When the captains of several English trading vessels were killed by Indians in the region, Massachusetts Bay launched an attack on the Pequots. In many ways, the Pequot War of 1637 was the Puritans' Wessagussett: a terrifyingly brutal assault that changed the balance of power in the region for decades to come.

Much as Massasoit had done more than a decade before, a Mohegan sachem named Uncas used the conflict between the Indians and English as an opportunity to advance his own tribe. Before the Pequot War, Uncas was a minor player in the region. But after pledging his loyalty to the Puritans, he and his people were on their way to overtaking the Pequots as the most powerful tribe in Connecticut.

The Narragansetts were less enthusiastic in their support of the English. The Pequots were their traditional enemies, but they were reluctant to join forces with Uncas and the Mohegans. Only after Roger Williams, the founder of Rhode Island, personally asked for help on Massachusetts Bay's behalf did Narragansett sachem Miantonomi agree to assist the Puritans against the Pequots.

The Puritans attacked a Pequot fortress on the Mystic River in

◆ *An engraving showing the Puritans' 1637 attack on the Pequot fort in Mystic, Connecticut.*

southern Connecticut near the Rhode Island border. After setting the Indians' wigwams on fire, the soldiers shot and hacked to pieces anyone who attempted to escape. By the end of the day, approximately four hundred Pequot men, women, and children were dead. "It was a fearful sight to see them thus frying in the fire and the streams of blood quenching the same," William Bradford wrote, "and horrible was the stink and scent thereof; but the victory seemed a sweet sacrifice, and they gave the praise thereof to God."

Bradford saw the killing as the work of the Lord. The Narragansetts, however, saw nothing divine in the slaughter. As Roger Williams observed, Native American warfare was more about the bravery and honor of the fighters than the body count, and usually only a handful of warriors were killed in battle. Prior to the attack on the Pequot fort in Mystic, sachem Miantonomi had tried to get Williams to promise that no women and children would be killed. Unfortunately, Williams, who had been thrown out of Massachusetts Bay just two years before for his unorthodox religious views, had been unable to make any kind of deal with the Puritans. As the flames devoured every living thing in the

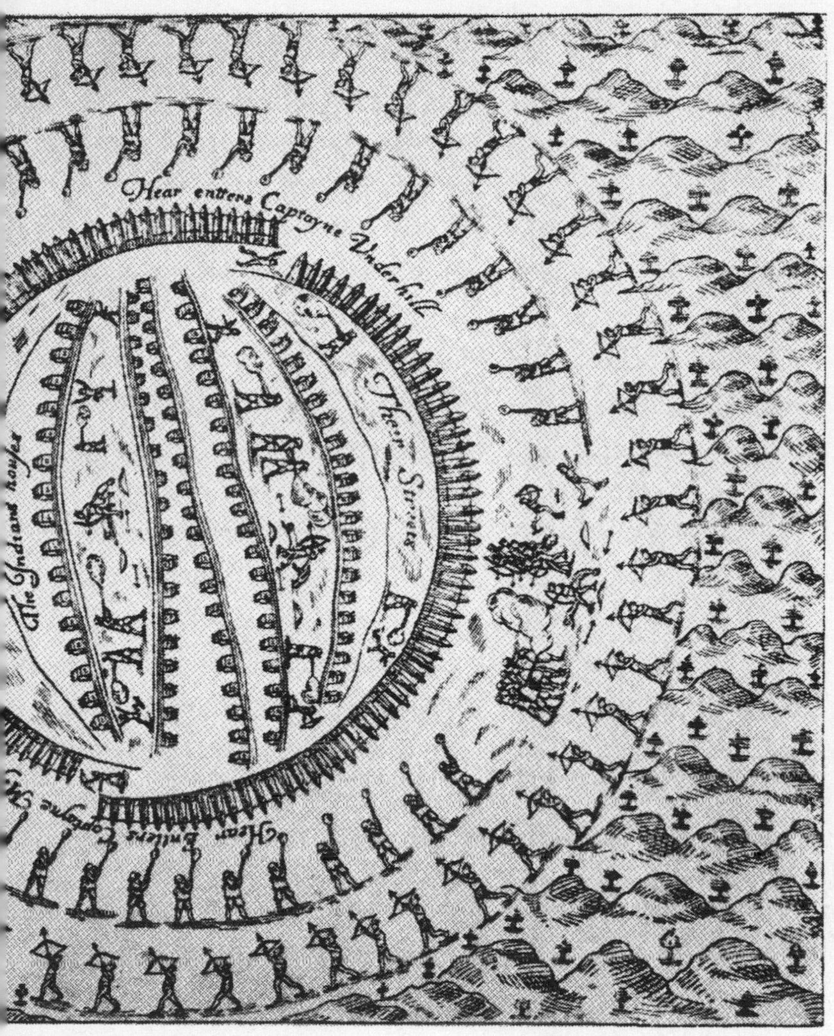

village, the Narragansetts angrily protested the slaughter, claiming "it is too furious, and slays too many men." With the Pequot War, New England was introduced to the horrors of European-style genocide.

◆ ◆ ◆ Before the massacre, the Pequots had urged the Narragansetts to join them against the Puritans, claiming that the English would soon "overspread their country" and force them off their own lands. In the years ahead, the Narragansett sachem Miantonomi would come to realize that the Pequots had been right. By the late 1630s, when he saw that there were more Puritans in Massachusetts Bay than Native Americans in all of New England, he decided to eliminate the English threat before the Narragansetts suffered the same fate as the Pequots.

In 1642, he traveled to the Montauks on Long Island in hopes of persuading them to join the Narragansetts against the English. To accomplish this, he proposed that all Indians work together to retake New England. Miantonomi's speech to the Montauks included an insightful account of the ecological problems that had come to New England: "You know our fathers had plenty of deer and skins, our plains were full of deer, as also our woods, and of turkeys, and our coves full of fish and fowl. But these English having gotten our land, they with scythes cut down the grass, and with axes fell the trees; their cows and horses eat the grass, and their hogs spoil our clam banks, and we shall all be starved." Miantonomi knew from experience that to pick a fight with the Puritans was to fight to the death. He proposed that they now "kill men, women, and children, but no cows," since the Indians would need the English livestock for food.

But instead of joining with Miantonomi and the Narragansetts, the Montauks reported his speech to the English. And in the end, Miantonomi was unable to follow his own advice. Instead of attacking the English, he attacked Uncas and the Mohegans. Like Massasoit before him, Uncas had used his allegiance with the English to increase his power and influence, and by 1643, Miantonomi had had enough of him. After an assassination plot against Uncas failed, Miantonomi

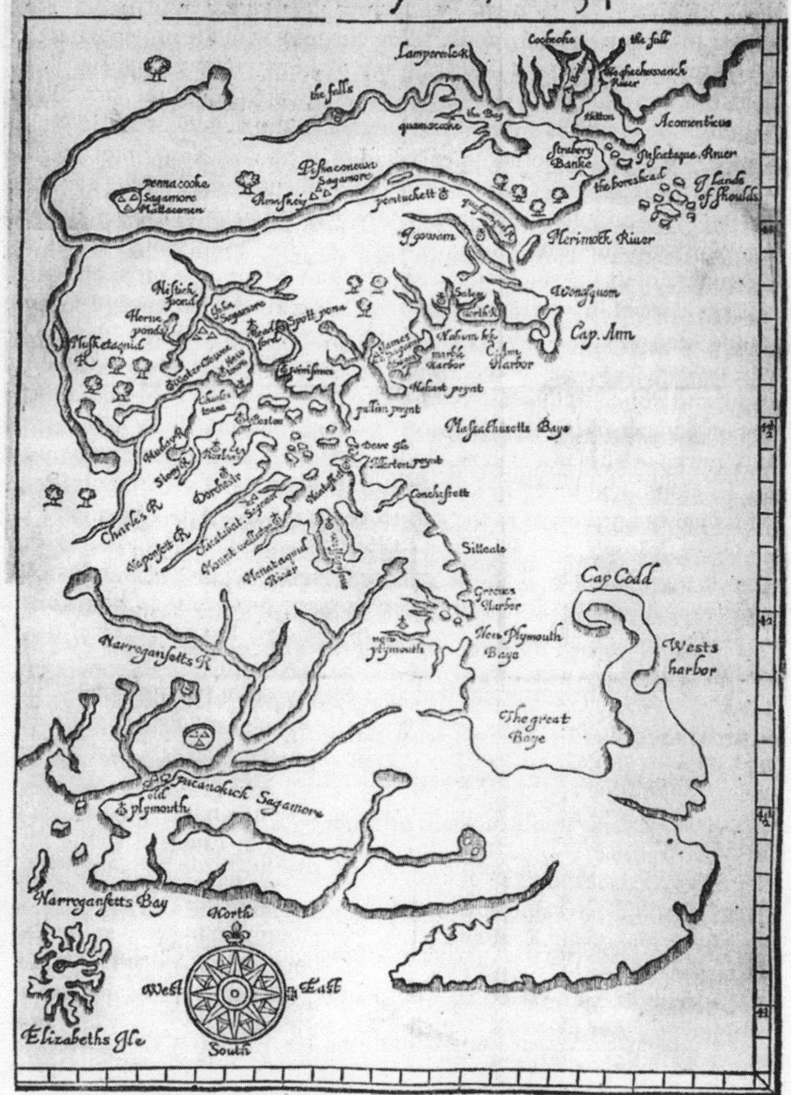

◆ *A 1634 map of New England.*

and a thousand of his warriors launched an assault on the Mohegans.

Before the attack, Miantonomi put on a protective iron corselet, like the English wore in battle. But instead of saving his life, the armor led to his death. When the fighting turned against the Narragansetts and the sachem was forced to flee, he staggered under the weight of the metal breastplate and was easily captured.

At the same time as the Narragansetts and the Mohegans were fighting, it had become clear to many New Englanders that the English colonies had to act as one body in their dealings with the Indians. So they established the United Colonies of New England. Each colony had its own representatives, called "commissioners." Noticeably missing from the union was Roger Williams's Rhode Island—the only non-Puritan colony in New England.

According to John Quincy Adams, the United Colonies of 1643 was "the model and prototype of the North American Confederacy of 1774," which, in turn, became the basis of the United States. More than a hundred years before the colonies' war with England, the United Colonies of New England showed the importance of looking beyond local concerns and prejudices. If Miantonomi had succeeded in creating the same kind of confederacy for the Native Americans of the region, the history of New England might have been very different.

Miantonomi was still being held prisoner by Uncas when the commissioners of the United Colonies met for the first time in Hartford, Connecticut, on September 7, 1643. Uncas asked the commissioners what he should do with the Narragansett sachem. After long discussions, they decided to let Uncas do as he wished.

There is evidence that the Miantonomi tried one last time to unite the Native peoples of New England by proposing that he marry one of

Uncas's sisters. It was, however, too late to make up. On the path between Hartford and Windsor, Connecticut, Uncas's brother walked up behind Miantonomi and "clave his head with a hatchet." For the time being, the threat of a united Native assault against Puritan and Pilgrim New England had been laid to rest.

ELEVEN
The Ancient Mother

◆ ◆ ◆

BY THE EARLY 1640s, the Great Migration to the New World had come to an end as England was torn apart by civil war. Many settlers returned to England to join in Parliament's efforts to overthrow King Charles. With the king's execution in 1649, England became a Puritan state—unimaginable just a decade before. Bradford felt compelled to turn to an early page in his history of Plymouth and write, "Full little did I think, that the downfall of the bishops, with their courts, canons, and ceremonies, etc. had been so near, when I first began these scribbled writings . . . or that I should have lived to have seen, or hear of the same; but it is the Lord's doing, and ought to be marvelous in our eyes!"

Until this spectacular turn of events, it had been possible for a Puritan to believe that America was where God wanted them to be. Now it seemed that England was the true center stage. In addition, the English civil war hurt the region's economy. Pilgrims, who had watched the prices of their cattle and crops skyrocket over the last decade, were suddenly left with a surplus that was worth barely a quarter of what it was in the 1630s. More than a few New Englanders decided that it was time to return to the mother country, and one of those was Edward Winslow.

Winslow had emerged as Plymouth's main diplomat, whether negotiating with Massasoit or with the government back in England. In 1646, Winslow sailed for London on another diplomatic mission. His talents were noticed by Oliver Cromwell, head of the Puritan regime, and the Pilgrim diplomat soon became caught up in England's struggles. To Bradford's bitter regret, Winslow never returned to Plymouth. In 1654,

Cromwell sent Winslow to the West Indies; a year later, he died from yellow fever off the island of Jamaica and was buried at sea with full honors.

◆ ◆ ◆ By the time Bradford received word of Winslow's passing, Elder William Brewster had been dead for more than a decade. A year later, in 1656, Miles Standish died in his home in Duxbury. At that point, Bradford was sixty-eight years old. He had come to America not to establish a great and powerful colony but to create a tightly knit religious community. For that to happen, everyone was supposed to live together and worship in the same church. But as early as the 1630s it had become apparent that the soil around the original Plymouth settlement was not the best. Many inhabitants also claimed they needed more land to accommodate the growing herds of cattle. To the governor's dismay, many of his closest friends, including Brewster, Winslow, Standish, and John Alden, had left Plymouth to found communities to the north in Duxbury and Marshfield. Thomas Prence, one of the colony's rising stars, who first served as governor in 1634, also moved to Duxbury, then helped found the town of Eastham on Cape Cod.

At the root of this trend toward town building was, Governor Bradford insisted, a growing hunger for land. For Bradford, land had been a way to create a community of Saints. For an increasing number of Pilgrims and especially for their children, land was a way to get rich. Bradford claimed that the formation of new towns was "not for want or necessity" but "for the enriching of themselves," and he predicted it would be "the ruin of New England."

It was difficult for Bradford to lose Winslow, Brewster, and the others. For as the new towns prospered and grew, Plymouth, the village where it had all begun, fell on hard times. "And thus was this poor church left,"

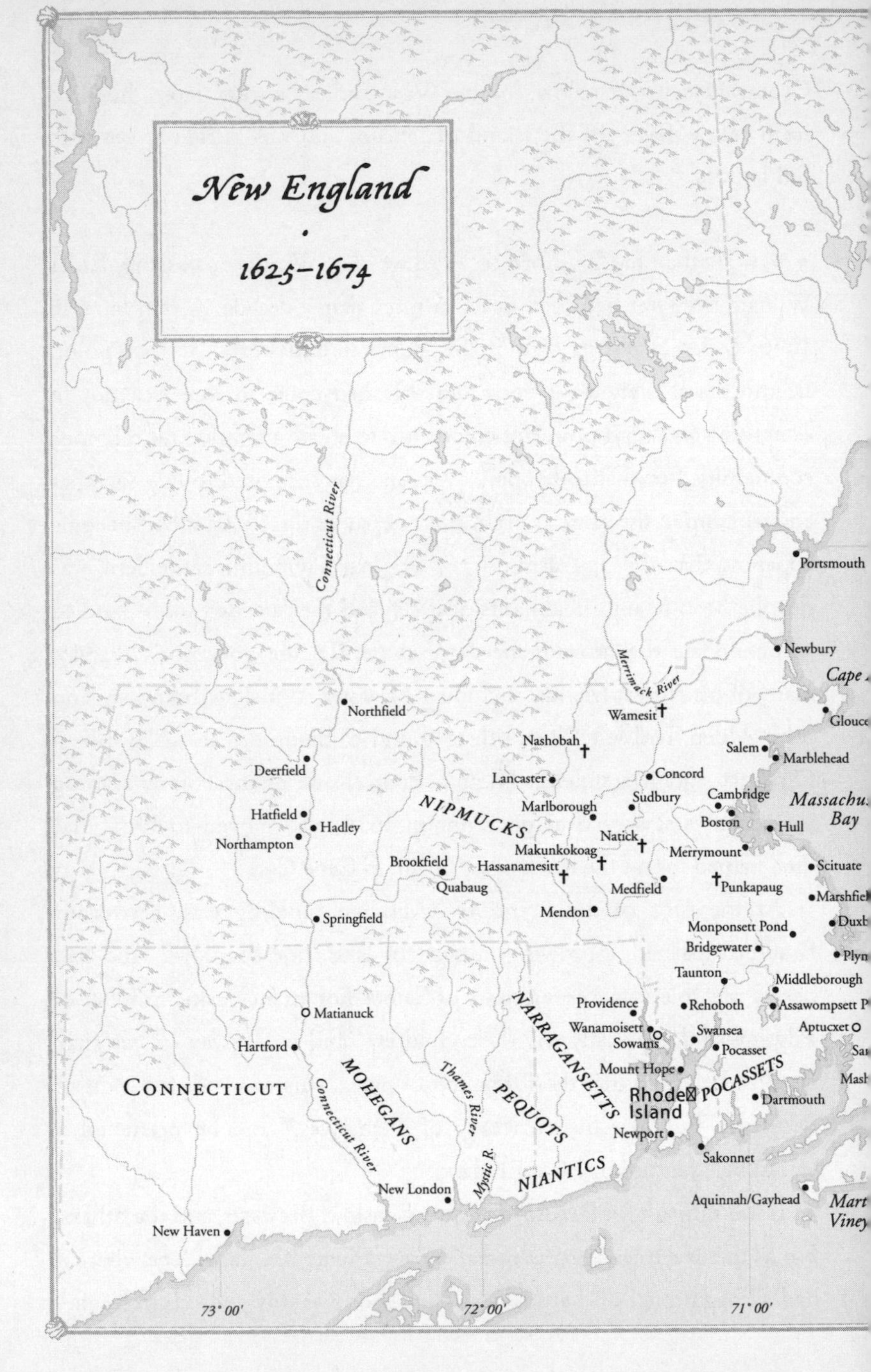

New England
1625–1674
Connecticut River
Portsmouth
Newbury
Cape
Merrimack River
Northfield
Wamesit
Glouce
Nashobah
Salem
Marblehead
Deerfield
Lancaster
Concord
Sudbury
Cambridge
Massachu
Bay
NIPMUCKS
Marlborough
Hatfield
Boston
Hull
Hadley
Northampton
Natick
Makunkokoag
Merrymount
Brookfield
Hassanamesitt
Scituate
Quabaug
Medfield
Punkapaug
Marshfie
Mendon
Springfield
Monponsett Pond
Dux
Bridgewater
Plym
Taunton
Middleborough
NARRAGANSETTS
Providence
Rehoboth
Assawompsett P
Matianuck
Wanamoisett
Aptucxet
Sowams
Swansea
Hartford
Pocasset
MOHEGANS
Thames River
Mount Hope
POCASSETS
Mash
CONNECTICUT
Connecticut River
PEQUOTS
Rhode
Island
Dartmouth
Newport
Sakonnet
NIANTICS
Mystic R.
New London
Aquinnah/Gayhead
Mart
Viney
New Haven
73° 00'
72° 00'
71° 00'

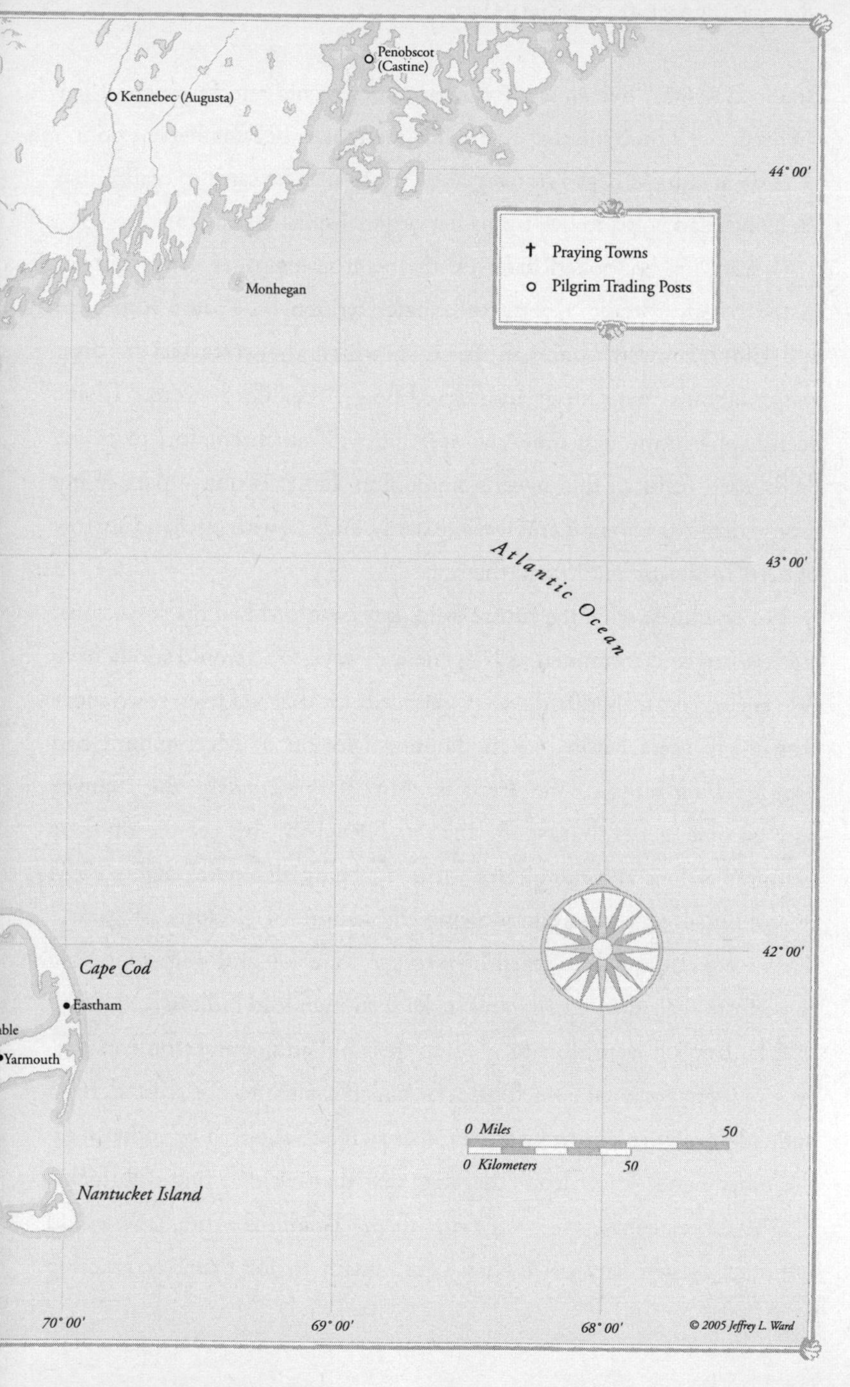
Penobscot
(Castine)
Kennebec (Augusta)
44° 00'
Praying Towns
Pilgrim Trading Posts
Monhegan
Atlantic Ocean
43° 00'
42° 00'
Cape Cod
Eastham
ble
Yarmouth
0 Miles 50
0 Kilometers 50
Nantucket Island
70° 00'
69° 00'
68° 00'
© 2005 Jeffrey L. Ward

Bradford wrote, "like an ancient mother grown old and forsaken of her children. . . . Thus, she that had made many rich became herself poor."

A deep sadness began to overtake Bradford as he came to realize that Plymouth had failed to live up to her original spiritual mission.

Late in life, he looked back on the manuscript pages of his history of the colony. Beside a copy of a letter written by Pastor Robinson and Elder Brewster back in 1617, in which they referred to their congregation's "most strict and sacred bond," Bradford wrote, "I have been happy in my first times, to see, and with much comfort to enjoy, the blessed fruits of this sweet communion, but it is now a part of my misery in old age, to find and feel the decay, and . . . with grief and sorrow of heart to lament and bewail the same."

No one knew what the future held, but Bradford had his suspicions. If New England continued its "degenerate" ways, God would surely have his vengeance. In Bradford's view, the seeds for this had been sown more than thirty years before, when Thomas Morton of Merrymount had begun selling guns to the Indians. Almost immediately, the Natives had become better huntsmen than the English "by reason of their swiftness of foot and nimbleness of body, being also quick-sighted and by continual exercise well knowing the haunts of all sorts of game." They were also quick to learn how to use a musket and were soon able to perform their own repairs and make their own lead bullets.

The English were slow to give up their old and cumbersome matchlock muskets for the newer flintlocks, which came into use around 1630 and didn't require a burning wick (or "match") to shoot. The Indians, on the other hand, knew from the start that they wanted only flintlocks. "[T]hey became mad (as it were) after them," Bradford wrote, "and would not stick to give any price they could attain to for them; accounting

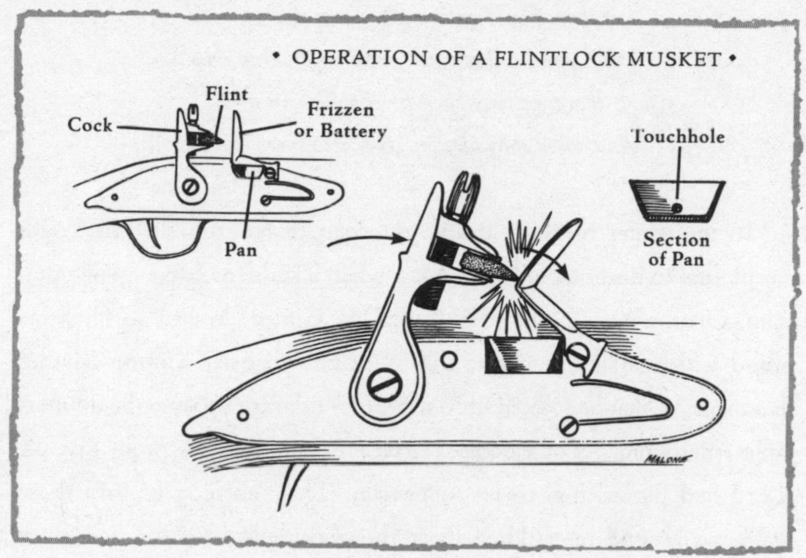

their bows and arrows but baubles in comparison of them." Suddenly the English were no longer the technological superiors of the Native Americans, and when they ran into "the Indians in the woods armed with guns in this sort, it was a terror unto them."

Over time, however, the English became accustomed to the sight of an Indian with a gun. Indians armed with flintlocks brought in more game and furs to English trading posts. And besides, if the Indians did not get their weapons from the English, they could easily buy them from the French and the Dutch. Selling guns and ammunition was a highly profitable business, and Plymouth eventually came to approve the sales.

From Governor Bradford's perspective, the arming of the Indians showed that New England was headed for a fall. And it was the gun-toting Indians who would be "the rod" with which the Lord punished his people:

For these fierce natives, they are now so fill'd
With guns and muskets, and in them so skill'd
As that they may keep the English in awe,
And when they please, give unto them the law.

In the winter of 1657, Bradford began to feel unwell. His health continued to decline until early May, when a sudden change came upon him. On the morning of May 8, "[T]he God of heaven so filled his mind with ineffable consolations," Puritan historian Cotton Mather later wrote, "that he seemed little short of Paul, rapt up unto the unutterable entertainments of Paradise." Here at long last was proof that the Lord had picked him to go to heaven. That morning he told those gathered around his sickbed that "the good spirit of God had given him a pledge of happiness in another world, and the first-fruits of his

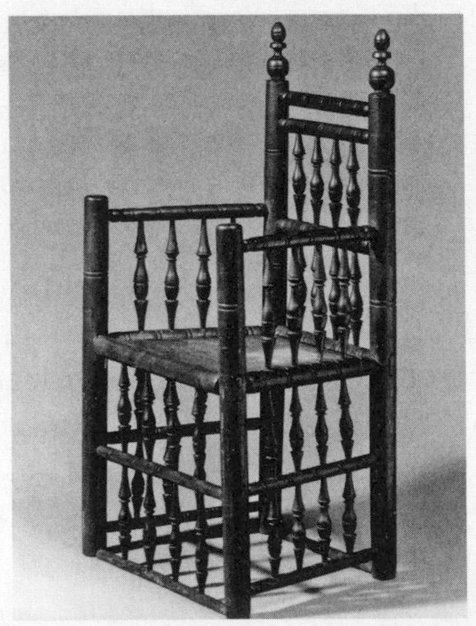

• *A chair once owned by William Bradford.*

eternal glory." He died the next day, "lamented by all the colonies of New England, as a common blessing and father to them all."

◆ ◆ ◆ In the forty years since the voyage of the *Mayflower,* the Native Americans had experienced huge changes, but they had continued to draw strength from traditional ways. The Pokanokets still hunted much as their fathers had done, but instead of bows and arrows, they now used the latest flintlock muskets. Inside their wigwams made of reed mats and tree bark were English chests in which they kept bracelets, rings, and strings of wampum beads. Attached to their buckskin breeches were brass bells that tinkled as they walked.

Given the spirituality of the Native Americans, it was perhaps inevitable that many of them also showed an interest in the Englishmen's religion. The Pilgrims had done little to convert the Indians to Christianity, but for the Puritans of Massachusetts Bay, it was a priority from the start. The colony's seal, created even before their arrival in the New World, showed a Native American saying, "Come over and help us."

The Puritans believed a Christian must be able to read God's word in the Bible, and early on, efforts were made to teach the Indians how to read and write. A handful of Native Americans even attended the newly founded Harvard College. In the 1650s, the missionary John Eliot translated the entire Old and New Testaments into a phonetic version of the Massachusetts language, titled *Mamusse Wanneetupanatamwe Up-Biblum God.*

Eliot created a series of Native communities known as Praying Towns. In addition to teaching the "Praying Indians" about Christianity, Eliot hoped to turn them from their traditional ways. But as was true with their use of flintlocks and jewelry, the Indians never wholly abandoned their

◆ *Painting of missionary John Eliot, circa 1660.*

former identities. Instead of replacing the old ways, Christianity became, for many Indians, the way for Native culture to endure.

For sachems in the seventeenth century, however, Christianity threatened their power. As increasing numbers of Indians turned to God, especially on Martha's Vineyard and Cape Cod, there were fewer left to supply Massasoit with the steady stream of tribute on which he had traditionally depended.

◆ ◆ ◆ When it came to borrowing from the English, the Indians had demonstrated tremendous creativity and enthusiasm. The English were much more reluctant to borrow from the Indians, yet they did adopt some Native ways, particularly when it came to food. Ever since the Pilgrims stumbled across the buried corn on Cape Cod, maize had been an essential part of every New Englander's diet. It has been estimated that the Indians ate between 280 and 340 pounds of corn per person per year, and the English were not far behind. Hominy and johnnycakes, which became staples of early American diets, are adaptations of Native recipes. Over the years, the English pottage that Massasoit had craved on his sickbed had become more like the Indians' own succotash: a soupy mishmash of corn, beans, and whatever fish and meat were available. When it came to harvesting corn, the English adopted the Native husking bee celebration, a communal tradition in which a young man who came across a red ear of corn was allowed to demand a kiss from the girl of his choice.

When the Pilgrims had first settled at Plymouth, there had been forty miles between them and Massasoit's village at Sowams. By 1655, there were just a few miles between the Pokanokets' headquarters and the closest English homes at Wannamoisett. An intimacy existed between the English and Indians that would have been almost unimaginable to later generations of Americans. The English hired their Indian neighbors as farmhands; they traded with them for fish and game. Inevitably, a mixture of English-Indian languages developed, and it became second nature for an Englishman to greet a Native acquaintance as *netop*, or friend.

Still, intermarriage between the two races was virtually nonexistent, and without children to provide them with a genetic and cultural common ground, the Indians and English would always have difficulty understanding each other's point of view. But while relations between the Indians and English were by no means perfect throughout the midpoint of the seventeenth century, the leaders on both sides worked hard to settle their differences. As they all understood, it was the only way to avoid a war.

◆ *Massasoit's pictogram from a 1657 land deed.*

◆ ◆ ◆ In the fall of 1657, a few months after the death of William Bradford, Massasoit, now approaching eighty years of age, signed his last Plymouth land deed. At the bottom of the parchment, he sketched an intricate pictogram. What looks like the upper portion of a man floats above what could be his legs with only a wavy line connecting the two. Whatever it actually shows, the pictogram gives a sense of distance and removal. With this deed, Massasoit disappears from the records of Plymouth Colony, only to reappear in the records of Massachusetts Bay as leader of the Quabaugs, a subgroup of the Nipmucks based more than fifty-five miles northwest of Pokanoket.

For years, the Pokanokets had maintained a close relationship with the Quabaugs, who lived with other subgroups of the Nipmucks between the Connecticut River to the west and the English settlements outside Boston to the east. As early as 1637, Massasoit came before officials in Boston as leader of the Quabaugs, and some historians think that twenty years later, in 1657, he moved to live among them. The move not only distanced the old sachem from Plymouth, it gave his eldest son, Wamsutta, who was nearly forty years old, a chance to establish himself as the Pokanokets' new leader.

Wamsutta had already begun to show signs of independence. In 1654, he sold Hog Island in Narragansett Bay to the Rhode Islander Richard

Smith without the written approval of either his father or the Plymouth commissioners. Just a few months later, Wamsutta refused to part with land his father had agreed to sell to the town of Taunton. Displaying a disregard for the Plymouth authorities, Wamsutta proclaimed that he was unwilling to surrender lands that the owners "say is granted by the court of Plymouth." Named as a witness to the document is John Sassamon—an Indian who represented everything Massasoit had come to fear and distrust.

John Sassamon had been one of the missionary John Eliot's star pupils. He had learned to read and write English, and in 1653, he attended Harvard College. For years, he had worked in Eliot's mission, and now he was Wamsutta's interpreter and scribe. In the spring of 1660, perhaps at Sassamon's urging, Wamsutta appeared before the Plymouth court—not to approve a sale of land but to change his name. The record reads:

> At the earnest request of Wamsutta, desiring that in regard his father is lately deceased, and he being desirous, according to the custom of the natives, to change his name, that the Court would confer an English name upon him, which accordingly they did, and therefore ordered, that for the future he shall be called by the name of Alexander of Pokanoket; and desiring the same in the behalf of his brother, they have named him Philip.

From that day forward, Massasoit's sons were known, at their own request, by Christian names. It was a new era.

◆ ◆ ◆ Except for his son's mention of his death in the Plymouth records, we know nothing about the circumstances of Massasoit's passing. It is difficult to believe that he could be buried anywhere but Pokanoket. One thing we do know is that late in life he began to share Governor Bradford's concerns about the future. At some point before his death, he took his two sons to the home of John Brown in nearby Wannamoisett. There, in the presence of Brown and his family, Massasoit stated his hope "that there might be love and amity after his death, between his sons and them, as there had been betwixt himself and them in former times."

It was somewhat unusual that Massasoit had chosen to make this pronouncement not in the presence of William Bradford's successor as governor, Thomas Prence, but in the home of an English neighbor. But as the sachem undoubtedly realized, if conflicts should one day arise between his people and the English, it was here, in the borderlands between Plymouth and Pokanoket, where the trouble would begin.

TWELVE
The Trial

◆ ◆ ◆

THE PILGRIMS HAD been driven by deeply held spiritual beliefs. They had sailed across a vast and dangerous ocean to a wilderness where, against impossible odds, they had made a home. The second generation of settlers grew up under very different circumstances. Instead of their spiritual beliefs, it was the economic rewards of *this* life that increasingly became the focus of the Pilgrims' children and grandchildren. Most Plymouth residents were farmers, but there was much more than agriculture driving the New England economy. The demand for fish, timber, grain, and cattle in Europe, the West Indies, and beyond was huge, and by the 1650s, New England merchants had established the pattern of transatlantic trade that existed right up to the American Revolution.

By the early 1660s, one of the foremost citizens of Plymouth Colony was Josiah Winslow, son of *Mayflower* passenger Edward Winslow. Josiah was one of the few Plymouth residents to have attended Harvard College, and he had married the beautiful Penelope Pelham, daughter of Harvard treasurer and assistant governor of Massachusetts Herbert Pelham. In 1662, even though he was only thirty-three years old, Josiah had taken over Miles Standish's role as Plymouth's chief military officer.

Being Edward Winslow's son, Josiah had come to know the Indians well. By the 1660s, many colonists, particularly the younger ones like Winslow, felt that their survival no longer depended on the support of the Indians. Forgetting the debt they owed the Pokanokets, without

◆ *Penelope and Josiah Winslow in 1651.*

whom their parents would never have survived their first year in America, some of the Pilgrims' children were less willing to treat Native leaders with the tolerance and respect their parents had once offered Massasoit.

For his part, Massasoit's son Alexander had shown a combativeness of his own. First he had ignored Massasoit's agreement with the colony and sold Hog Island to the Rhode Islander Richard Smith. Then, in the spring of 1662, word reached Plymouth that Alexander had done it again. He had illegally sold land to yet another Rhode Islander. There were also unsettling rumors that the sachem had spoken with the Narragansetts about joining forces against the English. So the Plymouth authorities summoned him to appear before them. When Alexander failed to show up, Governor Thomas Prence instructed Major Josiah Winslow to bring him in.

◆ ◆ ◆ Winslow headed out in July of 1662 with ten well-armed men, all of them on horseback, trotting along the same old Indian trail that their forefathers had once walked to Pokanoket. They were about fifteen miles inland from Plymouth when they learned that Alexander was nearby at a hunting and fishing lodge on Monponsett Pond in modern Halifax, Massachusetts.

It was still morning when Winslow and his men arrived at the Indians' camp. They found the sachem and about ten others, including his wife, Weetamoo, eating their breakfast inside a wigwam. Their muskets were left outside in plain view. Winslow ordered his men to seize the weapons and to surround the wigwam. He then went inside to have it out with Alexander.

The Pokanoket sachem spoke to Winslow through an interpreter, John Sassamon's brother Rowland, and as the conversation became more heated, the major insisted that they move outside. Alexander was outraged that Plymouth officials had chosen to treat him in such a rude manner. If there had been any truth to the rumor of a conspiracy with the Narragansetts would he be here, casually fishing at Monponsett Pond?

Winslow reminded the sachem that he had neglected to appear, as promised, before the Plymouth court. Alexander explained that he had been waiting for his friend Thomas Willett, a Plymouth resident with close ties to the Indians, to return from Manhattan so that he could speak to him about the matter.

By this point, Alexander had worked himself into a raging fury. Winslow took out his pistol, held the weapon to the sachem's chest, and said, "I have been ordered to bring you to Plymouth, and by the help of God I will do it."

Understandably stunned, Alexander was on the verge of exploding, when Sassamon asked that he be given the chance to speak to his sachem alone. After a few minutes of tense conversation, it was announced that Alexander had agreed to go with Winslow, but only as long as "he might go like a sachem"—in the company of his attendants.

It was a hot summer day, and Winslow offered Alexander the use of one of their horses. Since his wife and the others had to walk, the sachem said that "he could go on foot as well as they," provided that the English kept a reasonable pace. In the meantime, Winslow sent a messenger ahead to organize a hasty meeting of the magistrates in Duxbury.

The meeting seems to have done much to calm tempers on both sides. What happened next is somewhat unclear, but soon after the conference, Alexander and his entourage spent a night at Winslow's house in Marshfield, where the sachem suddenly fell ill. The sachem's attendants asked that they be allowed to take him back to Mount Hope. Permission was granted, and Alexander's men carried him on their shoulders till they reached the Taunton River in Middleborough. From there he was taken by canoe back to Mount Hope, where he died a few days later.

It was an astonishing and disturbing sequence of events that showed just where matters stood between the English and Indians in Plymouth Colony. In 1623, Edward Winslow had earned Massasoit's undying love by doing everything in his power—even scraping the sachem's tongue—to save his life. Thirty-nine years later, Winslow's son had burst into Alexander's wigwam, waving a pistol. Within a week, the Pokanoket leader was dead.

In years to come, the rumors would grow: that Alexander had been marched unmercifully under the burning summer sun until he had sickened and died; that he had been thrown in jail and starved to death.

In an effort to stop the rumors, one of the men who'd accompanied Winslow—William Bradford's son William Jr.—provided an account of the incident in which he insisted that Alexander had accompanied Winslow "freely and readily." But Alexander's younger brother Philip became convinced that Winslow had poisoned the sachem. Intentionally or not, Winslow had lit the slow-burning fuse that would one day ignite New England.

◆ ◆ ◆ For days, hundreds, perhaps thousands of Indians gathered at Mount Hope to mourn the passing of Alexander. Then the despair

◆ *The "Seat of Philip" at the eastern shore of Mount Hope.*

turned to joy as the crowds celebrated his brother Philip's rise to supreme sachem of the Pokanokets.

On the eastern shore of Mount Hope is the huge rock from which the peninsula gets its name. More than three hundred feet high, Mount Hope provides panoramic views of Narragansett and Mount Hope bays. There is a legend that Philip once stood upon the top of Mount Hope and, turning west, hurled a stone all the way across the peninsula to Poppasquash Neck, more than two miles away. It is a tradition that reflects the sense of power and strength that many Pokanokets may have projected upon their new leader, who was just twenty-four years old in August 1662. That summer, the "flocking multitudes" at Mount Hope caused the Plymouth magistrates to fear that Philip had gathered a council of war. Only a few weeks after hauling his brother into court, Governor Prence made the same demand of Philip.

The young sachem who appeared at Plymouth on August 6, 1662, was not about to bow before the English. As Philip made clear in the years ahead, he considered himself on equal terms with none other than King Charles II. All others—including Governor Prence and the lying Major Josiah Winslow—were "but subjects" of the king of England and unfit to tell a fellow monarch what to do. Philip's "ambitious and haughty" attitude at the Plymouth court that day moved one observer to refer to him mockingly as "King Philip"—a nickname he never claimed for himself but that followed the sachem into history.

No matter how confident Philip appeared that day in court, he knew that now was not the time to accuse the English of murdering his brother. So instead of accusing Winslow of the deed—something he did not say openly to an Englishman until near the outbreak of war thirteen years later—Philip told the members of the court exactly what they wanted to hear. He promised that the "ancient covenant" that had existed between his father and Plymouth remained unchanged. He even offered his younger brother as a hostage if it might ease the magistrates' concerns, but it was decided that this was not necessary. As far as Governor Prence was concerned, relations with the Indians were once again back to normal.

◆ ◆ ◆ Over the next few years, as Philip settled into his new role as leader of the Pokanokets, New England grew more and more crowded. Both the English and the Indians depended on agriculture, and only about 20 percent of the land was suitable for farming. Adding to the pressure for land was the rapid rise of the English population. The first generation of settlers had averaged seven to eight children per family, and by the 1660s, those children wanted farms of their own.

The English were not the only ones whose world was changing. The Indians of Philip's generation had grown up amid the boom times of the fur trade and had come to regard expensive Western goods as an essential part of their lives. But now, with the virtual extinction of the beaver and the loss of so much land, this new generation of Native Americans was beginning to face a future with fewer opportunities.

The pressure was particularly intense in Plymouth. Unlike Massachusetts Bay and Connecticut, which had large tracts of land to the west that could still be settled, the Indians and English in Plymouth had almost nowhere left to go. Pushed south to the neck of Mount Hope, Philip and his people were hemmed in from nearly every side.

As Philip knew, losing land had a direct impact on his people. If the Pokanokets were to survive as an independent tribe, they must hold on to what land his father and brother had not yet sold. Soon after

◆ *Paul Revere's engraving of King Philip.*

becoming sachem, he and Governor Prence agreed to a seven-year halt on the sale of Indian land. It was an extraordinary agreement that marked a dramatic change from the past, and Philip instructed John Sassamon to write the governor a letter. "Last summer [Philip] made that promise with you," Sassamon wrote, "that he would not sell no land in seven years time. . . . [H]e would have no English trouble him before that time."

But Philip soon changed his mind. The following year, in April 1664, Philip agreed to sell a piece of land bordering the towns of Bridgewater, Taunton, and Rehoboth for a record £66 (roughly $12,000 today)—almost twice the amount his father had received for the Pokanoket homeland of Sowams. Philip had at least succeeded in getting the English to pay a decent price for his land. In a way, he was doing just what his father had done forty years before—adapting to the inevitable forces of change.

◆ ◆ ◆ By 1667, Philip was five years into his reign as sachem of Mount Hope. Almost thirty years old, he and his wife, Wootonekanuske, had just had a son, and the birth of the boy appears to have caused Philip to draft a will. When Philip's interpreter, John Sassamon, read the will back to him, all seemed as the sachem had intended. But, as it turned out, Sassamon had written something else entirely.

Instead of leaving his lands to his intended heirs, Philip had, according to the will written by Sassamon, left his lands to his interpreter, a trick like Squanto's almost forty years earlier. When Philip discovered what his trusted interpreter had done, Sassamon, it was reported, "ran away from him." Soon Sassamon was back with his former mentor, John Eliot, working as a teacher and minister to the Praying Indians.

Sassamon's betrayal was just one setback in what proved to be a difficult year for the Pokanoket sachem. That spring, Plymouth governor Prence heard a disturbing rumor. Spies from Rehoboth, partway between Plymouth and Mount Hope, reported that Philip had been talking about joining forces with the French and Dutch against the English. Not only would this allow the Indians to get back their lands, Philip had claimed, but it would enable them to "enrich themselves with [English] goods." Once again, it was time to send Major Josiah Winslow to Mount Hope.

Once at Mount Hope, Winslow took away the Pokanokets' guns, then found an Indian who told him that Philip had indeed been talking about a possible conspiracy against the English. Described as "one of Philip's sachem's men," the witness told of Philip's plan with so many specific details that Winslow felt the accusation was "very probably true." Philip must once again appear before the Plymouth court.

From the outset, Philip claimed that he had been set up, "pleading how irrational a thing it was that he should desert his long experienced friends, the English, and comply with the French and Dutch." Should the English decide to withdraw "their wonted favor," he said, it would be "little less than a death to him, gladding his enemies, grieving and weakening his friends."

In the end, the Plymouth magistrates decided that even if Philip's "tongue had been running out," he was not about to attack anybody. Instead, they were now concerned that this accusation had so weakened Philip that he was in danger of being rejected by his own people. From the colony's point of view, it was better to have a weak leader in place among the Pokanokets than a sachem who might rally his people against them. "[N]ot willing to desert [Philip] and let him sink," the court decided to continue its official backing of Philip and return the confiscated weapons. But this did not stop the magistrates from charging the sachem £40 ($8,000 today) to help pay for Winslow's fact-gathering mission. As the magistrates knew all too well, the only way the sachem was going to pay the fine was to sell the English some more of his peoples' land.

Philip had begun with the best of intentions, but by the end of the 1660s, he was on his way to a huge sell-off of Native land, aided by his brother's former friend Thomas Willett. From 1650 to 1659, there had been a total of fourteen Indian land deeds registered in Plymouth court; between 1665 and 1675, there would be seventy-six deeds.

Governor Prence and Major Winslow were proud of the strategy they had developed to deal with the Indians in the colony. With the help of Willett, the governor served as Philip's main contact, while Winslow built a relationship with the sachem of the Massachusetts to the north. It was a division of alliances that the two officials modeled on how Governor Bradford and Captain Standish had handled Squanto and Hobbamock in 1622.

But while Bradford and Standish's strategy appears to have worked reasonably well, Prence and Winslow's approach proved far less effective when Prence died in 1673 and Winslow became governor. With Prence gone, Philip was now forced to deal with the one official he absolutely hated above all others. Not only was Winslow linked to his brother's death, he had proven himself to be one of Plymouth's most aggressive purchasers of Indian real estate. By the time he became governor in 1673, Winslow had come to embody Plymouth's policy of increasing antagonism toward the colony's Native Americans.

It may have been true that from a strictly legal standpoint there was nothing wrong with how Winslow and the other Plymouth officials acquired large amounts of Pokanoket land. And yet, the process removed the Indians from their territory as effectively—and as cheaply—as driving them off at gunpoint. Philip had to do something to stop the long series of losses that had come to be identified with his leadership.

◆ ◆ ◆ In March 1671, Hugh Cole of Swansea reported that Indians from all over the region were meeting at Mount Hope. At one point, Philip led a group of sixty armed warriors on a march up the peninsula to the edge of the English settlement. Josiah Winslow reported the rumor that in addition to winning the support of the Narragansetts, Philip had hatched a plot to kidnap the Plymouth governor. Though not a shot had yet been fired, many in Plymouth believed that after years of rumors, war had finally come to the colony.

Some New Englanders dared to suggest that the Indians were not entirely to blame for the threatened revolt and that Plymouth was guilty of treating the Pokanokets badly. In an attempt to prove otherwise, Plymouth magistrates invited a group from Massachusetts Bay to attend a meeting with Philip at the town of Taunton on April 10, 1671.

Philip and a large group of warriors—all of them armed and with their faces painted—cautiously approached the Taunton town green, where an equal number of Plymouth militiamen, armed with muskets and swords, marched back and forth. Fearful that he was leading his men into a trap,

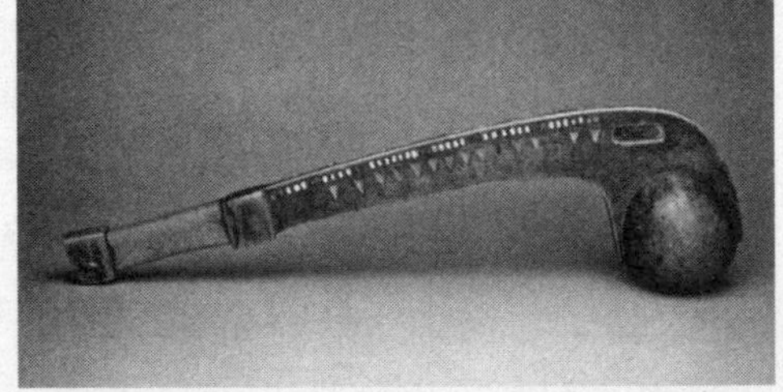

◆ *Solid maple war club, inlaid with white and purple wampum, reputed to have been King Philip's.*

Philip insisted that they be given several English hostages before he entered the town. Tensions were so high that many of the colony's soldiers shouted out that it was time for them to attack. Only at the angry insistence of Massachusetts Bay officials were the Plymouth men made to stop. Finally, after the exchange of several more messages, Philip and his warriors agreed to meet inside the Taunton meetinghouse—the Indians on one side of the aisle, the colonists on the other.

It did not go well for Philip. Once again, the Plymouth magistrates bullied him into submission, insisting that he sign a document in which he acknowledged the "naughtiness of my heart." He also agreed to surrender all his warriors' weapons to the English. According to the Puritan historian William Hubbard, one of Philip's own men was so ashamed by the outcome that he flung down his musket, accused his sachem of being "a white-livered cur," and vowed that "he would never [follow Philip] again or fight under him." Yet another warrior who was the son of a Nipmuck sachem left Taunton in such a rage that he was moved to kill an Englishman on his way back to his home in central Massachusetts. He was eventually tried and hanged on Boston Common, where his severed head was placed upon the gallows.

In the months that followed, the colony required that the Indians from Cape Cod to Nemasket sign documents restating their loyalty to Plymouth. The magistrates also insisted that Philip and his warriors turn over all their remaining weapons. When Philip refused, it seemed once again as if war might break out. Fearful that Plymouth was about to drive the Pokanokets and, with them, all of New England into war, the missionary John Eliot suggested that Philip come to Boston to speak directly with Massachusetts Bay officials.

As the missionary had said might happen, the sachem received a much more sympathetic welcome in Boston than he had ever been given in

Plymouth. Philip then agreed to meet with Plymouth officials again on September 24, 1671, as long as a delegation from Massachusetts Bay was also in attendance.

But by the time Philip appeared in Plymouth, the officials from Massachusetts Bay had changed their position: Plymouth was right, and the Pokanokets were wrong. The treaty Philip was subsequently forced to sign was a total and embarrassing surrender. He was required once again to turn over all his weapons, and pay a fine of £100. Even worse, he was now a subject of Plymouth and had to pay the colony an annual tribute of five wolves' heads. Plymouth had given Philip no options: If he was to survive as sachem of the Pokanokets, he must now go to war.

◆ ◆ ◆ Philip was disarmed but hardly defeated. He immediately began to make plans for obtaining more muskets. But to pay for the new weapons, he was going to need money—and lots of it.

In August of 1672, Philip took out a mortgage on some land along the Taunton River to pay off a debt of £83; soon after, he sold a four-mile-square piece of land in the same area for £143 (approximately $32,000 today)—the largest price ever paid for a piece of Indian real estate in Plymouth. Philip, it appears, had launched into a strategy of selling land for weapons. It didn't matter to him that he was about to sell almost every parcel of land he owned, because it was all to fund a war to win those lands back. By 1673, Philip had sold every last scrap of land surrounding his territory.

Playing into Philip's strategy was English greed. Rather than wonder how he and his people could possibly survive once they'd been confined to a reservation at Mount Hope, or question where all this money was going, the English went ahead and bought more land—even agreeing to pay for the rights to fish in the waters surrounding Mount Hope when it meant that the Pokanokets might no longer be able to feed themselves.

◆ ◆ ◆ The Pokanokets represented just 5 percent of the total Indian population of New England. If Philip was to have any hope of winning a war, he needed a significant number of the other tribes to join him. He knew he could probably count on the Pocassets and the Nemaskets, who were both led by his relatives, but it was questionable whether the Indians on Cape Cod and the islands, where Christianity had made large inroads, would follow him into war. Closer to home, the Massachusetts, who were so cozy with Winslow, would never join him. Uncas and the Mohegans, along with the remnants of the Pequots, also had strong ties to the English. The Nipmucks, on the other hand, were the Pokanokets' ancient and trustworthy friends, a relationship strengthened by Massasoit's final years with the Quabaugs.

There were two important unknowns. To the south of Pocasset were the Sakonnets, led by the female sachem Awashonks. The Sakonnets' loyalties were difficult to determine, as were the Narragansetts', the traditional foes of the Pokanokets. Some progress had been made in establishing a common ground between the two tribes, but the Narragansetts were too large to speak with a single voice. Their young warriors were anxious to fight, but the tribe's older, more cautious sachems were reluctant to go to war.

In putting together a pan-Indian force to fight the English, Philip was attempting to accomplish what not even the great Narragansett sachem Miantonomi had been able to pull off in the 1640s. Miantonomi had been known for his bravery in battle, while Philip appears to have had a different sort of charisma. His growing desperation and anger over how he'd been treated by Plymouth Colony made him extremely attractive to many Indians across the region, all of whom had experienced some version of the Pokanokets' problems with the English. If they did not band together now, the opportunity might never come again.

For their part, the English remained confident that Philip had committed himself to peace. Instead of being concerned by the Pokanokets' growing desire for guns and ammunition, they saw it as a financial opportunity. Incredibly, in the fall of 1674, Plymouth magistrates voted to repeal a law prohibiting the sale of gunpowder and ammunition to the Indians.

Then, in January of 1675, John Sassamon, the Harvard-educated Indian who had once served as Philip's interpreter, paid a visit to Josiah Winslow.

◆ ◆ ◆ Although Philip considered him dishonest, Sassamon was nonetheless the son-in-law of Philip's sister Amie. In fact, he lived on land given to him by Amie's husband, Tuspaquin, known as the Black Sachem of Nemasket. Despite his connection to Native royalty, Sassamon was working once again for the missionary John Eliot and was minister to a group of Praying Indians in Nemasket.

In January, Sassamon informed Josiah Winslow that Philip was on the verge of war. This was not what the governor of Plymouth wanted to hear. Even when Sassamon warned that his life would be in danger if anyone learned that he had spoken with the governor, Winslow's reaction was to dismiss the claim as yet another Indian rumor.

At forty-three, Winslow was no longer the bold young man who had shoved a pistol in Alexander's chest. His health had become a concern (he may have had tuberculosis), and the prospect of a major Indian war was simply not part of the future he saw for Plymouth.

Not long after his meeting with the governor, Sassamon's dead body was discovered beneath the ice of Assawompsett Pond in modern Lakeville, Massachusetts. Left lying on the ice were his hat, his musket, and several ducks he had shot. It certainly appeared as if Sassamon had accidentally fallen through the ice and drowned. But when the Indian who found the body pulled it from the pond, no water poured from his mouth—an indication that Sassamon had been dead before he went through the ice. The body was also bruised and swollen around the neck and head.

When word of Sassamon's death reached Winslow, the governor of Plymouth finally began to believe that the Pokanokets might be up to something. An investigation was launched, and in March Philip voluntarily appeared in court to answer any questions the officials might have. Strenuously denying his involvement in Sassamon's death, the sachem insisted that this was an Indian matter and not the concern of the Plymouth government. The court, however, continued its investigation and soon found an Indian who claimed to have witnessed the murder. Conveniently hidden on a hill overlooking the pond, he had seen three Indians—Tobias, one of Philip's senior counselors; Tobias's son; and one other—seize Sassamon and violently twist his neck before shoving his lifeless body beneath the ice. On the strength of this testimony, a trial date was set for June 1.

As the date of the trial approached, Philip's brother-in-law Tuspaquin bailed out Tobias. This enabled Tobias to speak with Philip, who was concerned that he would be the next one on trial. To no one's surprise,

Philip chose not to attend the hearing. Instead, he remained at Mount Hope, where he surrounded himself with warriors and marched to within sight of the border of Swansea, a town founded just eight years before that abutted the Pokanokets' lands at Mount Hope. Reports began to filter in to Plymouth that large numbers of "strange Indians" were making their way to the Pokanoket homeland.

The last thing Philip wanted was to go to war before all was ready. They did not have enough muskets, bullets, and especially gunpowder. But events were quickly spinning beyond any single person's control. If the English insisted on putting Tobias and the others on trial, he might have no choice.

A panel of eight judges, headed by Winslow, ran the trial. There were twelve English jurors assisted by six Praying Indians. Winslow later claimed they were the "most indifferentest, gravest, and sage Indians," but this did little to alter Philip's belief that the verdict had already been decided.

According to English law in the seventeenth century, two witnesses were required to convict someone of murder. But the English had only a single witness, and as it came out in the trial, before supposedly witnessing the murder, he had been forced to give up his coat to Tobias to pay off a gambling debt. Even so, all eighteen members of the jury found Tobias and the others guilty. It was a shocking miscarriage of justice.

The executions were scheduled for June 8. As the condemned were brought to the gallows, all three Indians continued to maintain their innocence. Tobias was hanged first, followed by his friend. But when it came time to execute Tobias's son, the rope broke. Whether this was by accident or was planned, it had the desired effect. As the young Indian struggled to his feet, with the still-twitching bodies of his father and family friend suspended in the air above him, he was given the chance to save his life. So he changed his story, claiming that the other two had indeed killed Sassamon while he looked on helplessly. With the boy's confession, the authorities now had the number of witnesses the law required, even if it was after the fact.

Traditionally, a condemned man had his life spared after a failed execution. But a month later, with war raging across the colony, Tobias's son was taken from his cell and shot to death with a musket.

◆ ◆ ◆ The trial had been a travesty of justice—and an insulting challenge to the authority of the Pokanoket leader. Now, it seemed, was the time for Philip to take the opportunity given him by the English and lead his people triumphantly into battle.

◆ ***The site of King Philip's village on the eastern shore of the Mount Hope Peninsula in the early 1900s.***

His warriors were surely ready for it. Young, with little to lose and everything to gain, the fighting men of the Pokanokets now had the chance to win back their people's land. It was a year ahead of Philip's original schedule, but the season was right. The trees and underbrush were thick with new leaves, providing the cover the warriors needed when attacking the English. The swamps, which the Indians traditionally used as sanctuaries in times of war, were still mucky with spring rain, and the English soldiers could never enter them. If they waited until midsummer, it would be too late. They did not have the stores of gunpowder they had hoped to have in a year's time, nor the firm commitments they had planned to get from the other tribes, but there was nothing they could do about that now. They needed to strike soon and furiously.

Despite all the evidence to the contrary, Governor Winslow remained hopeful that the present troubles would blow over. But except for writing a single letter to Philip in the weeks after the trial for Sassamon's murder, he failed to take an active role in stopping a possible outbreak of violence. Puritan historians later insisted that Philip pushed his people into the conflict. The English residents of Swansea told a different story. According to an account recorded in the early part of the following century, Philip and his counselors "were utterly averse to the war" in June 1675. Swansea resident Hugh Cole later told how Philip sent him word that "he could not control his young warriors" and that Cole should abandon his home and seek shelter on Aquidneck Island. Another tradition claimed that when Philip first heard that one of his warriors had killed an Englishman, he "wept at the news."

He had reason to weep. Even with recent recruits from neighboring tribes, his fighting force amounted to no more than a few hundred poorly equipped warriors. Even worse, they were situated on a peninsula. If they were unable to fight their way north into the heart of Plymouth Colony, their only means of escape from Mount Hope was by water.

But the English had weaknesses of their own. Unlike the Indians, who traveled across the countryside as the seasons changed, the English lived in houses that were fixed permanently to the ground. As a consequence, all their possessions—including clothing, furniture, food, and livestock—were there for the taking. As they were about to discover, an Indian war was the worst fate imaginable for the English of Plymouth Colony.

PART III

WAR

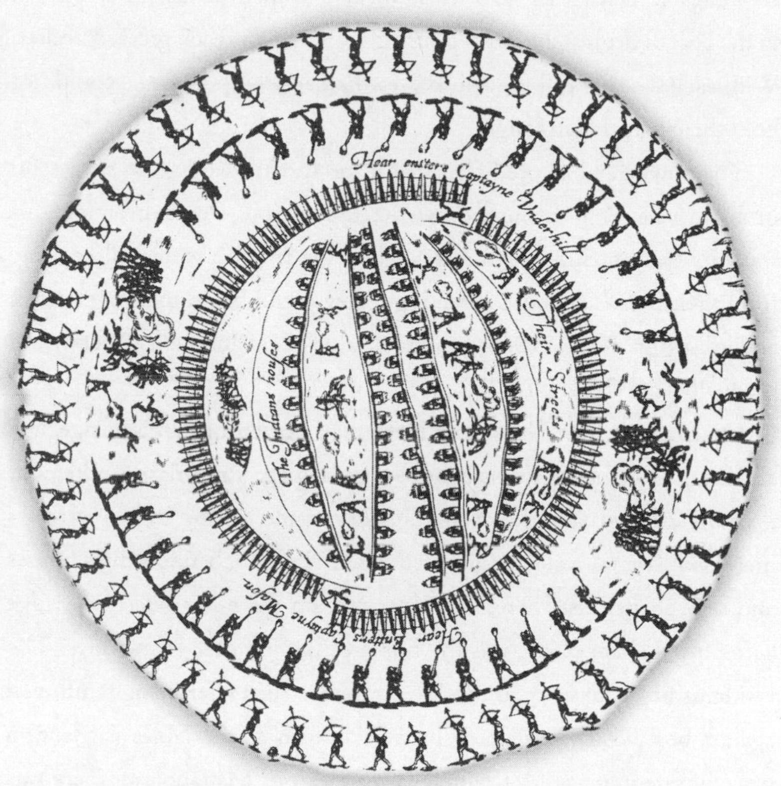
Hear enstere Captayne Underhill
The Indians houses
Their Streets
Hear Entters Captayne Mason

THIRTEEN
Kindling the Flame

◆ ◆ ◆

By the middle of June 1675, the Pokanokets' war dance had entered its third week. The warriors had their faces painted, their hair "trimmed up in comb fashion," according to a witness, "with their powder horns and shot bags at their backs" and with muskets in their hands. They danced to the beat of drums, the sweat pouring from their already greased bodies. With each day, the call for action grew fiercer. Philip knew he could not hold them back much longer.

The powwows had predicted that if the Indians were to be successful in a war, the English must draw the first blood. Philip promised his warriors that on Sunday, June 20, when the English would all be away from their homes at church meetings, they could begin pillaging houses and killing livestock, thus beginning a game of cat and mouse that would gradually lead the English into war.

On Mount Hope Neck, just a few miles north of Philip's village, was a cluster of eighteen English houses at a place known as Kickemuit. As June 20 approached and the hostility of the nearby Indian warriors increased, several residents decided it was time to abandon their homes and seek shelter elsewhere. To the north, on the other side of a bridge across the Palmer River, was the home of the minister John Miles. The residents began to flock to this large house, which after being reinforced against possible Indian attack became known as the Miles garrison, a place of safety in war. A few miles to the east in Mattapoisett, there was also the Bourne garrison, a large stone structure that soon contained sixteen men and fifty-four women and children.

On the morning of Sunday, June 20, seven or eight Indians approached a man from Kickemuit who had not yet abandoned his home. The Indians asked if they could use his grinding stone to sharpen one of their hatchets. The man told them that since it was the Sabbath, "his God would be very angry if he should let them do it." Soon after, the Indians came across an Englishman walking up the road. They stopped him and said "he should not work on his God's Day, and that he should tell no lies." Intimidated by the Indians, the last residents of Kickemuit left for the shelter of the garrisons. By day's end, two houses had been burned to the ground.

Governor Winslow heard the news that night, and by the morning of Monday, June 21, he had ordered towns across the colony to assemble their militia at Taunton, from where they would be sent to Swansea. He also sent a message to officials in Boston, asking for help, but there was no reason to assume that Massachusetts Bay would rush to Plymouth's defense. There were many in that colony who were critical of Plymouth's treatment of the Pokanokets. And for those with long memories, Plymouth had been so slow to come to the Bay Colony's aid during the Pequot War that the Plymouth militia had missed the fighting.

◆ ◆ ◆ In only a few days' time, companies of militiamen had begun to arrive at Taunton. The elderly James Cudworth was named the army's commander, with Major William Bradford, the fifty-five-year-old son of the former governor, as his second-in-command.

Since they'd just arrived on the scene, Cudworth and Bradford were as ignorant as everyone else as to the movements of the Pokanokets. There was one man, however, who had firsthand knowledge of the territory to the south and the Indians surrounding Mount Hope Bay. Just the year before, Benjamin Church, a thirty-three-year-old carpenter,

◆ *An engraving of Benjamin Church that appeared in a nineteenth-century edition of his narrative.*

had become the first Englishman to settle in the southeastern tip of Narragansett Bay at a place called Sakonnet, home to the female sachem Awashonks and several hundred of her people.

Instead of being intimidated by the fact that he was the only

Englishman in Sakonnet, Church enjoyed the chance to start from scratch. "My head and hands were full about settling a new plantation," he later remembered.

From the beginning, Church had known that his future at Sakonnet depended on a strong relationship with sachem Awashonks, and over the course of the last year, the two had become good friends. In early June, she sent him an urgent message. Philip was about to go to war, and he demanded that the Sakonnets join him. Before she made her decision, Awashonks wanted to speak with Church.

Church quickly discovered that six of Philip's warriors had come to Sakonnet. Awashonks explained that they had threatened to make the Plymouth authorities turn against her by attacking the English houses and livestock on her side of the river. She would then have no alternative but to join Philip. Church recommended instead that Awashonks ask Plymouth for protection from the Pokanokets. He promised to leave immediately for Plymouth and return as soon as possible with instructions from the governor.

Just to the north of the Sakonnets in modern Tiverton, Rhode Island, were the Pocassets, led by another female sachem, Weetamoo. Even though she was Philip's former sister-in-law, the relationship did not necessarily mean she had to join him. Church decided to stop at Pocasset on his way to Winslow's home in Duxbury.

He found her, alone and very upset, on a hill overlooking Mount Hope Bay. She had just returned by canoe from Philip's village. War, Weetamoo feared, was inevitable. Her own warriors "were all gone, against her will, to the dances" at Mount Hope. Church advised her to go immediately to Aquidneck Island, just a short canoe ride away, for her safety. As he had told Awashonks, he promised to return in just a few days with word from Governor Winslow.

But Church never got the chance to make good on his promise. Before he could return to Weetamoo and Awashonks, the fighting had begun.

◆ ◆ ◆ Church had been in Plymouth speaking with Governor Winslow when the call for the militia had gone out, and he had immediately reported to Taunton. As the army prepared to march to Swansea, Major Bradford asked Church to lead the way with a small group of soldiers. Church and his company, which included several "friend Indians," moved so quickly over the path to Swansea that they were able to kill, roast, and eat a deer before the main body of troops caught up with them. Church was already discovering that he enjoyed the life of a soldier. As he later wrote in a book about his experiences during the war, "I was spirited for that work."

But Church still had much to learn about military tactics. His mission had been to provide protection to the soldiers behind him. By sprinting to Swansea, he had left the army open to an Indian ambush. While Church bragged about the speed of his march south, his commanding officers may have begun to realize that this was a soldier who might be too reckless to be trusted.

Over the next few days, more and more soldiers arrived at Swansea. In addition to strengthening the Miles garrison, a temporary barricade was built to provide the growing number of soldiers with protection from possible attack. But no direct action was taken against the Indians. Since hundreds of Native warriors were said to be with Philip, Cudworth felt that his own force had to match the Indians' numbers before they could march on Mount Hope.

With each passing day, the Indians' taunting of the English increased. Church and his company could hear their whoops and the crackle of

◆ *The Miles garrison in the early twentieth century.*

gunfire as the Native warriors slaughtered cattle and robbed houses. But so far, no English men or women had been injured. By the morning of Wednesday, June 23, some residents had grown bold enough to return to their houses to retrieve goods and food.

That day, a father and son left the garrison and came upon a group of Indians ransacking several houses. The boy had a musket, and his father urged him to fire on the Indians. One of the Indians fell, then picked himself up and ran away. Later in the day, some Indians approached the garrison and asked why the boy had shot at one of their men. The English responded by asking whether the Indian was dead. When the Indians said yes, the boy snidely replied, "It was no matter." The soldiers tried to calm the now enraged Indians by saying it was "but an idle lad's word." But the truth of the matter was that the boy had given the warriors exactly what they wanted: the go-ahead to kill.

Thursday, June 24, proved momentous in the history of Plymouth. Reports differ, but all agree that it was a day of horror and death in Swansea. At least ten people, including the boy and his father, were killed by the Indians. Some were ambushed on their way back from prayers at the meetinghouse. One couple and their twenty-year-old son stopped at their home to get some provisions. The father told his wife and son to return to the garrison while he finished collecting corn. But as the father left the house, he was attacked by Indians and killed. Hearing gunshots, the son and his mother returned to the house. Both were attacked and in what became a common fate in the months ahead, they were scalped.

For the next few days, Church and the other soldiers remained cooped up at the garrison as their commanders waited for reinforcements to arrive from Massachusetts Bay. In a clear attempt to mock the soldiers, the Indians had the nerve to approach the garrison itself. Two soldiers sent to draw a bucket of water from a nearby well were shot and carried away. They were later discovered with "their fingers and feet cut off, and the skin of their heads flayed off." Even worse, the Indians succeeded in killing two of the garrison's sentries "under the very noses of most of our forces."

On the night of June 26, a total eclipse of the moon was witnessed all across New England. Several soldiers claimed they saw a black spot in the moon's center resembling "the scalp of an Indian." All agreed that an "eclipse falling out at that instant of time was ominous."

Finally on Monday, June 28, with the arrival of several Massachusetts companies from Boston, the number of soldiers had reached the point that Cudworth was willing to attack the Indians. In addition to a troop of horsemen under Captain Thomas Prentice and a company of foot soldiers under Captain Daniel Henchman, there was a rowdy bunch of volunteers under the command of Captain Samuel Moseley.

The English had not yet fought a single battle, but Moseley, a sea captain, was already something of a hero. In April, he had led a successful assault on some Dutch pirates off the coast of Maine. In June, several of the captured sailors were put on trial and condemned to death, but with the outbreak of war, they were let free as long as they were willing to fight the Indians under Moseley. In addition to this group of pirates, which included a huge Dutchman named Cornelius Anderson, Moseley had a wild gang of servants and apprentices from Boston.

To a pious group of farm boys and merchants from Plymouth, Moseley's men seemed as savage as the Indians themselves. To Benjamin Church, Moseley was destined to become a bitter rival.

The attack on the Indians was scheduled for the following day, but some of the new arrivals, led by quartermasters John Gill and Andrew Belcher, asked to go out immediately and "seek the enemy in their own quarters." Some Indians on the opposite side of the river were taking great delight in shooting at the garrison. It was time to put these heathens in their place.

Permission was granted, and twelve troopers prepared to take it to the enemy. In addition to William Hammond of nearby Rehoboth, who was to act as their scout, the troopers asked Benjamin Church to join them. They quickly set out across the bridge, all of them knowing that an audience of several hundred English soldiers was watching their every move.

Almost as soon as they crossed the bridge, about a dozen Indians hidden in some nearby bushes started firing at them. In an instant, Hammond, the scout, was, if not dead, nearly so. Belcher was hit in the

◆ *Massachusetts governor John Leverett wearing an ox-hide buff coat.*

knee and his horse was shot out from under him, while Gill was slammed in the gut. Fortunately, he'd worn a protective coat of quarter-inch-thick ox hide, known as a buff coat, which he had lined with several pieces of well-placed parchment, and suffered only a severe bruise.

The troopers were so terrified by the attack that they turned their horses around and galloped back for the garrison, leaving Hammond dazed and dying and Belcher trapped beneath his horse. As the troopers clattered across the bridge, Church "stormed and stamped, and told them 'twas a shame to run and leave a wounded man there to become a prey to the barbarous enemy."

By this time, Hammond had fallen down dead off his horse, and with the assistance of Gill and only one other man, Church attempted to save Belcher's life. Church jumped off his horse and loaded both Belcher and Hammond onto the horses of the other two. As they retreated to the garrison, Church went after Hammond's horse, which was wandering off toward the Indians. All the while, he shouted out to those at the garrison "to come over and fight the enemy." But no one appeared willing to join him.

The Indians had had a chance to reload and were now blasting away at Church as he continued to yell at his army on the other side of the river.

Every one of the Indians' bullets missed, although one ball did strike the foot of a soldier watching from the safety of the garrison. Church decided he had better join his cowardly companions before the Indians had a chance to reload and fire once again. He started back across the bridge, but not without proclaiming, "The Lord have mercy on us if such a handful of Indians shall thus dare such an army!"

◆ ◆ ◆ It was an awful night. As a cold wind lashed the Miles garrison with rain and Moseley's men mocked the troopers with "many profane oaths," a soldier from Watertown lost control of himself. Screaming "God is against the English!" he ran crazily around the garrison—"a lamentable spectacle"—until he was finally calmed down.

The next morning, Moseley and his pirates led the way across the bridge. Having learned to fight on a ship's deck, these sailors were, it turned out, much better adapted to fighting Indians than the militiamen, who were trained in old-fashioned warfare and still carried heavy, ineffective matchlocks instead of flintlocks. Ten of the enemy could be seen on the opposite side of the river, about a half mile away, shouting insults at the English. "[N]ot at all daunted by such kind of alarms," Moseley and his men "ran violently down upon them over the bridge, pursuing them a mile and a quarter on the other side."

Moseley's men chased the Indians until they had disappeared into a swamp, killing, it was later reported, about a half dozen of them. In the meantime Church was forced to participate in a more traditional military operation. Fanning out in two wings, the troopers created a long line meant to clear the area of Indians while protecting the foot soldiers in the middle. Unfortunately, the center of the line was, in Church's judgment, "not well headed." With the rain making it hard to see, some of the soldiers mistook their comrades for the enemy. One of the troopers, a twenty-year-old soldier named Perez Savage, who "boldly held up his colors in the front of his company," was shot not once but twice, one ball harmlessly piercing the brim of his hat and the other hitting him in the thigh. With the weather getting worse by the moment and no Indians in sight (although several officers insisted that Savage had been hit by Native fire), it was decided to return to the garrison for the night.

The next day, the English forces were in no hurry to march on Mount Hope, where as many as five hundred Native warriors were said to be waiting for them. Not until noon did the English head out once again across the bridge. The previous day they had ventured only a mile and a half into enemy territory; this time they continued on to the English settlement at Kickemuit. Tensions were already high among the militiamen. What they saw at Kickemuit made them only more nervous about what lay ahead.

The abandoned houses had all been burned. But even more disturbing were the pieces of paper seen fluttering in the air, paper that soon proved to be the torn pages of a Bible. For this overwhelmingly Puritan force, it was shocking to know that the Indians had ripped apart this most sacred of books and scattered God's words to the winds "in hatred of our religion."

Then, three miles later, they discovered the remains of eight Englishmen, killed five days earlier at the nearby settlement of Mattapoisett. The Indians had placed the men's heads, scalps, and hands on poles and planted them beside the road in a "barbarous and inhuman manner bidding us defiance." The body parts were quickly buried, and the soldiers continued on.

Two miles later, they reached the Pokanokets' village. One of the first to arrive was the giant Dutch pirate Cornelius Anderson. It was clear that the Indians had left in a hurry. Cooking utensils had been left scattered on the ground, and at Philip's own wigwam the Dutchman found what several local residents recognized as the sachem's hat—a hat that Anderson placed triumphantly on his own huge head.

Spreading out almost as far as the eye could see was an estimated thousand acres of Indian corn. Soon the soldiers began uprooting every stalk. If they could not defeat the Indians in battle, they would do their best to starve them to death.

Church knew immediately what had happened. Philip and his people had escaped by canoes across the sound to Pocasset—not an easy feat since the waters surrounding Mount Hope were supposedly being guarded by ships from Rhode Island. Once in Pocasset, Philip had met up with Weetamoo, who now had no choice but to join her brother-in-law.

Church recognized it as a brilliant move. Not only did Philip now have "a more advantageous post," he was stronger than he'd ever been. Church's commanders, however, chose to see Philip's escape from Mount Hope as "a mighty conquest." They had driven the Pokanokets from their homeland.

Church urged his superiors to pursue Philip immediately. If the sachem escaped again from Pocasset, the whole region might soon be at war. But the Plymouth commander James Cudworth insisted that they must first search every inch of the Mount Hope Peninsula for Indians. Then it was decided that the army should build a fort on the site of Philip's village to make sure the Pokanokets did not return to Mount Hope. From Church's perspective, it was nothing but busywork to delay the time when the English must finally face the Indians in battle. "'Twas rather their fear than their courage," Church wrote, "that obliged them to set up the marks of their conquest."

While the Plymouth forces built a useless fort, the Massachusetts Bay

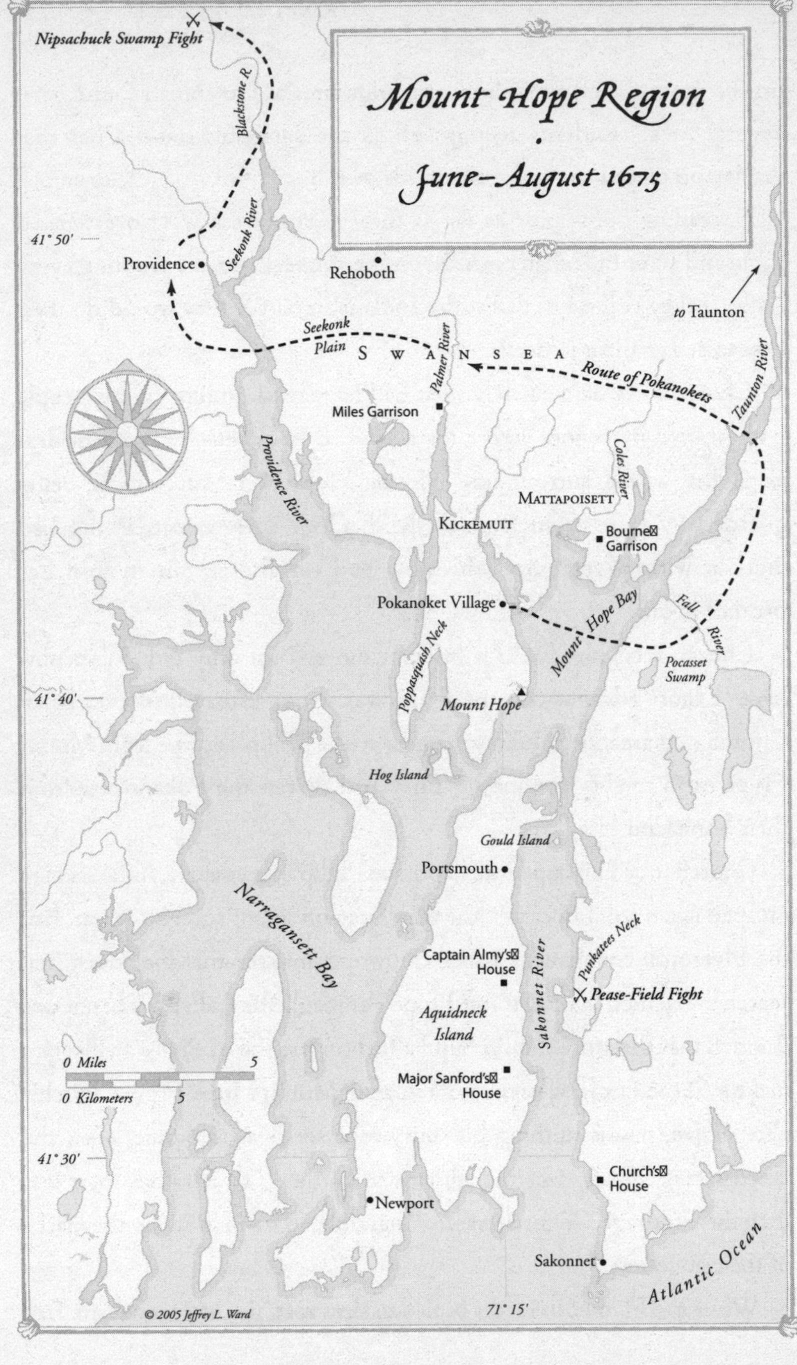
Mount Hope Region
June–August 1675
Nipsachuck Swamp Fight
Blackstone R.
Seekonk River
41° 50'
Providence
Rehoboth
to Taunton
Seekonk
Plain
SWANSEA
Palmer River
Route of Pokanokets
Taunton River
Miles Garrison
Providence River
Coles River
Mattapoisett
Kickemuit
Bourne
Garrison
Pokanoket Village
Mount Hope Bay
Fall
River
Poppasquash Neck
Pocasset
Swamp
41° 40'
Mount Hope
Hog Island
Gould Island
Portsmouth
Narragansett Bay
Punkatees Neck
Captain Almy's
House
Sakonnet River
Pease-Field Fight
Aquidneck
Island
0 Miles 5
0 Kilometers 5
Major Sanford's
House
41° 30'
Church's
House
Newport
Sakonnet
Atlantic Ocean
© 2005 Jeffrey L. Ward
71° 15'

authorities committed an even larger mistake. Instead of sending Moseley and the others after Philip, they decided it was time to turn their attention to the Narragansetts. There were concerns that the tribe might be preparing to join Philip in the war. Some of the Pokanokets' women and children, it was rumored, had sought shelter with the Narragansetts.

In truth, however, there was no clear evidence that the tribe might attack the English. The Narragansetts, like all the other tribes in New England, were watching Philip's rebellion very closely. In the beginning, they assumed the conflict was just between Philip and Plymouth. With the arrival of soldiers from Massachusetts Bay, the Narragansetts began to realize that the English saw the rebellion differently. Even though Massachusetts Bay had no complaints against Philip, the Puritans had quickly come to their neighbors' defense. Even Rhode Island, which both Plymouth and Massachusetts normally ignored, had offered to help. "[The Narragansetts] demanded why the Massachusetts and Rhode Island rose and joined with Plymouth against Philip," Roger Williams wrote on June 25, "and left not Philip and Plymouth to fight it out. We answered that all the colonies were subject to one King Charles, and it was his pleasure and our duty and engagement for one Englishman to stand to the death by each other in all parts of the world."

For his part, Church had not given up on his original hope of winning both Weetamoo and Awashonks over to the English side. He was convinced that if he'd been able to speak to the sachems before the fighting began, they would not have joined Philip. But even if it was too late to keep the Pocassets and Sakonnets out of the war, it was a waste of time to stay at Mount Hope.

One other officer agreed with Church that it was time to move into Pocasset. Matthew Fuller was the army's surgeon general. Although he was, in his own words, too "ancient and heavy" to be chasing

Indians, he asked Church if he'd go with him to Pocasset. Church responded that "he had rather do anything in the world than stay there to build the fort." So on the night of Thursday, July 8, after taking the ferry that ran from the southern tip of Mount Hope to Aquidneck Island, which was part of Rhode Island and remained free of violence throughout the war, Fuller, Church, and just thirty-six men were transported by boat to the shores of Pocasset.

◆ ◆ ◆ While Fuller went north with half the men, Church took the other half south toward his home in Sakonnet. With any luck, he might make contact with Awashonks. Several hours later, his men began to complain that they had not yet found any of the Indians he had promised them. As they made their way along the shore of the Sakonnet River, Church assured them "that if it was their desire to see Indians, he believed he should now soon show them what they should say was enough."

On Punkatees Neck, between a hill of dense forest and the stony shore of the Sakonnet River, they found a newly planted field of peas. They also saw two Indians walking through the field toward them. When the Indians turned and started to run, Church called out that he only wanted to talk and would not hurt them. But the Indians continued to run.

There was a fence between the field and the woods, so Church and his men followed the Indians over the fence and into the woods. Suddenly the darkness erupted with the roar of dozens of muskets firing simultaneously. Like many other English officers would do in the months ahead, Church had led his men into an ambush.

Church glanced back, "expecting to have seen half of them dead." But all his men were still standing and firing blindly ahead. Church ordered them to stop firing. If they shot all at once, the Indians might charge them with their hatchets while they reloaded. It was time to retreat to the field.

As soon as they reached the fence, Church ordered those who had not yet fired their muskets to hide behind the fence while the others moved into the field and reloaded. If the Indians should chase them to the fence, there would be a trap waiting for them. Church was quickly learning how to use the Indians' own tactics of hiding and surprise against them.

But when Church looked back to the heavily wooded hill from which they'd just come, he immediately began to change his strategy. From where he stood, the wooded hill appeared to be moving. He soon realized that the rise of land was completely covered with Indians, "their bright guns glittering in the sun" as they poured out of the woods and onto the field. The field bordered the Sakonnet River, and the Indians were attempting to surround the Englishmen before they reached the water's edge.

Near the water were the ruins of a stone wall. Church ordered his men to run across the field and to the wall before the Indians reached it. He also told them to strip down to their white shirts so that any boats across the river would know that they were Englishmen and rescue them. Soon they were all dashing across the field, the Indians' bullets cutting through the leaves of the pea plants as they threw themselves over an old hedge and tumbled down the bank to the wall beside the shore.

Unfortunately, it was not much of a wall. As the Indians took up positions around them, using the ruins of an old stone house and any available stumps, rocks, trees, and fence posts for protection, Church and his men were left wide open to shots from the north and south. They grabbed whatever rocks they could find and began widening the wall.

But their biggest problem was not a lack of protection—it was their lack of gunpowder. Church estimated that they were up against several hundred Indians, and there were only twenty of them. Once they ran out of powder, the Indians would fall on them in a moment, and they would all be massacred.

Church marveled at how his men "bravely and wonderfully defended themselves" in the face of such a huge force. All afternoon, beneath a hot sun, Church and his men held their ground as the Indians whooped and shouted. With night approaching, one of Church's soldiers said he could see a sloop sailing toward them from a tiny island several miles up the river. "Succor is now coming!" Church shouted. He recognized the ship as belonging to Captain Roger Goulding, "a man," he assured them, "for business."

The sloop glided with the breeze down to the English soldiers. Captain Goulding proved as trustworthy as Church had claimed. He anchored his vessel and floated his canoe out to Church and his men. The sails and hull of his sloop were soon riddled with bullet holes, but Goulding stayed put.

The canoe was so tiny that only two men could fit in it at a time. It took ten slow trips back and forth, but at least there was a growing number of soldiers in the sloop to provide cover for those in the canoe. Finally, only Church was left ashore. As he prepared to climb into the canoe, he realized that he had left his hat and cutlass at a nearby well, where he had stopped to get a drink of water at the beginning of the siege. When he told his men that he was going back to get his things, they begged him to get into the canoe. But Church refused to listen to them; he must have his hat and sword.

Since he was the only Englishman left, all the Indians' guns were aimed at him as he made his way to the well, which today bears his name. A stream of bullets flew through the air, but none hit Church. On returning to the canoe, with the hat on his head and the cutlass at his side, he fired his musket one last time. Just as he settled into the canoe, a bullet grazed his hair, but he reached the sloop unharmed.

It had been a remarkable day. For six hours, twenty men had held off three hundred Indians (a number that was later confirmed by the Indians themselves) without suffering a single death. Church looked to this event for the rest of his life as proof of "the glory of God and His protecting providence." But he'd also learned something else during what came to be known as the Pease Field Fight: When it came to Awashonks and the Sakonnets, the time for diplomacy was over.

◆ ◆ ◆ On Monday, July 19, 1675, a combined Plymouth-Massachusetts force crossed the bay for Pocasset. Running along the eastern shore of the bay was a seven-mile-long cedar swamp, beside which Philip had reportedly camped with Weetamoo. For the English it would be a day of confusion and fear as they chased the Pokanokets and Pocassets into the depths of what Major William Bradford described as a "hideous swamp." Samuel Moseley once again led the charge. Moseley and his pirates were assisted by a pack of dogs, but even they weren't very helpful in the Pocasset Swamp.

Almost as soon as Moseley's men entered the swamp, five of them were dead, the bullets flying, it seemed, from the trees themselves. The Indians quickly retreated deeper into the swamp, deserting close to a hundred wigwams made of bark so green that they were impossible to burn. The English came upon an old man who was unable to keep up with the others and who told them that Philip had just been there.

For the next few hours, they wandered through the swamp but soon discovered, in Hubbard's words, "how dangerous it is to fight in such dismal woods, when their eyes were muffled with the leaves, and their

◆ *Pocasset Swamp as it appeared in the early twentieth century.*

arms pinioned with the thick boughs of the trees, as their feet were continually shackled with the roots spreading every way in those boggy woods." Several soldiers accidentally shot at their own men, and as darkness came on, all of them gladly gave up and retreated to more solid ground.

That night, Major Cudworth, the leader of the Plymouth forces, decided that he had had enough of swamps. They would do as they had done on Mount Hope: Instead of pursuing the enemy, they'd build a fort. Cudworth and his fellow officers thought that they now had Philip and Weetamoo trapped. If they carefully guarded the swamp and prevented the Indians from escaping, they could starve them out.

In addition to the soldiers stationed at forts on Mount Hope and in Pocasset, Cudworth suggested that there be a small "flying army," whose purpose was to prevent the Indians from "destroying cattle and fetching in [a] supply of food, which being attended, will bring them to great straits." If this strategy worked, the war would effectively be over. Since there was now no need for a large army, most of the companies from Massachusetts Bay, including Moseley's, were sent back to Boston.

There was evidence, however, that Philip was not the only Indian sachem at war. A week earlier, on July 14, what appeared to have been Nipmucks from Massachusetts had attacked the town of Mendon, twenty miles to the west of Boston, and killed six people. Closer to home, Philip's brother-in-law Tuspaquin, the Black Sachem, had burned down Middleborough, while the sachem Totoson from the Buzzards Bay region just to the west of Cape Cod had attacked the town of Dartmouth, burning houses and killing several people. While yet another "losing fort" was being built at Pocasset, Church accompanied the 112 Plymouth soldiers sent to aid Dartmouth.

What seems never to have occurred to Major Cudworth, who led the expedition to Dartmouth himself, and to Captain Henchman, who was left to build the Pocasset fort, was that Totoson's attack might have been a diversion. On July 30, word reached Henchman that the Indians he was supposedly guarding in the Pocasset Swamp were no longer there. Philip and several hundred Pokanokets and Pocassets had managed to escape to the north and make their way across a shallow part of the Taunton River. They were now hurrying west and to the north toward Nipmuck country.

A messenger was sent to Rehoboth, where the minister, Noah Newman, began to organize a party of volunteers to pursue Philip. Also in Rehoboth was a group of approximately fifty newly arrived Mohegan Indians under the command of Uncas's son Oneco. The Mohegans' decision to remain loyal to the English was one of the few pieces of good news the colonies received in the summer of 1675, and Uncas's son eagerly joined the chase.

By sunset of July 31, the English and Mohegans had pursued Philip across the Seekonk River into the vicinity of modern North Providence. The trail headed northwest for another ten or so miles, and with it now almost totally dark, several Mohegan scouts were sent up ahead. They reported hearing the sounds of wood being chopped as Philip's men made camp. Leaving their horses behind, the English and Mohegans continued on foot another three miles until they reached a region known as Nipsachuck.

It had been hoped that Captain Henchman and his men, who had sailed from Pocasset to Providence, would have joined them by now. But even without reinforcements, they decided it was time to fight the enemy. As they prepared to attack just before dawn, five Pocassets from Weetamoo's camp, apparently out looking for food, stumbled upon them. Shots were fired, and the battle began.

The fighting lasted until nine in the morning, when Philip's and Weetamoo's men were forced to retreat into a nearby swamp. They had suffered a major loss—twenty-three men including Nimrod, one of Philip's bravest warriors, were dead—while the English had lost only two men.

Philip had lost even more men to desertion, and he and his sixty or so remaining warriors were almost ready to surrender as they huddled at the edge of the Nipsachuck Swamp. They were starving, exhausted, and almost out of gunpowder, with several hundred women and children depending on them for protection. But instead of pursuing the enemy, Captain Henchman, who had not arrived from Providence until after the fighting was over, decided to wait until the Mohegans had finished taking plunder from the bodies of the dead. Not until the next morning did he order his men to break camp and pursue Philip.

By then it was too late. Both Weetamoo and Philip had managed to escape. They hadn't gone far when Weetamoo, who had been a reluctant ally of Philip's since the very beginning of the war, decided to leave her brother-in-law. Many of the women and children were unable to go much farther. Even if it might mean capture, the Pocasset sachem decided that she and two hundred women and children, along with a handful of their husbands and fathers, would look for safety among the nearby Narragansetts to the south. Philip's forces, now down to just forty warriors and a hundred or so women and children, continued north until they were met by several Nipmuck warriors, who led them to a remote, well-guarded village at Menameset.

◆ ◆ ◆ Three times Philip had avoided what seemed like certain capture, but he had been driven from his homeland. His original fighting force of approximately 250 warriors was down to 40, only 30 of whom had guns. The Pokanokets were, for all practical purposes, defeated. Yet by fighting his way out of Plymouth Colony, Philip had a chance to transform a local fight into a regionwide war.

The Pokanokets were in bad shape, but the Nipmucks were ready to take up the fight. Just a few days before, they had destroyed the frontier town of Brookfield, Massachusetts. On Friday, August 6, Philip was greeted by three of the Nipmucks' most powerful sachems. Philip still possessed a coat made of wampum, and he used it to good effect. Unstringing the valuable white and purple shell beads, he gave a large amount of wampum to each of the sachems.

In the months ahead, Philip continued to cut "his coat to pieces" as he secured the cooperation of sachems from Connecticut to modern Maine. "[B]y this means," William Hubbard wrote, "Philip . . . kindl[ed] the flame of war . . . wherever he [went]."

FOURTEEN
Fuel to the Enemy

◆ ◆ ◆

THE WAR THAT had begun in New England's oldest colony spread with terrifying speed to the newest and most distant settlements in the region. The frontier of Massachusetts, which included the Connecticut River valley and modern New Hampshire and Maine, soon erupted into violence.

The war in Massachusetts had truly begun on August 2 with the Nipmucks' attack on the town of Brookfield, one of the most isolated settlements in the colony. Brookfield had just twenty houses and was a day's journey from its nearest neighbor, Springfield. As happened often in the months ahead, the fighting began with an ambush. Diplomats from Boston, hoping to establish peace with the Nipmucks, were suddenly attacked from a hillside overlooking the forest path. Eight English, including three residents of Brookfield, were killed, with just a handful of survivors managing to ride back to town. Soon after their arrival, several hundred Nipmucks descended on Brookfield, and one of the most legendary sieges in the history of New England was under way.

For two days, eighty people, most of them women and children, gathered in the home of Sergeant John Ayres, one of those killed in the ambush. When the Indians were not burning the rest of the town to the ground, they were firing on the house with guns and flaming arrows, forcing the English to chop holes through the roof and walls so that they could put out the fires. At one point, the Nipmucks loaded a cart full of flaming rags and pushed it up against the side of the house. If not for a sudden shower of rain, the house would surely have caught fire.

◆ *Nineteenth-century engraving of the English coming to the rescue at the end of the Indian assault on Brookfield.*

Finally, on the night of August 3, fifty troopers under the command of Major Simon Willard came to the rescue, and the Nipmucks dispersed.

With the attack on Brookfield, people throughout the western portion of the colony began to fear that they would be next, especially when the Nipmucks moved on Lancaster on August 22 and killed eight English. On August 24, a council of war was held at the town of Hatfield on the Connecticut River, where concerns were raised about the loyalty of the neighboring Indians. A force of one hundred English was sent out, and the Indians, many of whom did not want to go to war, had no choice but to join the fight against them. What became known as the battle of South Deerfield resulted in the deaths of nine English and twenty-six Indians as the war quickly spread up and down the river valley.

On September 3, Richard Beers was sent with thirty-six men to evacuate the town of Northfield. Unaware of the Indians' use of hiding as a tactical weapon, Beers led his men into an ambush and twenty-one were killed. On September 17, a day of public humiliation and prayer was declared in Boston. Colonists were told to refrain from "intolerable pride in clothes and hair [and] the toleration of so many taverns." But the Lord remained unmoved.

The following day proved to be, according to Hubbard, "that most fatal day, the saddest that ever befell New England." Captain Thomas Lathrop was leading seventy-nine people away from the town of Deerfield. They were about to cross a small stream when several of the soldiers

◆ *Nineteenth-century engraving of the Native American attack on Deerfield, Massachusetts.*

put down their guns to gather some ripe autumn grapes. At that moment, hundreds of Indians burst out of the forest. Fifty-seven English were killed, turning the brown waters of what was known as Muddy Brook bright red with blood. From then on, the stream was called Bloody Brook.

For the Indians, it was an astonishingly easy triumph. "[T]he heathen were wonderfully animated," the historian Increase Mather wrote, "some of them triumphing and saying, that so great a slaughter was never known, and indeed in their wars one with another, the like hath rarely been heard of." But the fighting was not over yet.

Captain Samuel Moseley and his men happened to be nearby, and they heard gunshots. By this time, Moseley was widely known as Massachusetts Bay's most ferocious Indian fighter. Moseley believed that the only good Indian was a dead Indian, so he refused to trust Native scouts and had nothing but contempt for the colony's Praying Indians. In August, he disregarded orders and burned the wigwams of the friendly Penacooks in New Hampshire; soon after, he seized a group of Praying Indians on false charges, strung them together by the neck, and marched them into Boston for punishment. Since Moseley was related to the governor and was now a popular hero, he felt free to do anything he wanted. He also enjoyed shocking the authorities back in Boston. That fall, he happily wrote that he had ordered a captive Indian woman "be torn in pieces by dogs."

There was no Englishman the Indians hated more, and when Moseley took the field at Bloody Brook, the Nipmuck warriors shouted, "Come on, Moseley, come on. You want Indians. Here are enough Indians for you."

For the next six hours, Moseley and his men put up a tremendous fight. Moseley ordered his vastly outnumbered men to remain together as

◆ *Nineteenth-century engraving of the ambush at Bloody Brook.*

a unit as they marched back and forth through the Natives, firing their muskets relentlessly. After hours of fighting, Moseley was forced to ask his two lieutenants to take the lead while he, according to Hubbard, "took a little breath, who was almost melted with laboring, commanding, and leading his men through the midst of the enemy." If not for the arrival of Major Robert Treat and some friendly Mohegans at dusk, Moseley and his men might have all been killed. The next day, sixty-four Englishmen were buried in a single mass grave.

Less than a month later, on October 5, the Indians fell on Springfield. By day's end, thirty-two houses and twenty-five barns had been burned; several mills had been destroyed and tons of provisions. In all of Springfield, only thirteen out of seventy-five houses and barns were left standing.

In this climate of growing fear, the presence of the Praying Indians' self-contained villages within a thirty-mile radius of Boston became unacceptable to most New Englanders. When the minister John Eliot and Captain Daniel Gookin, superintendent to the Praying Indians, dared to defend the Indians against charges of disloyalty, they received death threats. Finally, Massachusetts authorities decided to relocate the Praying Indians to a camp on Deer Island in Boston Harbor.

On the night of October 30, hundreds of Praying Indians gathered at a dock on the Charles River. The ships left at midnight, and in the months ahead, many of these Indians died of starvation and exposure on the bleak shores of Deer Island.

That fall, Boston was overrun with English refugees from towns along the Connecticut River. With food running low, Major Samuel Appleton was told to stop any more people from leaving their settlements without official permission.

Adding to the fears and frustrations of the English was the elusiveness of the man who had started the conflict. By November, Philip had become an almost mythic figure to the Puritans, who imagined he was responsible for every burning house and lifeless English body. In the years to come, stories sprang up in the river valley of how Philip moved from cave to cave and mountaintop to mountaintop, watching with satisfaction as fire and smoke arose from the towns along the Connecticut River.

The truth, however, was less romantic. Instead of being everywhere, Philip spent much of the summer and fall near the modern Massachusetts-Vermont state border. While he and his handful of poorly armed warriors may have participated in some of the victories that season, Philip was not the mastermind behind any plan of Native attack. Indeed, there is no proof of his presence at a single battle in the fall of 1675. Rather than looking to the Pokanoket sachem for direction, the Nipmucks and the river valley Indians, as well as the Abenakis in New Hampshire and Maine, were fighting this war on their own.

With Philip having vanished like smoke into the western wilderness, and with unrest and fear growing by the day among the English, colonial authorities needed a foe they could see and fight. To the south was the largest tribe in the region: the Narragansetts. To date, their sachems had signed two different treaties swearing their loyalty to the English. However, many New Englanders believed that the Narragansetts were simply waiting. Come spring, when the leaves had returned to the trees, they would surely attack. "[T]his false peace hath undone this country," wrote one Providence resident on October 20.

The colonial forces demanded that the Narragansetts turn over the Pokanokets and Pocassets who were in their midst—especially the female sachem Weetamoo. When an October 28 deadline came and went and no Indians had been surrendered, the decision was made. "The sword having marched eastward and westward and northward," Increase Mather wrote, "now beginneth to face toward the south."

The United Colonies of Massachusetts, Connecticut, and Plymouth decided to raise the largest army New England had ever seen. In December, one thousand soldiers, representing close to 5 percent of the region's male English population, would invade the colony of Rhode Island, which refused to participate in the attack. The leader of this huge force was to be Plymouth's own Josiah Winslow. Serving as General Winslow's trusted aide was none other than Benjamin Church.

◆ ◆ ◆ In early December, Church and Winslow rode together to Boston. After meeting with Massachusetts officials, they headed to Dedham Plain, where more than 450 soldiers and horse troopers were assembling as similar groups gathered in Taunton, Plymouth, and New

London. In all, 527 soldiers came from Massachusetts, 158 from Plymouth, and 325 from Connecticut. The Massachusetts forces were under the command of Major Appleton, a veteran of the war in the western frontier. The Connecticut forces were under Major Treat, another veteran commander, and Plymouth's two companies were under captains William Bradford and John Gorham.

December 2 was declared a day of prayer throughout New England. According to Increase Mather, "the churches were all upon their knees before the Lord, the God of Armies, entreating his favor and gracious success in the undertaking." On December 8, Winslow and his soldiers departed from Dedham. The next day, the army arrived at Seekonk along the Seekonk River. Winslow ordered Church to sail directly for their next destination, Smith's garrison in Wickford, Rhode Island, while he led the troops on the land route through Providence. That way Church could prepare for his arrival; it also gave Church the chance to share a boat ride with Samuel Moseley.

By this time in the war, Moseley was almost as mythic a figure as Philip himself, while Church, with the exception of the Pease Field Fight, had accomplished almost nothing. For his part, Church wanted to prove that he was as skilled at capturing Indians as anyone in New England. So instead of remaining at Smith's garrison in Wickford to await Winslow, Church teamed up with some "brisk blades" from Rhode Island and set out that night in search of Indians. It was a cold December night, but they had the benefit of a nearly full moon. By sunrise the next day, Church and his men had returned to the garrison with eighteen captive Indians. As it turned out, Moseley had also been out that night, and he, too, had captured eighteen Indians.

Winslow and his army had already arrived by the time Church and Moseley returned to Wickford. "The general, pleased with the exploit,"

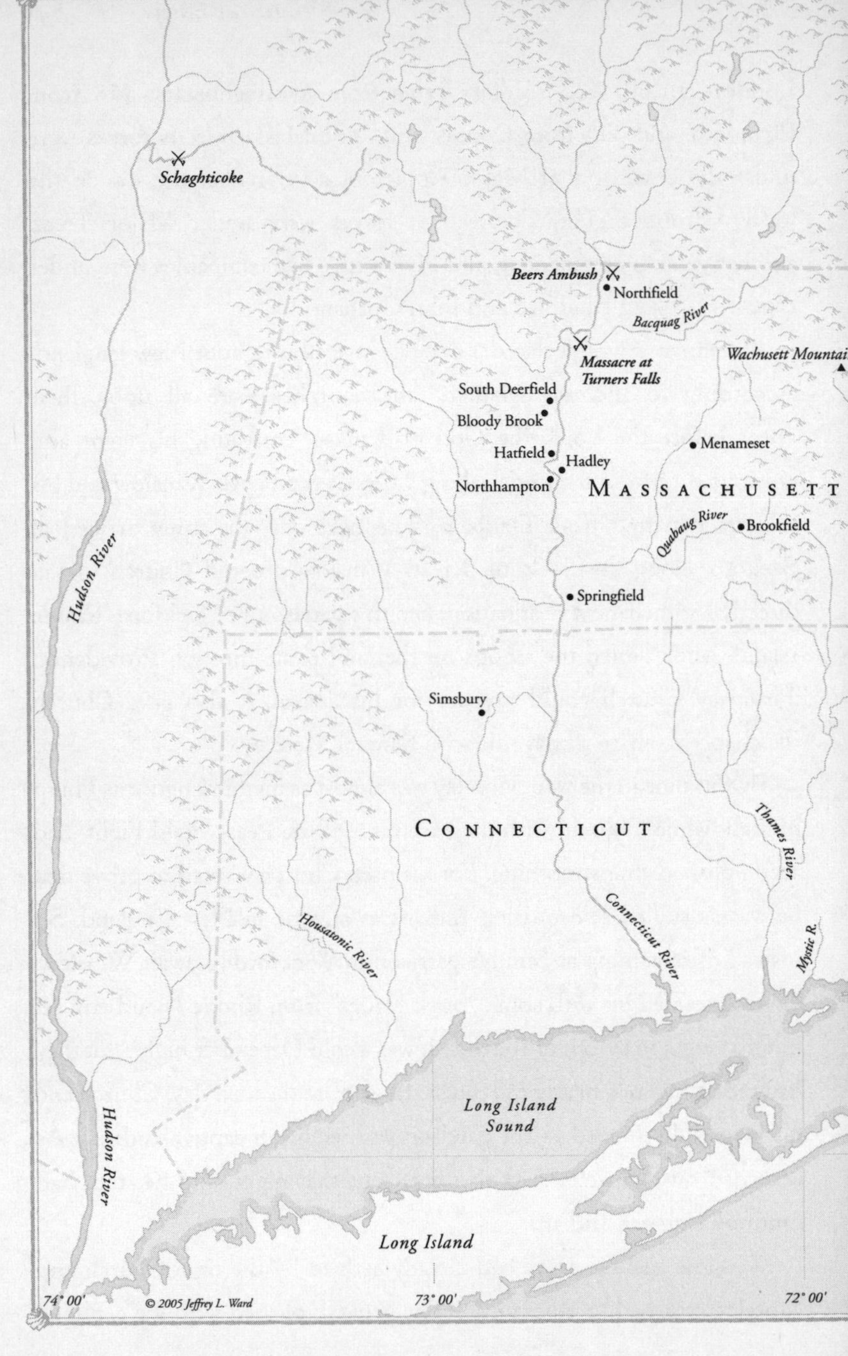
Schaghticoke
Beers Ambush
Northfield
Bacquag River
Massacre at
Turners Falls
Wachusett Mountain
South Deerfield
Bloody Brook
Menameset
Hatfield
Hadley
Northhampton
MASSACHUSETTS
Quabaug River
Brookfield
Hudson River
Springfield
Simsbury
CONNECTICUT
Thames River
Connecticut River
Housatonic River
Mystic R.
Long Island
Sound
Hudson River
Long Island
74° 00'
© 2005 Jeffrey L. Ward
73° 00'
72° 00'

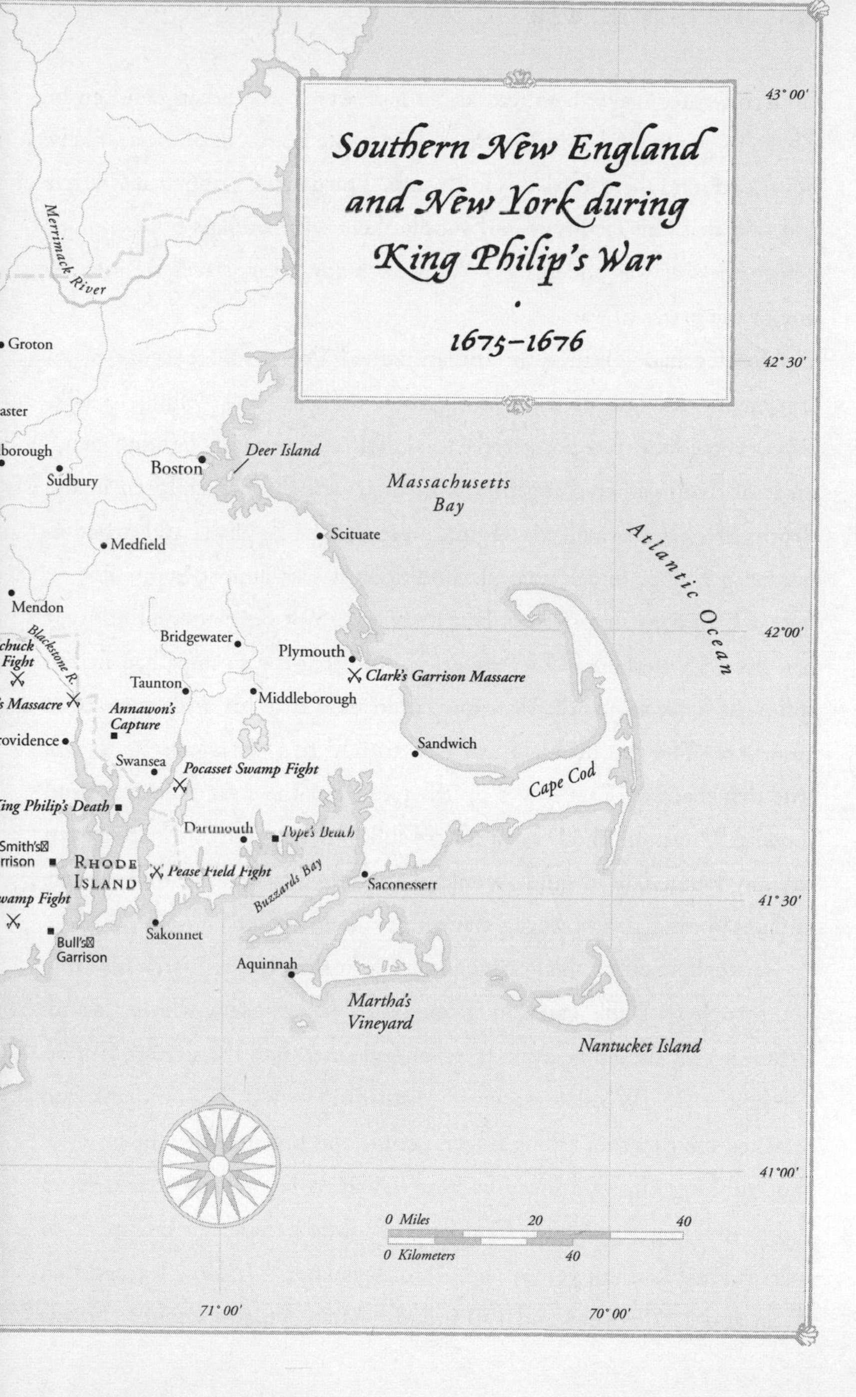
Southern New England and New York during King Philip's War
1675–1676
43° 00'
42° 30'
42° 00'
41° 30'
41° 00'
71° 00'
70° 00'
Merrimack River
Groton
caster
lborough
Sudbury
Boston
Deer Island
Massachusetts Bay
Atlantic Ocean
Scituate
Medfield
Mendon
Blackstone R.
Bridgewater
Plymouth
Clark's Garrison Massacre
Taunton
Middleborough
's Massacre
Annawon's Capture
Providence
Swansea
Pocasset Swamp Fight
Sandwich
Cape Cod
King Philip's Death
Dartmouth
Pope's Beach
Smith's Garrison
Rhode Island
Pease Field Fight
Buzzards Bay
Saconessett
Swamp Fight
Sakonnet
Bull's Garrison
Aquinnah
Martha's Vineyard
Nantucket Island
0 Miles 20 40
0 Kilometers 40

Church wrote, "gave them thanks." There were two Indian children in Church's group, and Winslow decided to make a present of these "likely boys" and send them to friends in Boston. The general grinned at Church and said that "his faculty would supply them with Indians boys enough before the war was ended." As Winslow made clear, slaves were to be one of the prizes of war.

Moseley had captured an Indian named Peter, who because of an argument with one of the Narragansett sachems was willing to talk. Peter claimed the tribe possessed a total of three thousand "fighting men," most of them gathered together with their women and children in the depths of a giant swamp to the southwest. As the English had learned in pursuing Philip, under normal conditions it was almost impossible to fight the Indians in a swamp. But these were not normal conditions. It had been a bitterly cold December, so cold that the swamps had frozen solid. As a consequence, Winslow could now take his army just about anywhere. The real problem was how to find the Narragansetts. It was true that there were no leaves on the trees, but the swamplands around modern Kingston, Rhode Island, were still so dense with bushes that even the most experienced guide would have difficulty leading them to the Indians' base. Peter, however, claimed he could find it.

For them to attack the Narragansetts, Winslow had to march his army south to Jireh Bull's garrison in modern Narragansett, Rhode Island. From there it should be a six- to seven-mile march to the swamp. But on December 15, Winslow received disturbing news. The Indians had attacked the garrison, killing fifteen people and burning it to the ground, thus robbing him of a location from which to launch the attack. Even more troubling was that the Connecticut soldiers under the command of Major Treat had not yet arrived. Two days later, Winslow learned that Treat and 300 English and 150 friendly Mohegan and Pequot Indians had come to the burned-out shell of Bull's garrison. Winslow's force set out to the south, arriving at the garrison around five in the evening on December 18.

The next day was a Sunday, but Winslow decided he had no choice but to attack. Otherwise his entire army might freeze and starve to death. Most of his men had only enough food to last them a single day. With the garrison in ruins, his army had no shelter during one of the coldest nights in New England's history. Plus it had begun to snow. "That night was very snowy," one of the captains wrote. "We lay a thousand in the open field that long night." By morning, the snow was two to three feet deep. Even before the men headed out at 5 A.M., the hands of many were so frostbitten that they were unable to work their muskets.

For eight hours they marched without stop through the snow, with Moseley's company in the lead and with the soldiers from Connecticut taking up the rear. Finally, around 1 P.M., they came to the edge of a dense swamp. Indians began to fire from the trees and bushes, and Peter announced that they had arrived at their destination. Winslow appears to have had no real plan of what to do next. Two Massachusetts companies pursued the Indians into the swamp "without," Hubbard wrote, "staying for word of command, as if everyone were ambitious who should go first."

They had not gone far when they came upon a huge wooden fort. No one had ever seen anything quite like it. Set on a five-acre island and containing approximately five hundred wigwams and thousands of Indians, the fort combined elements of Native and European design. In addition to an outside wall of tree trunks, the fort was surrounded by a sixteen-foot-thick "hedge" of clay and brushwork. At the fort's corners and exposed points were flankers and what the English described as

blockhouses—structures made of tree branches from which the Indians could fire at anyone attempting to climb the wall. The fort had a single point of entry, where a massive tree trunk lay across a moatlike sheet of frozen water. Any Englishman who attempted to cross the tree trunk would be shot by the Indians long before he made it into the fort. They had to find another way in.

Peter, their Indian guide, was not sure whether there was, in fact, another entrance. But in a remote corner of the fort there was a section

◆ *Illustration of the Great Swamp Fight, December 1675, at the Narragansett fort. The artist apparently believed that every English soldier had an identical goatee, mustache and hat!*

that appeared to be unfinished. Instead of vertical logs and a thick clay barrier, there was a section of horizontally laid tree trunks that was just four feet high and wide enough for several men to climb over and into the fort at a time. But what soon became known as the "trees of death" was probably not, as the English assumed, an unfinished portion of the fort. It may have been an intentional feature designed to lure the English to a single point. On either side of the gap were flankers, where Indians armed with muskets could shoot any soldiers who dared to climb over the opening; there was also a blockhouse directly across from the opening, which gave those inside the chance to kill anyone who managed to enter the fort.

In the end, the fort proved who the true aggressors in this conflict were. Instead of joining the Pokanokets and Nipmucks, the Narragansetts had spent the fall and winter doing everything in their power to defend themselves against an unprovoked Puritan attack. If ever there was a defensive structure, it was this fort, and now a thousand English soldiers were about to do their best to wipe out a community of more than three thousand Indian men, women, and children, who asked only to be left alone.

As soldiers spread themselves along the edge of the fort and fired their muskets, the Massachusetts companies, led by captains Isaac Johnson and Nathaniel Davenport, prepared to go in. With the officers leading the way, they charged the four-foot-high section of the fort. As soon as Johnson reached the logs, he was shot dead. Captain Davenport was hit three times, and after handing his musket to his lieutenant, died of his wounds. The fire from the flankers and blockhouse was so fierce that those soldiers who were not already dead fell on their faces and waited for reinforcements.

It was now time for captains Moseley and Joseph Gardner to give it a

try. Moseley later bragged that once inside the fort he saw the muskets of fifty different Indians all aimed at him. Moseley survived the attack, but his men were unable to make any significant progress into the fort.

Next came Major Appleton and Captain James Oliver. Instead of a wild rush, they organized their men into "a storming column." Crying out, "[T]he Indians are running!" Appleton's and Oliver's men were able to push past their comrades from Massachusetts Bay and take the flanker on the left side of the entrance. In addition to reducing the deadliness of the Indians' fire by approximately a third, the capture of the flanker provided the soldiers with some much-needed protection.

Holding back his own Plymouth companies, Winslow sent in the soldiers from Connecticut. One of the flankers had been taken, but no one had told the Connecticut officers of the danger presented by the blockhouse directly opposite the entrance. Major Treat and his men ran right into fire so deadly that four of five Connecticut captains were killed. The soldiers were, in Hubbard's words, "enraged rather than discouraged by the loss of their commanders," and pushed on into the fort.

As the fighting raged on, Benjamin Church began to regret his decision not to lead a company of his own. "[I]mpatient of being out of the heat of the action, he importunately begged leave of the general

◆ *Nineteenth-century engraving of the attack on the Narragansett fort during the Great Swamp Fight.*

that he might run down to the assistance of his friends." Winslow reluctantly yielded to his request, provided that Church take some soldiers with him. Thirty Plymouth men instantly volunteered, and Church and his company were on their way into battle.

Church had no sooner entered the fort than he saw "many men and several valiant captains lie slain." There were also many Indian bodies, with more than fifty corpses piled high in a corner of the fort. To his left, fighting amid the wigwams, was a friend of Church's, Captain Gardner of Salem. Church called out to Gardner, and the two men exchanged glances when the captain suddenly slumped to the ground. Church ran up to him and, seeing blood trickle down Gardner's cheek, lifted up his cap. Gardner looked up at Church but "spoke not a word." A bullet had passed through his skull, and before Church could say anything, Gardner was dead.

Studying the wound, Church realized that the bullet had come from an English musket. As soldiers pulled Gardner's body from the battle, Church sent word back to Winslow that English soldiers were being killed by their comrades behind them. With between three hundred and four hundred soldiers inside this extremely small space, the English were as much a threat to themselves as were the Narragansetts, who, after several hours of fighting, were beginning to run out of gunpowder.

Church could see that many of the warriors had started to abandon the fort, leaving large numbers of Native women, children, and old people trapped in their wigwams. Instead of running away, the warriors had taken up positions amid the bushes and trees of the swamp outside and were firing back on the English soldiers inside the fort.

It was clear to Church that the fort had been effectively taken. It was now time for him to take care of the Indians in the swamp. Church led his men out of the fort to a dense clump of bushes just a few yards behind a group of Narragansetts, who were preparing to fire in unison at the fort. As the Indians stood up in a group to shoot, Church and his men gave them such an "unexpected clap on their backs" that those who were not dead were soon running in confusion. About a dozen of them even ran back *into* the fort and took refuge in the blockhouse.

Church and his men quickly followed. They were running toward a group of Indians concealed inside another blockhouse within the fort when Church was suddenly hit by three pieces of lead. The first bullet buried itself harmlessly into a pair of mittens rolled up inside his pocket; the second cut through his breeches but only nicked him in the side; it was the third bullet that almost killed him—slicing into his thigh before bouncing off his hipbone. As Church fell to the ground, he made sure to fire his gun and wound the Indian who had shot him.

His men rushed to his side and began to carry him out of the fort. With the enemy on the run, the order now came to burn down the fort. In his weakened state, Church tried to protest—there were valuable supplies of corn and meat inside, as well as hundreds of Native women and children. But he was shouted down by Moseley, who had suddenly appeared from the edge of the swamp. And while Winslow, the Plymouth governor, might have been named commander of this army, Moseley and Massachusetts Bay were apparently in charge. The fort, along with all its provisions and perhaps hundreds of Native women, children, and elderly, was set on fire.

Many accounts of the battle focus on the bravery of the English officers and soldiers but make little mention of the slaughter that followed the taking of the fort. It must have been a horrendous and terrifying scene as Narragansett women and children screamed and cried amid the gunshots and the flames.

Sometime after five o'clock, the order was given to begin the long march back to Wickford. It was the worst night of the soldiers' lives. They had spent the previous night trying to sleep on an open field in the midst of a snowstorm; that morning they had marched for eight hours and then fought for another three; now they were slogging their way through the snow—eight hundred men lugging the bodies of more than two hundred of the dead and wounded. "And I suppose," Church wrote, "everyone that is acquainted with the circumstances of that night's march, deeply laments the miseries that attended them, especially the wounded and dying men."

The first ones reached the Smith garrison at 2 A.M. Winslow and his entourage became lost and did not arrive at Wickford until seven in the morning. Twenty-two of the army's wounded died during the march.

The next afternoon, thirty-four English corpses were buried in a mass grave; six more died over the next two days. Those wounded who survived the march, including Church and Captain William Bradford (who had been injured in the eye), were shipped to Newport on Aquidneck Island for medical treatment.

The battle became known as the Great Swamp Fight, and more than 20 percent of the English soldiers had been either killed or wounded—double the casualty rate of the American forces at D-day in World War II. Of all the colonies, Connecticut had suffered the most. Major Treat (who was the last man to leave the fort) reported that four of his five captains had been killed and that eighty of his three hundred soldiers were either dead or wounded. This makes for a casualty rate of almost 30 percent—roughly equivalent to the Confederate losses at Antietam on the bloodiest day of the Civil War. Major Treat insisted that his men return to Connecticut, and despite the outraged objections of Winslow and his staff, who were already debating another strike against the

Narragansetts, the Connecticut forces marched for Stonington on December 28.

But as Winslow knew all too well, his army was not about to go anywhere. One supply ship had managed to make it to Wickford, but the rest of the vessels were trapped in the ice of Boston Harbor. The awful weather meant that it took five days before Bostonians heard the news of the army's hard-fought victory.

It cannot be denied that the assault was a major defeat for the Narragansetts. Somewhere between 350 and 600 Native men, women, and children were either shot or burned to death that day. And yet there were still thousands of Narragansetts left alive. If they could make their way north to Nipmuck country, the number of enemy Indian warriors would be more than doubled. Instead of saving New England, Winslow's army had only increased the danger.

Two young sachems were left to lead what remained of the tribe: Canonchet, who had traveled to Boston that fall to negotiate with Puritan officials, and Quinnapin, who had married the Pocasset sachem Weetamoo. Before he had abandoned the fort, Canonchet had been careful to leave a message for the English. In the final minutes of the battle, as the soldiers moved from wigwam to wigwam with torches in their hands, one of them found the treaty Canonchet had signed in Boston. The Puritans took this as proof that the Narragansetts were fully aware that they broke their treaty with the English, but as Canonchet now knew for sure, it was a piece of parchment that had been worthless from the start.

◆ ◆ ◆ In the weeks ahead, Church lay in a bed in Newport, sick with fever, as his body fought off the infections from his wounds. The weather outside remained brutally cold—so cold that eleven of the replacement soldiers sent from Boston during the first week of January died of exposure before they reached Winslow's army at Wickford.

However, in the middle of January, the temperature began to rise. A thaw unlike anything seen in New England since the arrival of the Pilgrims melted the snow and ice. It was just what the Narragansetts had been waiting for. The English could no longer track them in the snow and the Indians could now dig for groundnuts. The time had come for the Narragansetts to make a run for it and join Philip and the Nipmucks to the north.

On January 21, Winslow received word that the Indians were "in full flight." Not until almost a week later, on January 27, did the army—which had grown to fourteen hundred with the return of Major Treat's Connecticut forces—begin its pursuit.

By this time, Benjamin Church had also returned. He was not yet fully recovered, but he agreed to join in what was hoped to be the knockout punch against the Indians. Reports claimed that there were four thousand of them, including eighteen hundred warriors, marching north. If they should reach the wilderness of Nipmuck country, New England was in for a winter and spring of violence and suffering.

About ten miles north of Providence, Winslow's soldiers came upon a pile of sixty horse heads. The Narragansetts were killing and eating anything they could get their hands on. Unfortunately, this left little food for the English, who were almost as poorly provisioned as the Indians. On a few occasions, the soldiers leading the English army were able to catch a glimpse of the rear of the Narragansetts only to watch the Indians disappear into the forest as soon as they came under attack.

Without enough food and with no way to engage the enemy, the morale of the English soldiers got worse with each day, and desertions became widespread. The temperature started to fall once again, and illness swept through the English ranks.

By February 5, what has become known as the Hungry March had reached the town of Marlborough at the eastern fringes of Nipmuck country. Without enough food, Winslow decided that he had no choice but to disband his army. Church returned to his pregnant wife, Alice, and their son, Thomas, who had been staying with family and friends in Duxbury.

The march had been a complete disaster. Back in December, colonial officials had hoped to wipe the Narragansetts off the face of the earth. Instead, they had sent thousands of them running into the arms of the enemy.

FIFTEEN

Keeping the Faith

◆ ◆ ◆

SICK, DESPERATE, AND quickly becoming irrelevant to the war he had started, Philip and his small band of warriors headed more than fifty miles west to the Hudson River valley. In late December, they made camp at Schaghticoke on the Hoosic River, an eastern branch of the Hudson. It was here in the colony of New York, where some of the original Dutch settlers still actively traded with the Indians and where the Hudson River provided access to the French to the north, that Philip hoped to stage his triumphant return to the war.

That fall, Philip had met with a French official on his way back to Canada after a visit to Boston. The Frenchman had presented the sachem with an ornate brass gun and pledged his country's support in the war against the English. Specifically, he had promised Philip three hundred Indian warriors from Canada and all the ammunition he needed.

Philip was, once again, following in his father's footsteps. He, too, was attempting to strengthen his tribe through an alliance with a European power. There was no guarantee that the French would be any more trustworthy than the English in the long run, but at least for now Philip would have the warriors and ammunition he desperately needed. So he and his men, led by his main captain, Annawon, set up winter headquarters at Schaghticoke and waited for the French and their Native allies.

By February, Philip's forces had reportedly grown to twenty-one hundred, which included six hundred "French Indians with straws in their noses." Although this figure was undoubtedly exaggerated, Philip had succeeded in gathering one of the largest forces of Indian warriors in the region.

But there was another Native group to consider. The Mohawks, a powerful subset of the Iroquois, lived near Albany and were the most feared warriors in the Northeast. In addition to being the traditional enemies of the Indians of southern New England, like the Pokanokets and Nipmucks, they had a special hatred of the French and their Indian allies to the north. Yet if Philip could somehow make the Mohawks his allies, he would be in a position to bring the New England colonies to their knees.

Philip was not the only one seeking an alliance with the Mohawks. The governor of New York, Edmund Andros, also hoped to get them on his side. Unlike the Puritan magistrates, who viewed all Indians as potential enemies, Andros saw the Mohawks and the rest of the Iroquois as a powerful independent group that must be dealt with diplomatically rather than through force. Andros and the Iroquois were in the midst of creating what became known as the Covenant Chain, a partnership between the colony and the Iroquois that would stand for generations. It became Andros's mission to persuade the Mohawks that Philip and the tribes to the east were a threat to that alliance.

Sometime in late February, the Mohawks attacked Philip's forces in Schaghticoke. By all accounts, it was a rout. On March 4, Governor Andros witnessed the triumphant return of the Mohawks to Albany. In addition to plenty of prisoners, they proudly showed all the scalps of the Indians they had killed.

Once again, Philip's forces had been decimated and were on the run. This time they headed east, back to the Connecticut River. The future of the war was in others' hands.

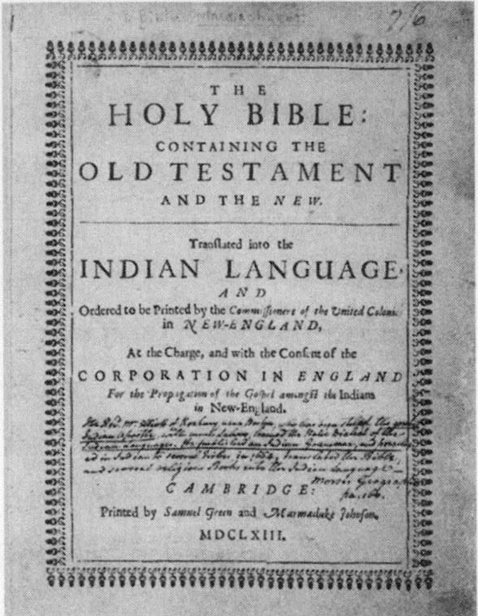

THE
HOLY BIBLE:
CONTAINING THE
OLD TESTAMENT
AND THE *NEW*.

Translated into the
INDIAN LANGUAGE
AND
Ordered to be Printed by the *Commissioners of the United Colonies* in *NEW-ENGLAND*,
At the Charge, and with the Consent of the
CORPORATION IN *ENGLAND*
For the Propagation of the Gospel amongst the Indians in New-England.

CAMBRIDGE:
Printed by *Samuel Green* and *Marmaduke Johnson*.
MDCLXIII.

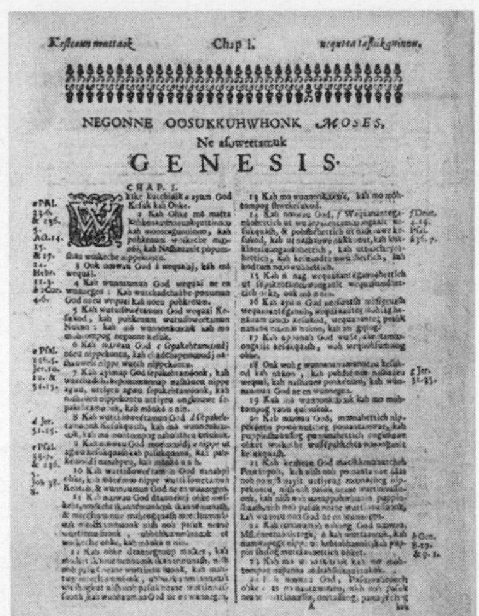

Chap I.

NEGONNE OOSUKKUHWHONK *MOSES*,
Ne asoweetamuk
GENESIS.

CHAP. I.

◆ *The title page and first page of Genesis from John Eliot's Bible, translated into the Wampanoag language for the Praying Indians.*

◆ ◆ ◆ His name was Job Kattenanit. He was a Praying Indian who had been sent to Deer Island. Before he had been transported to the island, his village had been attacked by the Nipmucks, who'd taken his three children captive. By December, Job, who was a widower, was desperate to find his children, so he and another Praying Indian named James volunteered to become spies for the English. Their mission was to join the Nipmucks at Menameset, the village near Brookfield to which Philip had fled after escaping from Plymouth, and learn anything they could about the Indians' plans for the winter. If Job was lucky, he might also make contact with his three children. It was a dangerous task to be sure, but James and Job could truthfully tell the Nipmucks that they had been so abused by the English that they had no choice but to leave Deer Island.

James was the first to report back to the English on January 24. He said that the Nipmucks had at first threatened to kill him and Job, but a sachem who had fought with James against the Mohawks several years earlier spoke in his defense, and they had been allowed to live. Job had found his children, who were all still alive, and he had decided to remain with them at Menameset for as long as possible. James reported to Daniel Gookin, the superintendent of the Praying Indians, that the Nipmucks had "rejoiced much" when they learned that the Narragansetts had been forced to join their struggle. Now that most of the English towns along the Massachusetts portion of the Connecticut River had been abandoned, the Indians planned to attack the settlements to the east, beginning with Lancaster. James even knew the details of how the Nipmucks planned to do it. First they would destroy the bridge that was the only entrance to the town. Knowing that there was no way for English reinforcements to reach it, the Indians could easily burn the settlement.

Much of what James said was confirmed by other reports, but the Massachusetts authorities chose to ignore his warnings as the untrustworthy testimony of just another Indian. Then, at ten o'clock on the night of February 9, Daniel Gookin was awakened by an urgent pounding on the door of his home in Cambridge.

It was Job. Like James before him, he had traveled with "rackets on his feet" through the snow of the western frontier. He was starving, exhausted, and fearful of what might happen to his children, whom he had been forced to leave with the Nipmucks, but he felt a responsibility to tell Gookin that everything James had reported was true. Four hundred Nipmucks and Narragansetts were about to descend on Lancaster, and there was very little time. The attack was scheduled to begin the next day, February 10, at daybreak.

Gookin leaped out of bed and sent a messenger to Marlborough, where Captain Samuel Wadsworth and about forty troops were stationed. The messenger rode all that night, and by morning Wadsworth and his men were riding furiously for Lancaster, about ten miles away. As both James and Job had predicted, the bridge had been set on fire, but Wadsworth and his troops were able to get their horses across it. Up ahead the English soldiers could see smoke rising into the sky and hear the shouts of the Indians and the firing of muskets. The attack had already begun.

◆ ◆ ◆ Mary Rowlandson was thirty-eight years old and the mother of three children—Joseph, eleven; Mary, ten; and Sarah, six. In a few years' time she would be the author of *The Sovereignty and Goodness of God*, an account of her capture by the Indians that became one of America's first bestsellers. But on February 10, 1676, she was simply the wife of Lancaster's minister, John Rowlandson, who was away in Boston begging the Puritan authorities to provide his town with some protection.

On the morning of February 10, the residents of Lancaster had taken the precaution of gathering in five different garrisons, one of which included the Rowlandson home, which was built beside a hill, with a barn nearby. When the Indians attacked at daybreak, there were between forty and fifty men, women, and children assembled in the Rowlandson garrison.

First they heard the musket fire in the distance. When they looked cautiously out the windows, they could see that several houses were already burning. They could hear shouts and screams as the Indians worked their way from house to house until suddenly they, too, were under attack.

Dozens of Indians climbed up on the barn roof and on the hill behind the house and began firing on the garrison "so that the bullets seemed to fly like hail." In no time at all, three of the men stationed at the windows had been hit, one of them quite badly in the jaw. Soon enough, the roof of the house was on fire. "Now is the dreadful hour come," she remembered. "Some in our house were fighting for their lives, others wallowing in their blood, the house on fire over our heads, and the bloody heathen ready to knock us on the head if we stirred out." Mothers and children were "crying out for themselves and one another, 'Lord, what shall we do?' "

With six-year-old Sarah in her arms and her other two children and a niece gathered around her, Mary decided "to go forth and leave the house." But as they approached the doorway, the Indians unleashed a round of "shot so thick that the bullets rattled against the house as if one had taken a handful of stones and threw them." Mary and the children paused, but with the flames roaring behind them, they had no choice but to push ahead, even though they could see the Indians waiting for them with their muskets, hatchets, and spears. Her sister's husband John, already wounded, was the first to die. The Indians shouted and began to strip his body of clothes as they continued firing at anyone who dared leave the house. Mary was then hit in the side, the bullet passing through her and into Sarah's abdomen. Her nephew William's leg was broken by a bullet, and he was soon killed with a hatchet. "Thus were we butchered by those merciless heathen," she wrote, "standing amazed, with the blood running down to our heels." Rowlandson's oldest sister, who had not yet left the house and had just seen her son and brother-in-law killed, cried out, "Lord let me die with them!" Almost immediately, she was struck by a bullet and fell down dead across the entrance of the house.

An Indian grabbed Rowlandson and told her to come with him. Indians had also seized her children Joseph and Mary and were pulling them in the opposite direction. Meanwhile, Captain Wadsworth and his troopers had just arrived, and the Indians had decided it was time to leave. Mary begged for her children but was told that if she went along quietly,

◆ *A 1771 woodcut depicting the attack on Mary Rowlandson's house.*

they would not be harmed. She and twenty-three others were taken prisoner that day and so began what she later described as "that grievous captivity."

◆ ◆ ◆ They spent the first night on a hill overlooking the smoking ruins of Lancaster. An empty house stood on the hill, and Rowlandson asked if she and her injured daughter might sleep inside. "What, will you love Englishmen still?" mocked the Indians, who celebrated by feasting on roasted cattle while Rowlandson and the others were given nothing to eat. "Oh the roaring and singing and dancing and yelling of those black creatures in the night," she remembered, "which made the place a lively resemblance of hell."

They left early the next morning. Rowlandson's wounds had become infected, making it impossible for her to carry her daughter. One of the

Indians had a horse, and he offered to hold Sarah, who whimpered, "I shall die, I shall die" as Rowlandson staggered behind "with sorrow that cannot be expressed." That night she sat in the snow with her daughter in her lap. "[T]he Lord upheld me with His gracious and merciful spirit," she remembered, "and we were both alive to see the light of the next morning."

That afternoon they arrived at the great Nipmuck gathering spot of Menameset. There Rowlandson met Robert Pepper, a captive now for more than five months. Pepper told her to lay oak leaves on her wound, a Native remedy that had helped his injured leg and would also cure Rowlandson. But there was nothing to be done for little Sarah, who had caught a deadly fever. "I sat much alone with a poor wounded child in my lap," she wrote, "which moaned night and day, having nothing to revive the body or cheer the spirits." Finally on February 18, nine days after being shot, Sarah died.

That night, Rowlandson slept in the snow with Sarah in her arms. The next morning, the Indians buried her child on the top of a nearby hill. "I have thought since of the wonderful goodness of God to me," Rowlandson wrote, "in preserving me in the use of my reason and sense, in that distressed time, that I did not use wicked and violent means to end my own miserable life." Instead, she went in search of her other two children.

There were more than two thousand Indians gathered at Menameset. Rowlandson had learned that her ten-year-old daughter Mary was somewhere nearby. That day as she wandered from wigwam to wigwam, she found her daughter. But when Mary began to sob uncontrollably, the girl's Indian master told Rowlandson that she must leave—"a heart-cutting word to me."

"I could not sit still in this condition," she remembered, "but kept walking from one place to another." She prayed to the Lord that He would show her "some sign, and hope of some relief." Soon after, she heard her son's voice.

Joseph Rowlandson had been taken to a village about six miles away. But his master's wife had agreed to bring him all the way to Menameset to look for his mother, and "with tears in his eyes, he asked me whether his sister Sarah was dead . . . and prayed . . . that I would not be troubled in reference to himself." It was too brief a visit, but Rowlandson could not help but interpret her son's appearance as God's "gracious answer to my earnest and unfeigned desire."

The next day, February 22, several hundred warriors returned from a raid on the town of Medfield, twenty miles southwest of Boston. There had been about two hundred soldiers in the town, but even they were not enough to prevent the Indians from burning close to fifty houses and killing more than a dozen inhabitants. Even worse, the Indians had the nerve to leave a note. "Know by this paper, that the Indians that thou hast provoked to wrath and anger, will war this twenty-one years if you will; there are many Indians yet, we come three hundred at this time. You must consider the Indians lost nothing but their life; you must lose your fair houses and cattle."

When the war party returned to Menameset, the warriors shouted a total of twenty-three times to indicate how many English had been killed. "Oh! The outrageous roaring and hooping that there was," Rowlandson wrote. "Oh, the hideous insulting and triumphing that there was over some Englishmen's scalps that they had taken." One of the Indians had brought back a Bible from the raid, and he offered it to Rowlandson. She immediately turned to chapter 30 of Deuteronomy and read, "though we were scattered from one end of the earth to the other, yet the Lord would gather us together, and turn all those curses upon our enemies." It was a wonderful gift for the grieving Englishwoman. "I do not desire to live to forget this Scripture," she remembered, "and what comfort it was to me."

Rowlandson's master was the Narragansett sachem Quinnapin. Her mistress was Quinnapin's new wife, Weetamoo, the sachem from Pocasset. After reluctantly joining her brother-in-law Philip, she had fled to the then-neutral Narragansetts. By marrying Quinnapin, who already had two wives but none as important as the Pocasset sachem, Weetamoo was now partners with the Pocassets' traditional enemy. After the Great Swamp Fight, all of them were in this together.

By the middle of February, word had reached Menameset of the Mohawk attack on Philip. The Pokanoket sachem and what was left of his forces were heading to a village site well to the north on the Connecticut River. It was time for the Nipmucks and Narragansetts to meet with Philip and plan for the spring attack. When their scouts informed them that a large Puritan army, including six hundred horsemen, was headed for Menameset, the Nipmucks and Narragansetts immediately broke camp and headed north.

Keeping two thousand Native men, women, and children ahead of an English army on horseback might seem impossible. But as Mary Rowlandson witnessed firsthand, the Indians' knowledge of the land and their talent for working together made them more than a match for the fastest English forces. As a small group of warriors headed south "to hold the English army in play," hundreds upon hundreds of Indians picked up their possessions and began to flee. "[T]hey marched on furiously, with their old and with their young. Some carried their old decrepit mothers, some carried one and some another. Four of them carried a great Indian upon a bier, but going through a thick wood with him, they were hindered and could make no haste; whereupon they took him upon their backs and carried him, one at a time, till they came to Bacquag River."

Known today as Miller's River, the waterway is an eastern branch of the Connecticut. "They quickly fell to cutting dry trees," Rowlandson wrote, "to make rafts to carry them over the river." Rowlandson and her master and mistress were among the first to cross the river. The Indians had heaped brush onto the log rafts to protect them from the frigid water, and Rowlandson was thankful that she made it across without wetting her feet, "it being a very cold time."

It was now the third week of her captivity, and Rowlandson's hunger was such that she ate what she had earlier called "filthy trash," from groundnuts and corn husks to the rotting meat of a long-dead horse. Rowlandson was often on the edge of starvation, but so were her captors, whose ability to find food in the winter landscape seemed nothing less than a miracle. "[S]trangely did the Lord provide for them," she wrote, "that I did not see (all the time that I was among them) one man, woman, or child die with hunger."

Now that she no longer had her daughter to care for, Rowlandson was expected to work. She was soon knitting a pair of white cotton stockings for her mistress, Weetamoo. As a sachem, Weetamoo wore both English and Native clothing. She was "a severe and proud dame . . . bestowing . . . as much time as any of the gentry of the land [in dressing herself neatly]: powdering her hair, and painting her face, going with necklaces, with jewels in her ears, and bracelets upon her hands."

Just as the last groups of Indians reached the north bank of the river, the English army, under the command of Major Thomas Savage, arrived at the southern bank. But instead of pursuing the Indians across the river, Savage chose to do as so many Puritan commanders had done before him and quit the chase. For Rowlandson, it was a crushing turn of events, but the Lord must have had his reasons. "God did not give them courage or activity to go after us," she wrote; "we were not ready for so great a mercy as victory and deliverance."

The Indians continued north for several days until they reached the Connecticut River near the town of Northfield. Philip, Rowlandson was told, was waiting for them on the opposite bank. "When I was in the canoe," she recalled, "I could not but be amazed at the numerous crew of pagans that were on the . . . other side. When I came ashore, they gathered all about me . . . [and] asked one another questions and laughed and rejoiced over their gains and victories." For the first time of her captivity, Rowlandson started to cry. "Although I had met with so much affliction," she wrote, "and my heart was many times ready to break, yet could I not shed one tear in their sight, but rather had been all this while in a maze, and like one astonished. But now I may say as Psalm 137, 'By the Rivers of Babylon . . . [I] wept.'"

One of the Indians asked why she was crying. Not knowing what to say, she blurted out that they were going to kill her. "'No,' said he, 'none will hurt you.'" Soon after, she was given two spoonfuls of cornmeal and told that Philip wanted to speak with her.

It was one of several conversations she would have with the Pokanoket sachem. Despite everything she had heard of Philip's evil nature, Rowlandson was treated with kindness and respect by the Native leader. In the weeks ahead, she would knit a shirt and cap for Philip's son and even be invited to dine with the sachem. "I went," she remembered, "and he gave me a pancake about as big as two fingers; it was made of parched wheat,

◆ *An elm bowl attributed to King Philip.*

• *Nineteenth-century depiction of Mary Rowlandson being taken across the Connecticut River toward Philip's forces.*

beaten and fried in bear's grease, but I thought I never tasted pleasanter meat in my life."

Later, in the midst of yet another extended journey, Rowlandson started to lose strength. As she slogged through the knee-deep mud of a swamp, Philip unexpectedly appeared at her side and offered his hand and some words of encouragement. In her book, Rowlandson faithfully records these acts of kindness on Philip's part. But nowhere does she suggest that the sachem was unfairly hated by her fellow Puritans. Rowlandson had lost her daughter and several other loved ones in the war Philip had started, and nothing—not a pancake or a hand offered in friendship—could ever bring them back.

On March 9, Philip met for the first time with Canonchet, the young leader of the Narragansetts. As they all knew, the victories they had so far won at Lancaster and Medfield were meaningless if they did not find a way to feed their people. They needed seed corn to plant crops in the spring. Hidden underground in Swansea was a large store of seed. Canonchet volunteered to lead a group of warriors and women back into

the very heart of Plymouth Colony to retrieve it. As the women returned with the seed to the Connecticut River valley, Canonchet would remain in Plymouth and bring the war back to where it had begun.

◆ ◆ ◆ On February 29, Benjamin Church attended a meeting of the Council of War at Governor Winslow's home in Marshfield. The raid on Medfield the week before had been followed by an attack on nearby Weymouth, and there were fears that the colony was about to be overrun with hostile Indians from the north. A member of the Council of War proposed that a militia company of sixty soldiers be sent to the farthest towns in the colony to defend against a possible Indian attack. The same official proposed that Church be the company's commander. But Church had a proposal of his own.

If the Indians returned to Plymouth, it was reasonable to assume that, in Church's words, "they would come very numerous." As Massachusetts had learned, it was a waste of time stationing militias in town garrisons. Although they helped to defend the settlement in the event of an attack, they did nothing to limit the Indians' activities. The only way to conduct the war was to "lie in the woods as the enemy did." And to do that, you not only needed a large force of several hundred men, you needed a large number of friendly Indians. "[I]f they intended to make an end of the war by subduing the enemy," Church insisted, "they must make a business of the war as the enemy did." He suggested that Plymouth officials should equip him with an army of three hundred men, a third of them Indians. Give him six weeks, he said, and he and his men would "do good service."

Because it included the use of a large number of Indians, Church's proposal shocked the Council of War. At that time in Plymouth Colony, fear of all Indians—hostile and friendly alike—was so high that just a few days before, the Council had voted to banish some Praying Indians to Clark's Island in Plymouth Harbor. Not surprisingly, the Council turned him down. But Church's words were not totally ignored. The man who agreed to serve instead, Captain Michael Pierce of Scituate, was given, in addition to sixty Englishmen, twenty "friend Indians" from Cape Cod.

Church decided then his first priority must be to make sure his pregnant wife, Alice, and their son, Tom, were safe. If the Indians should come in the numbers he expected, he knew that Duxbury, where they were now located, was likely to be a prime target. Even though it meant leaving the colony, he decided to take Alice and Tom to Aquidneck Island.

It was an unpopular decision with the authorities, from whom he needed a permit. Eventually, Church was able to convince Governor Winslow that he could be of some use to him "on that side of the colony," and he was given permission to relocate to Rhode Island. On March 9, they set out for Taunton, then proceeded by boat down the Taunton River to Mount Hope Bay and Aquidneck Island, before arriving safely at Captain John Almy's house in Portsmouth.

◆ ◆ ◆ For the English, March of 1676 was a terrible and terrifying month. Indians from across New England banded together for a devastating series of raids that reached from the Connecticut River valley to Maine and even into Connecticut itself, a colony that had, up until then, been spared from attack. But it was in Plymouth, on Sunday, March 26, where the English suffered one of the worst defeats of the war.

Captain Pierce and his force of sixty Englishmen and twenty Praying Indians were marching north along the east bank of the Blackstone River when they spotted some Indians. There were just a few of them, and when the Indians realized they were being followed, they turned to flee. Pierce's men eagerly chased them, only to discover that they had walked into an ambush. A force of five hundred Indians, apparently led by Canonchet, emerged from the trees. Pierce and his soldiers ran across the rocks to the west bank of the Blackstone, where another four hundred Indians were waiting for them.

Pierce ordered his company of eighty men to form a single ring, and standing back to back, they fought bravely against close to a thousand Indians, who according to one account "were as thick as they could stand, thirty deep." By the end of the fighting two hours later, fifty-five English, including Pierce, were dead, along with ten of the Praying Indians. Nine English soldiers either temporarily escaped the fighting or were taken alive and marched several miles north, where they were tortured to death at a place still known today as Nine Men's Misery.

Given the impossible odds, the Praying Indians would not have been blamed for trying to escape at the first sign of trouble. But one Indian named Amos stood at Pierce's side almost to the very end. Even after his commander had been shot in the thigh and lay dying at his feet, Amos continued to fire on the enemy. Finally, it became obvious that, in the words of William Hubbard, "there was no possibility for him to do any further good to Captain Pierce, nor yet to save himself if he stayed any longer." The Narragansetts and Nipmucks had all blackened their faces for battle. So Amos smeared his face with gunpowder and stripped off his English clothes to impersonate the enemy. After pretending to search the bodies of the English for anything valuable, he disappeared into the woods.

Amos was not the only Praying Indian to make a remarkable escape that day. As the fighting drew to a close, another Praying Indian turned to the English soldier beside him and told him to run. Taking up his tomahawk, the Indian pretended to be a Narragansett chasing his foe, and the two of them did not stop running until they had left the fighting far behind.

When word of the heroism of Pierce's Praying Indians began to spread, public opinion regarding the use of friendly Indians in combat started to shift. It still took some time, but New Englanders came to realize that instead of being untrustworthy and dangerous, Indians like Amos and the spies James and Job might in fact hold the secret to winning the war.

◆ ◆ ◆ Unlike Massachusetts and Plymouth, Connecticut had relied on friendly Indians from the start of the conflict. In addition to the Mohegans, there were the Pequots and the Niantics, a subset of the Narragansetts, who had remained loyal to the English. In early April, a Connecticut force under Captain George Denison was in the area of modern Pawtucket, Rhode Island, when they captured an Indian woman who told them that Canonchet was nearby. Over the course of the next few days, Denison's eighty or so Mohegans, Pequots, and Niantics competed with one another for the honor of capturing the great Narragansett sachem.

In the last few months, Canonchet had earned the reputation for

• *Canonchet Memorial in Narragansett, Rhode Island. Limestone statue sculpted in 1977.*

physical courage that had so far escaped the more famous Philip. Dressed in the silver-trimmed jacket the Puritans had given him during treaty negotiations in Boston, with a large wampum belt around his waist, the young sachem was known for his bravery in battle. Even the Puritans had to admit that Canonchet "was a very proper man, of goodly stature and great courage of mind, as well as strength of body." At considerable risk, he and thirty warriors had succeeded in collecting the seed corn from storage pits just north of Mount Hope. The corn had already been delivered to the Connecticut River valley, where the women would begin planting in May. He was now leading the army of fifteen hundred Indians that had destroyed Captain Pierce's company.

On April 9, Canonchet was resting at the foot of a hill near the Blackstone River with nine of his warriors, trading stories about the attack on Captain Pierce and his company, when he heard "the alarm of the English." He ordered two of his men to go to the top of the hill and report back what they saw, but the men never returned. A third warrior was sent, and he, too, disappeared. Only after two more men went to the top of the hill did Canonchet learn that "the English army was upon him."

Taking up his musket and blanket, the Narragansett sachem began to run around the base of the hill, hoping to sneak through the enemy forces and escape behind them. However, one of Denison's Niantic warriors saw the sachem moving swiftly through the woods, and the chase was on.

Canonchet soon realized that Denison's Indians were catching up to him. Hoping to slow them down, he stripped off his blanket, but the Indians refused to stop and pick up the valuable item. Canonchet then shook off his silver-trimmed coat, followed by his belt of wampum. Now the Indians knew they had, in Hubbard's words, "the right bird, which made them pursue as eagerly as the other fled."

Ahead was the Blackstone River, and Canonchet decided to try and cross it. But as he ran across the slick stones, his foot slipped, and he fell into the water and soaked his gun. Canonchet still had a considerable lead over his pursuers, but he now knew that flight was useless. According to Hubbard, "he confessed soon after that his heart and his bowels turned within him, so as he became like a rotten stick, void of strength." A few seconds later, a Pequot Indian named Monopoide caught up to the sachem, who surrendered without a fight.

The English offered to spare Canonchet's life if he helped them convince Philip and the others to stop the fighting. But he refused, "saying he knew the Indians would not yield." He was then taken to Stonington, where officials blamed him for dragging the Narragansetts into war. He responded that "others were as forward for the war as himself and that he desired to hear no more thereof." When told he'd been sentenced to die, he replied that "he liked it well, that he should die before his heart was soft or had spoken anything unworthy of himself." Just before his execution in front of a Pequot firing squad, Canonchet declared that "killing him would not end the war." He threw off his jacket and stretched out his arms just as the bullets pierced his chest.

Connecticut officials made sure that all three tribes of their friendly Indians shared in the execution. According to one account, "the Pequots shot him, the Mohegans cut off his head and quartered his body, and Ninigret's [Niantics] made the fire and burned his quarters; and as a token of their love and fidelity to the English, presented his head to the council at Hartford."

If the death of Canonchet did not end the war, it was, in Hubbard's words, "a considerable step thereunto." The Indians had lost a leader who had briefly united several groups of Native peoples into a

• *Reputed to be Ninigret II, son of the Niantic sachem who sided with the English during King Philip's War.*

powerful army. In the days and weeks ahead, dissension began to threaten the Indians as the English finally realized that using the Praying Indians was the best way to break apart the Nipmuck-Narragansett-Pokanoket alliance.

◆ ◆ ◆ By late March, a large number of Indians had gathered at Wachusett Mountain to the north of modern Worcester. The steep and rocky terrain protected them from the English yet was far enough east that they could easily attack the towns between them and Boston. On April 5, the Praying Indian Tom Doublet arrived at Wachusett with a letter from colonial officials in Boston. In addition to the possibility of starting peace negotiations, the letter mentioned the release of English prisoners.

On April 12, Doublet returned to Boston with the Indians' response. They were not ready yet to discuss peace: "you know and we know your heart great sorrowful with crying for you lost many many hundred men and all your houses and your land, and women, child and cattle . . . ; [you] on your backside stand." They were willing, however, to discuss the possibility of ransoming hostages. As a minister's wife, Mary Rowlandson was the Indians' most important captive, and she quickly became the focus of the negotiations.

In mid-April, Rowlandson, who was near the Connecticut River with Weetamoo, learned that she was wanted at Wachusett, where Philip and her master, Quinnapin, were already meeting with the Nipmucks. Before receiving this news, she had reached a new low. Her son was deathly ill, and she had heard nothing about her daughter. Without Quinnapin to help her, Rowlandson's relationship with Weetamoo—difficult from the start—had deteriorated to the point that the sachem had threatened to beat her with a log. "My heart was so heavy . . . that I could scarce speak or [walk along] the path," she remembered. But when she learned that she might soon be returned to the English, she felt a sudden burst of energy. "My strength seemed to come again," she wrote, "and recruit my feeble knees and aching heart."

Rowlandson arrived at Wachusett Mountain in the midst of preparations to attack the town of Sudbury. With the death of Canonchet, the

Indians urgently needed a major victory. They were winning the war, but they were very low on food. Even if they succeeded in growing a significant amount of corn, they couldn't harvest the crop until late summer. By June, the groundnuts would be gone. They needed to make peace with the English before the beginning of summer. Otherwise, no matter how great their military victories, they would begin to starve to death.

On April 17, Rowlandson became one of the few Westerners to witness a Native war dance. In the center of a large ring of kneeling warriors, who struck the ground with their palms and sang, were two men, one of whom held a musket and a deerskin. As the man with the gun stepped outside the ring, the other made a speech, to which the warriors in the ring cheered. Then the man at the center began to call for the one with the gun to return to the deerskin, but the outsider refused. As the warriors in the ring chanted and struck the ground, the armed man slowly began to yield and reentered the ring. Soon after, the drama was repeated,

◆ *An early-twentieth-century view of Wachusett Mountain.*

this time with the man holding two guns. Once the leader of the dance had made another speech and the warriors had "all assented in a rejoicing manner," it was time to attack Sudbury.

It was a great Native victory. Two different companies of English militia were successfully ambushed. The Indians killed as many as seventy-four men and suffered minimal losses. And yet, the Sudbury Fight failed to be the complete triumph the Indians had hoped for. "[T]hey came home," Rowlandson remembered, "without that rejoicing and triumphing over their victory, which they were wont to show at other times, but rather like dogs (as they say) which have lost their ears." Even though they had caused terrible damage to the English, there were still plenty of soldiers left to fight another day, and for the Indians the days were running out.

The negotiations with the English became more urgent. The sachems ordered Rowlandson to appear at their "General Court." They wanted to know what she thought she was worth. It was an impossible question, of course, but Rowlandson named the figure of £20, about $4,000 today. In the letter accompanying their ransom request, the sachems, led by the Nipmuck chief known as Sagamore Sam, tried to make amends: "I am sorry that I have done much wrong to you," the note read, "and yet I say the fate is lay upon you, for when we began quarrel at first with Plymouth men I did not think that you should have so much trouble as now is."

In early May, the Praying Indians Tom Doublet and Peter Conway arrived with the Englishman John Hoar from Concord. In addition to the ransom money, Hoar had brought along some provisions. It soon came out that Philip was against the ransoming of English captives, while the Nipmucks were for it. However, since Rowlandson was owned by Quinnapin, it was ultimately up to him.

Traditionally, Native Americans relied on ritual dances to help them make important decisions. The dance that day was led by four sachems and their wives, including Quinnapin and Weetamoo. Even though both of them had been almost constantly on the run for the last few months, the couple still wore the clothes of nobility. "He was dressed in his Holland shirt," Rowlandson wrote, "with great laces sewed at the tail of it; he had his silver buttons; his white stockings, his garters were hung round with shillings, and he had girdles of wampum upon his head and shoulders. She had a kersey [a twilled woolen fabric] coat and covered with girdles of wampum from the loins upward: her arms from her elbows to her hands were covered with bracelets; there were handfuls of necklaces about her neck and several sorts of jewels in her ears. She had fine red stockings and white shoes, her hair powdered and face painted red that was always before black."

The next morning, the sachems held another meeting. To Rowlandson's great joy, it was decided that she should be released. To this day, the place where she gained her freedom, marked by a huge boulder, is known as Redemption Rock. By sundown, Rowlandson, Hoar, and the two Praying Indians had reached her former home of Lancaster, where they decided to spend the night. "[A]nd a solemn sight it was to me," she wrote. "There had I lived many comfortable years amongst my relations and neighbors, and now not one Christian to be seen, nor one house left standing."

They reached Concord the next day around noon, and by evening they were in Boston, "where I met," Rowlandson recalled, "my dear husband, but the thoughts of our dear children, one being dead and the others we could not tell where, abated our comfort each to other." Over the course of the next few months, both their children were released, and they spent the rest of the war living among friends in Boston.

But Rowlandson found it difficult to leave her captivity behind. "I can remember the time when I used to sleep quietly without workings in my thoughts, whole nights together," she wrote, "but now is other ways with me. . . . [W]hen others are sleeping, mine eyes are weeping."

◆ ◆ ◆ With the success of Tom Doublet and Peter Conway in negotiating the release of Mary Rowlandson, and with more Massachusetts Bay officers using Praying Indians as scouts (even Samuel Moseley came to see the light), New Englanders began to realize that it was both stupid and inhumane to keep hundreds of loyal Indians as prisoners on Deer Island. In the middle of May, the Massachusetts General Court ordered that the Praying Indians be removed. "This deliverance . . . ," Daniel Gookin wrote, "was a jubilee to those poor creatures."

On May 18, Captain William Turner with 150 soldiers from Hatfield, Hadley, and Northampton attacked a large Native fishing camp on the Connecticut River. Although Turner and his men were ambushed during their retreat and more than forty Englishmen, including Turner, were killed, they had succeeded in killing hundreds of Indians. On June 9, the Nipmuck leader Sagamore Sam lost his wife in another English assault. The Nipmucks decided they had to make peace with the English.

Meanwhile, Philip, accompanied by Quinnapin and Weetamoo, left Wachusett Mountain and headed south into familiar territory. With his brother-in-law Tuspaquin, the Black Sachem of Nemasket, leading the way, Philip's people attacked towns throughout Plymouth and Rhode Island.

From his temporary home on Aquidneck Island, Benjamin Church could see the smoke rising from locations up and down Narragansett Bay. Communication was difficult in these dangerous times, and Church's family were all anxious for any word about their loved ones and friends.

On May 12, his wife, Alice, gave birth to a son named Constant in honor of her father.

A few days later, Church took up a knife and stick and began to whittle. He'd been out of the war for more than three months, and he wasn't sure what he should do now that his son had been born. Perhaps he should take up carpentry again. But as he whittled the stick, his hand slipped, and he badly cut two of his fingers. Church smiled. If he was going to injure himself, he might as well do it in battle.

It was time he returned to the war.

SIXTEEN
The Better Side of the Hedge

◆ ◆ ◆

ON TUESDAY, JUNE 6, Benjamin Church attended a meeting of the General Court in Plymouth. More than three months had passed since the Council of War had refused his request to lead a large group of Native Americans against Philip. Over that brief period of time, English attitudes toward the Praying Indians had changed just as the main fighting had shifted back to Plymouth Colony. Church sensed that his timing was just right.

As it so happened, the Council of War had decided to do almost exactly what Church suggested back in February. They planned to send out in a few weeks' time a force of three hundred soldiers, a third of them Indians, under the command of Major Bradford. Connecticut and the Bay Colony had also promised to provide companies that included significant numbers of Native scouts.

This was all good news, of course, but Church had no intention of serving under Bradford. Bradford was a trustworthy and loyal officer, but Church had his own ideas about how to fight the war. He wanted to find an army of his own.

◆ ◆ ◆ Two days later, Church was in a canoe with two Praying Indians headed back to Aquidneck Island. They were approaching the rocky shore of Sakonnet at the southeastern corner of Narragansett Bay. This was the home of Awashonks, the female sachem whom Church had known before the war. He was certain that if given the chance, Awashonks would have fought alongside the English. Instead, she'd taken her people across the bay to the Narragansetts. After the Great Swamp Fight, the Sakonnets had been forced north along with the Narragansetts and eventually made their way to Wachusett Mountain.

As Church and his two Indian guides approached the jagged rocks and pebble beach of Sakonnet, he saw some of the sachem's Indians fishing along the shore. The Sakonnets, Church realized, had returned home. Perhaps he could convince them to abandon Philip and serve under him.

After pulling the canoe up on shore, Church discovered that one of the Indians was an old friend named Honest George. George, who spoke English well, said that Church's suspicions were correct; Awashonks "had left Philip and did not intend to return to him any more." Church asked George to deliver a message to his sachem: in two days he would meet her and just two others at a well-known rock near the western shore of Sakonnet.

Church went to Newport and purchased a bottle of rum and a roll of tobacco to assist with his negotiations with Awashonks. On the morning of the next day, he and the two Cape Indians paddled to Sakonnet. As Church had hoped, he could see some Indians waiting on the bank. One of them was Honest George, and as soon as Church landed, Awashonks came down to the shore with her son Peter and her principal warrior, Nompash. The sachem shook Church's hand and gestured for him to follow her inland to a large rock at the edge of a meadow.

Almost as soon as the four of them gathered around the rock, "a great body" of Indians, all of them armed and with their faces covered in war paint, rose up out of the grass. After a brief pause, Church said that George had told him that Awashonks might be willing to consider peace. She agreed that such was indeed the case. "It is customary," Church replied, "when people meet to treat of peace to lay aside their arms and

◆ *Treaty Rock, circa 1900, where Sakonnet sachem Awashonks agreed to join forces with Benjamin Church.*

not to appear in such hostile form as your people do." Only after the warriors had placed their muskets in a large pile did Church begin the negotiations.

But first they had to share the rum. After drinking to the sachem's health, Church offered the rum to Awashonks. Church could tell by the way she had watched him drink that she suspected the liquor had been poisoned, but eventually she, too, tasted some of the rum, and Church began to talk.

The first thing the sachem wanted to know was why he had not returned a year ago, as promised, with a message from the governor. Church explained that the sudden outbreak of the war had made that impossible, and in fact, he had tried to contact her when he and a small group of men had come to Sakonnet only to become trapped in the Pease Field Fight. At the mention of this battle, the warriors rose up from the grass in a great "hubbub," with one of them shaking his wooden club angrily at Church.

Honest George explained that the warrior had lost his brother at the

Pease Field Fight and "therefore he thirsts for your blood." It was then that Nompash, Awashonks's chief warrior, stood up and commanded his men to be silent and "talk no more about old things." Church turned to Awashonks and said that he was sure the Plymouth authorities would spare their lives and allow them to remain at Sakonnet if they abandoned Philip. He mentioned the Pequots, a tribe that had once fought against the English but was now a trusted ally. He concluded by saying that on a personal level he sincerely looked forward to reclaiming "the former friendship" they had once enjoyed.

This was enough for Nompash. The warrior once again stood, and after stating the great respect he had for Church, bowed and proclaimed, "Sir, if you'll please to accept of me and my men, and will head us, we'll fight for you, and will help you to Philip's head before Indian corn be ripe."

Church had found his warriors. But now he had to secure the permission of Plymouth Colony.

◆ ◆ ◆ Once the Nipmucks decided they had to make peace with the English too, Philip was forced to flee from Wachusett Mountain. Since the Mohawks were now his enemy, he could not head to the west or the north, and the Mohegans were waiting for him in Connecticut to the south. He could only return to Plymouth Colony, where there was still plenty of corn hidden in underground storage pits.

Coming south with Philip were the sachems Quinnapin and Weetamoo, and by June, approximately a thousand Pokanokets, Narragansetts, and even some Indians from as far away as the Connecticut River valley had entered Plymouth Colony from the north. On June 16, they attacked Swansea and burned all but four garrisons to the ground. On June 26, the Indians turned their attention to Wannamoisett, the portion of Swansea first settled by the Brown and Willett families in the 1650s. By this time, Alexander's and Philip's old friend Thomas Willett had been dead almost two years. Willett's twenty-two-year-old son, Hezekiah, was living in a house that had a watchtower. Confident that no hostile Indians were nearby, Hezekiah ventured out with his black servant only to be shot and killed. The Indians cut off his head and, taking the servant captive, returned to their camp in triumph.

Hezekiah had been killed by Indians who were unaware of the Willetts' long-standing relationship with Philip and his brother. Before his death, Massasoit had instructed both his sons to be kind to John Brown and his family, and the sight of Hezekiah's severed head appears to have deeply saddened Philip. The black servant later told how "the Mount Hope Indians that knew Mr. Willett were sorry for his death, mourned, combed his head and hung peag [wampum] in his hair."

Philip had returned both to the land and to the people he had known all his life. Philip was at war with Plymouth, but from the beginning he had very mixed feelings about his relationship with the colony. In the weeks ahead, the war that ultimately bore his name drew him closer and closer to home.

◆ ◆ ◆ Church was having problems of his own. Soon after his meeting with Awashonks, he wrote a letter about the negotiations and gave it to the sachem's son Peter, who left for Plymouth to speak with the authorities. But on June 27, when Bradford's army arrived at Pocasset, Church had not yet received any word from Peter. Church told Bradford of the Sakonnets' willingness to join him in the fight against Philip, but Bradford would have none of it. He needed to have the official approval of Governor Winslow before he allowed Church to command a company of Sakonnets. Until he had that, Awashonks and her people had to go to Sandwich at the base of Cape Cod, where they would be beyond Philip's reach, and await the governor's decision.

Even though he was not happy with the major's orders, Church urged the Sakonnets to obey. He would go to Plymouth and find out what had happened to Peter. In a week, he promised, he would meet them in Sandwich with the approval from Governor Winslow. And so, with a Praying Indian leading them with a white flag of truce, the Sakonnets set out for Sandwich.

Before Church was able to go to Plymouth, he was forced to accompany Bradford's army on an unsuccessful hunt for Philip on Mount Hope. Not until Friday, July 7—several days past the deadline he had promised the Sakonnets—did Church finally reach Plymouth.

To his immense relief, he learned that Governor Winslow had accepted the agreement Church had reached with the Sakonnets. It

◆ *Engraving of Mount Hope as seen from the south.*

had taken a month to arrange, but it looked as if Church would at last have his own company of Indians.

He decided he needed only half a dozen or so Englishmen to round out his force, and in just a few hours he had assembled a group that included thirty-two-year-old Jabez Howland, son of *Mayflower* passenger John Howland, and Church's brother-in-law, twenty-eight-year-old Nathaniel Southworth. They mounted their horses and, after riding all that night, arrived in Sandwich just a few hours before daylight.

Unfortunately, the Sakonnets had departed several days before for parts unknown. Church feared that Awashonks had taken offense at yet another broken English promise; adding to his worries was the presence of hostile Indians in the region under the leadership of Totoson, the destroyer of Dartmouth and Clark's garrison in Plymouth. After a few hours' sleep, Church and his men set out to catch up with Awashonks and her people.

He thought it likely that they had headed back for home and were following the western shore of Buzzards Bay toward Sakonnet. After riding more than twenty-six miles, Church and his men came upon a panoramic view of a bay that today is the outer portion of New Bedford Harbor. Ahead, they "saw a vast company of Indians, of all ages and sexes, some on horseback running races, some at football, some catching eels and flatfish in the water, some clamming, etc." Church soon learned that these were indeed the Sakonnets and that Awashonks and her warriors were extremely pleased to see him once again.

They found the Sakonnet sachem at an open-sided shelter facing the bay. As Church and his men watched the red sun sink over the hills upon which the city of New Bedford would one day be built, the Sakonnets served them a supper that included "a curious young bass in one dish, eels and flatfish in a second, and shellfish in a third." By the time they'd finished eating, a large bonfire was lit, "all the Indians, great and small, gather[ing] in a ring round it."

Many of the Sakonnets had participated in the war dance witnessed by Mary Rowlandson prior to the Sudbury Fight. That night, they performed a similar ritual. Now, instead of preparing to fight *against* the English, they were preparing to fight *for* the people who once were considered their enemies. After each warrior had danced around the fire with a spear in one hand and a wooden club in the other and vowed to fight against the enemies of the English, Nompash stepped forward and announced to Church that "they were making soldiers for him."

In the weeks ahead, Church's Sakonnet warriors would take him to places that few Englishmen had been before. With the Sakonnets' help, Church's company would enter the forbidden swamps of the New England wilderness—the same places where, fifty-five years before, Massasoit had gathered his people after the arrival of the *Mayflower*.

We will never know what Massasoit's powwows had told him about the future, but we do know that his son Philip was encouraged by his own powwows' prophesy that he would never die at the hands of an Englishman. However, when Philip learned that the Sakonnets had joined the English, it was said to have "broke[n] Philip's heart." From that day forward, he was fighting not just the English—he was fighting his own people.

◆ ◆ ◆ Church and his Sakonnet recruits reached Plymouth the next day. He now attracted several new English volunteers, including Jabez Howland's brother Isaac, Caleb Cook, Jonathan Delano, and Jonathan Barnes.

In their late twenties and early thirties, many of these men were, like Church, either the sons or grandsons of the original Pilgrims. With the help of the Sakonnets, this group of *Mayflower* descendants was about to develop a new way to fight a war.

On the evening of July 11, Church's company of approximately two dozen men, more than half of them Indians, left Plymouth for Middleborough, where a mixed group of Pokanokets and Narragansetts had recently been sighted. Church realized he still had much to learn when it came to the methods of Indian warfare. As they made their way along the path to Middleborough, he asked the Sakonnets "[h]ow they got such advantage of the English in their marches through the woods." They replied that it was essential to keep the men widely separated or, as Church described, "thin and scattered." According to the Sakonnets, the English "always kept in a heap together"; as a result, it was as "easy to hit [a company of English soldiers] as to hit a house." Church soon discovered that spreading out his men had the added benefit of making his tiny army seem much larger than it actually was.

The Sakonnets also insisted that silence was essential when pursuing the enemy. The English constantly talked to one another, and it always alerted the Indians to their presence. Creaking leather shoes and even the swishing sound made by a pair of thick pants could be heard by the Indians. If some form of communication was required, they should use wildlife sounds, from birdcalls to the howling of a wolf.

They also had to learn how to track the enemy. The morning was the best time, since it was possible to trace a man's steps in the dew. But perhaps the most important lesson Church learned from the Sakonnets was never to leave a swamp the same way he had entered it. To do otherwise was to walk into an ambush.

◆ ◆ ◆ After a few hours' sleep in Middleborough, Church and his men set out after the enemy. Soon one of his Indian scouts reported that he'd found an Indian camp. Based on the Sakonnets' description of, in Church's words, "their fires and postures," he ordered his men to surround the camp. On his cue, they rushed at the enemy, "surprising them from every side so unexpectedly that they were all taken, not so much as one escaped."

One of the captured Indians, named Jeffrey, told Church there were a large number of Indians near Monponsett Pond, where Philip's brother Alexander had been seized back in 1662. Church decided to make Jeffrey a part of their company, promising "that if he continued to be faithful to

◆ *Nineteenth-century engraving of Captain Benjamin Church and his company. Although once again the depiction of the soldiers' clothing and facial hair is dubious, this image gives a good sense of the tactics Church learned about Indian warfare.*

him, he should not be sold out of the country [as a slave] but should become his waiting man." As it turned out, Jeffrey remained a part of the Church household for the rest of the Indian's life.

After delivering his prisoners to Plymouth, Church and his men were on their way to Monponsett, where they captured several dozen more Indians. Over the course of the next few weeks, Church's string of successes continued, and he soon became the talk of the colony. On July 24, Governor Winslow officially gave Church the power to grant mercy to those Indians who agreed to help him find more of the enemy, as he had done with Jeffrey. Church's recruits were soon convincing other newly captured Indians to do as they had done and come over to what he described as "the better side of the hedge."

It was a deal that was difficult to refuse, and much of its appeal depended on the company's captain. Church had the ability to bring even the most "treacherous dog" around to his way of thinking. "Come, come," he would say, "you look wild and surly and mutter, but that signifies nothing. These my best soldiers were a little while ago as wild and surly as you are now. By the time you have been but one day . . . with me, you'll love me too."

By the end of July, Church's little band of volunteers was routinely bringing in more Indians than all of Plymouth's and Massachusett Bay's companies combined. In his history of the war, Cotton Mather wrote, "[S]ome of [Church's] achievements were truly so magnanimous and extraordinary that my reader will suspect me to be transcribing the silly old romances, where the knights do conquer so many giants."

Church undoubtedly enjoyed the praise, and in his own account of the war, he does his best to portray himself as a swashbuckling knight of the woods. But as even he admitted, his successes would not have been possible without the presence of Bradford's more traditional army. Based in Taunton, Bradford's men chased Philip throughout the swamps and woods and several times came within minutes of taking the Pokanoket sachem. But, unlike Church's company, morale was a problem among Bradford's soldiers, and by the end of July, many of them had either deserted or found good excuses to return home.

On Sunday, July 30, Church took a brief break from the war to pray at the meetinghouse in Plymouth. But before the end of the service, the Reverend John Cotton was interrupted by a messenger from Josiah Winslow, who had just ridden in from Marshfield. The governor needed to speak with Captain Church immediately.

A "great army of Indians" had been seen gathering on the eastern shore of the Taunton River. If they succeeded in crossing the river, the towns of Taunton and Bridgewater would be in danger. Winslow requested that Church "immediately . . . rally what of his company he could."

Church gathered his company of eighteen Englishmen and twenty-two Indians and set out for Bridgewater. Meanwhile, a handful of the town's militia were already out on a mission of their own. They were approaching the Taunton River when they heard some suspicious noises. They soon discovered that the Indians had laid a huge tree across the river and were at that very moment beginning to cross over toward Bridgewater.

There were two Indians on the tree, an old man with the traditional long hair of a Native American and a younger man with his hair cut short in the style of a Praying Indian. One of the militiamen shot and killed the older Indian, and the younger one, who was lugging a container of gunpowder, tossed the powder into the bushes and escaped back into the forest on the eastern shore of the river.

The dead Indian turned out to be Akkompoin, Philip's uncle and one of the sachem's most trusted advisers. They later learned that the other Indian had been Philip himself. In an effort to disguise himself, he had cut off his hair, and for the moment at least, the change in hairstyle had saved his life.

Many of Philip's subjects were not so lucky that day. After more than a year of extreme hardship, they were exhausted, starving, and unhappy. Conditions had become particularly difficult in the last month. With the appearance of Church's company in early July, the swamps were no longer safe. With no way to protect their children, the Indians had been reduced to the most terrible measures a people can ever know. William Hubbard reported that "it is certainly affirmed that several of their young children were killed by themselves, that they might not be betrayed by their crying or be hindered with them in their flight."

The Bridgewater militiamen reported that the Indians they met on Monday, July 31, were so discouraged that many of them were helpless to defend themselves. According to one account, "Some of the Indians acknowledged that their arms shook and trembled so that they could not so readily discharge their guns as they would have done." Ten Indians were shot dead with loaded muskets in their hands, while fifteen others "threw down their guns and submitted themselves to the English." For many of the Indians, there was no reason left to fight.

◆ ◆ ◆ Early the next morning, Church and his company set out from Bridgewater. They had recruited several men from the local militia, and one of these "brisk lads" guided them to where the Indians had laid the tree over the river. Looking across, they saw an Indian sitting on the tree's stump—an unusual thing for a hostile Indian to be doing the morning after a confrontation with the Bridgewater militia. Church took aim, but his Native companion told him to hold his fire; he believed it might be a friendly Indian. Then the Indian, apparently hearing them, glanced in their direction, and the Sakonnet immediately realized it was Philip himself. He fired his musket, but it was too late. The sachem had rolled off the stump and escaped into the woods.

Church and his men ran across the tree and soon came upon a group of women and children that included Philip's wife and nine-year-old son. There was a fresh trail south, and the prisoners informed him that it had been left by sachem Quinnapin and his people, who had decided to return home to the western shore of Narragansett Bay. But where was Philip? The prisoners claimed that they did not know, "for he fled in a great fright when the first English gun was fired, and they had none of them seen or heard anything of him since."

Leaving some of his men with the prisoners, Church and the rest of the company headed down the trail, hopeful that they might overtake the enemy. But after several miles, Church realized that, given the importance of the prisoners he now had, he should get them back to Bridgewater before dark. His Sakonnets, however, were reluctant to give up the chase. They explained that Awashonks's brother had been killed by the Narragansetts, and they wanted revenge. Church named a Sakonnet called Lightfoot as their captain and "bid them go and quit themselves like men. . . . [A]way they scampered," Church wrote, "like so many horses."

The next morning, Lightfoot and his men returned with thirteen prisoners. They had caught up to the Narrangansetts and killed several of them and "rejoiced much at the opportunity of avenging themselves." Church sent the prisoners on to Bridgewater and, with the Sakonnets leading the way, resumed the search for Philip.

They came upon an abandoned camp that convinced them the Pokanokets were close at hand. Moving quickly through the woods, they discovered a large number of women and children who were too tired to keep up with the main body of Indians up ahead. The prisoners reported that "Philip with a great number of the enemy were a little before." It was getting late in the day, but Church didn't want to stop. He told the Sakonnets to inform their prisoners that "if they would submit to order and be still, no one should hurt them."

As night fell, they could hear the sounds of Philip's men chopping wood and setting up camp. Church told his men and prisoners that they were going to spend the night sitting quietly in the swamp. If any prisoner attempted to escape, Church would "immediately kill them all."

Just before daybreak, Church explained to the prisoners that he and his men were about to attack Philip. He had no one he could spare to guard them, but he told them that it was in their best interests not to escape. Once the fighting was over, they were to follow their trail and once again surrender themselves. Otherwise, they would all die.

He sent out two Sakonnet scouts. At the same time, it turned out, Philip sent two scouts of his own. Philip's men spotted the Sakonnets and were soon running back to camp, making "the most hideous noise they could invent." By the time Church and his men arrived, the Pokanokets had fled into a nearby swamp, leaving their kettles boiling and meat roasting on the fire.

Church left some of his men at the place where the Indians had entered the swamp, then led a group of soldiers around one side while Isaac Howland took another group around the other side. Once they had positioned men around the entire edge of the swamp, Church and Howland met at the farthest point just as a large number of the enemy emerged from inside the swamp.

Hopelessly outnumbered, Church and his handful of soldiers could easily have been massacred by the Pokanokets. Suddenly, a Sakonnet named Mathias shouted out in the Indians' own language, "If you fire one shot, you are all dead men!" Mathias went on to claim that they had a large force and had the swamp completely surrounded.

Many of the Pokanokets did as the other Indians had done just a day before: Astonished, they stood motionless as Church's men took the loaded muskets from their hands. Not far from the swamp was a dip in the land that Church compared to a "punchbowl." He directed the prisoners to jump down into the hollow, and with only a few men standing guard—all of them triple-armed with guns taken from the Indians—he ran back into the swamp to find Philip.

Almost immediately, Church found himself virtually face-to-face with the Pokanoket leader and several of his warriors. By this point, the sachem's behavior was entirely predictable. When cornered or confronted, Philip always ran. As Church and two Sakonnets fought the Pokanoket warriors, Philip turned and fled back to the entrance of the swamp.

This might have been the end of the sachem. But one of the men Church had left waiting in ambush outside the swamp was a notorious drunkard named Thomas Lucas. Whether or not he had just had a drink, Lucas was, in Church's words, not "as careful as he might have been about

◆ *Benjamin Church's sword.*

his stand." Instead of killing the enemy, Lucas was shot by the Pokanokets, and Philip escaped.

In the meantime, Church had his hands full in the swamp. Two enemy warriors surrendered, but the third, whom Church described as "a great stout surly fellow with his two locks tied up with red [cloth] and a great rattlesnake skin hanging to the back part of his head," refused to give up. This, it turned out, was the sachem Totoson.

While the Sakonnets guarded the others, Church chased Totoson. They were running through some dense bushes when the Indian tripped on a grapevine and fell flat on his face. Before he could get back up, Church raised the barrel of his musket and killed him with a single blow to the head. But as Church soon discovered, this was not Totoson. The sachem had somehow evaded him for the moment, and now, filled with rage, Totoson was coming up from behind, "flying at him like a dragon." Just in the nick of time, the Sakonnets opened fire. The bullets came close to killing Church, who claimed "he felt the wind of them," but they had succeeded in scaring off Totoson, who escaped into the swamp.

They had not captured Philip or, for that matter, Totoson, but Church's band of eighteen English soldiers and twenty-two Sakonnets had nonetheless managed one of the more spectacular feats of the war. Once the fighting had ended and they had rounded up all their prisoners, they discovered that they had taken a grand total of 173 Indians.

Church asked some of them if they could tell him anything about their sachem. "Sir," one of them replied, "you have now made Philip ready to die, for you have made him as poor and miserable as he used to make the English, for you have now killed or taken all his relations."

When they reached Bridgewater that night, the only place that could handle all the prisoners was the pound, a fenced-in area used to collect the town's herds of sheep and cattle. The Sakonnets were assigned guard duty, and Church made sure to provide both the guards and their prisoners with food and drink. "[T]hey had a merry night," Church remembered, "and the prisoners laughed as loud as the soldiers, not [having been] so [well] treated [in] a long time."

◆ ◆ ◆ By early August, most of the Indian leaders had been captured or killed, or had turned themselves in. On Sunday, August 6, two days after Church delivered his prisoners to Plymouth, Weetamoo and what remained of her Pocasset followers were near Taunton when a group of local militiamen attacked. The English took twenty-six prisoners, but Weetamoo escaped. Soon after, she tried to cross the Taunton River, but before she reached Pocasset on the eastern shore, her raft broke apart and she drowned.

Her naked body was discovered on the shore of Gardner's Neck, once the village site of her father, Corbitant. Not knowing who it was, an Englishman cut off the woman's head and sent it on to Taunton. Upon its arrival, the nameless head was placed upon a pole within sight of the Indians taken prisoner just a few days before. Soon enough, the residents of Taunton knew whose head it was. According to Increase Mather, the Pocassets "made a most horrid and diabolical lamentation, crying out that it was their Queen's head."

A few days later, Weetamoo's husband, Quinnapin, was taken captive, and on August 25, he was executed in Newport. A month later, Sagamore Sam and several other Nipmuck sachems who had been tricked into surrendering were also executed on the Common.

By that time, Totoson was dead. An old Indian woman later reported that after the sachem's eight-year-old son died from disease, Totoson's "heart became as a stone within him, and he died." The woman threw some brush and leaves over Totoson's body and surrendered herself to the authorities in Sandwich, where she, too, became ill and followed her sachem to the grave.

◆ ◆ ◆ In terms of the percentage of population killed, the English had suffered losses that are difficult for us to imagine today. During the forty-five months of World War II, the United States lost just under 1 percent of its adult male population; during the Civil War, the death rate was somewhere between 4 and 5 percent; during the fourteen months of King Philip's War, Plymouth Colony lost close to 8 percent of its men.

But the English losses appear almost tiny when compared to those of the Indians. Of a total Native population of approximately twenty thousand, at least two thousand had been killed in battle or died of their injuries; three thousand had died of sickness and starvation; a thousand

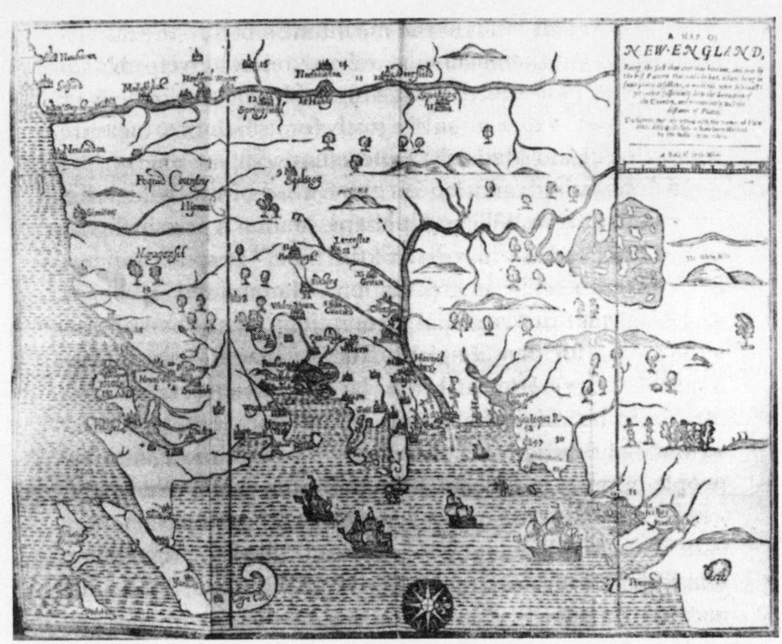

◆ *John Foster's 1677 map of New England.*

had been shipped out of the country as slaves, while an estimated two thousand eventually fled to join either the Iroquois to the west or the Abenakis to the north. Overall, the Native American population of southern New England lost somewhere between 60 and 80 percent of its people. Philip's local fight with Plymouth Colony had grown into a regionwide war that had done nearly as much as the plagues of 1616–19 to diminish New England's Native population.

In the end, the winner of the war was the side who was able to outlast the other. The colonies had suffered a series of terrible defeats, but they had England to provide them with food, muskets, and ammunition. The Indians had only themselves, and by summer they were without the food and gunpowder necessary to fight a war. By August, it had become obvious that the fighting was coming to a close. But as everyone knew, the war would not be over until Philip of Mount Hope had been taken.

◆ ◆ ◆ By Friday, August 11, most of the English forces from Plymouth Colony had been disbanded. Only Benjamin Church and his loyal Sakonnets were still out on patrol. They had just spent the day in Pocasset but had come up with nothing. Church decided he was going to visit his wife, Alice.

Church and his men took the ferry to Aquidneck Island. Alice and the boys were now staying at the home of the merchant Peleg Sanford in Newport, and Church and half a dozen of his company rode their horses the eight miles to Sanford's house. When she first glimpsed her husband, Alice was so overcome with surprise that she fainted. By the time she had begun to revive, Church noticed that two horsemen were approaching at great speed.

They proved to be Sanford and Church's old friend Captain Roger Goulding, the sailor who had saved him more than a year ago during the Pease Field Fight. They had news: An Indian had appeared earlier that day at the southern tip of the Mount Hope Peninsula. He reported that he had just fled from Philip, who had killed the Indian's brother for proposing that they surrender. The Indian was now on Aquidneck Island and willing to lead Church to Philip's camp.

Church turned to Alice and smiled apologetically. He and his men had not yet had the chance to unsaddle their horses. "[H]is wife," he later wrote, "must content herself with a short visit, when such game was ahead." Church asked Sanford and Goulding whether they wanted to come along. They quickly agreed, and soon the men were back on their horses and riding north toward Mount Hope.

◆ ◆ ◆ The Indian was waiting for them at the ferry. He was, according to Church, "a fellow of good sense, and told his story handsomely." Philip, the Indian reported, was on a little area of high ground surrounded by a swamp at the base of the rocky heights of Mount Hope. The sachem had returned to the center of his territory, and the Indian offered to lead Church to him "and to help kill him, that he might revenge his brother's death."

It was after midnight by the time they approached Philip's camp. In addition to Sanford and Goulding, Church had a few of his Plymouth regulars, including Caleb Cook, grandson of the *Mayflower* passenger Francis Cook, to fill out his veteran band of Sakonnets. There was also a Pocasset Indian named Alderman.

Church assigned Goulding to lead the group that would attack Philip's headquarters. With the Pokanoket to guide them, Goulding and his men would creep on their stomachs until they came within sight of the enemy. By that time, Church would have stationed the rest of his men around the edge of the swamp.

Experience had taught them that the Indians always built their shelters so that they were open to the swamp. They also knew that it was, in Church's words, "Philip's custom to be foremost in the flight." When Goulding and his men attacked, the sachem would immediately flee into the swamp, and Church and his men would be waiting for him.

It was always difficult to tell friend from foe in the early-morning darkness of a swamp, so Church told Goulding and his men to shout at the top of their lungs once the fighting began. The rest of them would fire on only those "that should come silently through the swamp."

◆ ◆ ◆ It had come down to just a handful of Philip's toughest and most loyal men. There was the young warrior who supposedly fired the first shot back in June of 1675. He would be one of the first to die that morning. There was also the great survivor: Annawon.

The old warrior had fought alongside Philip's father, Massasoit, decades before. It is likely that he had been one of the warriors to carry the dying Alexander on his shoulders back to Mount Hope. For more than a year now, he had been with Philip every step of the way. In just the last month alone, they had covered hundreds of miles as they crisscrossed their homeland, always on the run.

When the Indians had fallen asleep that night, their exhaustion had been mixed with more than the usual fear. After the brother of the executed warrior left, they all knew the English would be coming soon. As day approached, Philip awoke from a dream. They must leave immediately, he told Annawon and the others. In his dream, he had been captured by the English. They had been betrayed.

One of the warriors stood up. A musket fired, and the yelling began. Philip leaped to his feet, threw his powder horn and petunk (a pouch containing bullets) over his shoulder, and, with his musket in hand, started to run. It would be left to Annawon and the others to

◆ *The musket lock of the gun that supposedly killed King Philip.*

gather their belongings and hold the English off for as long as possible.

◆ ◆ ◆ The first noise of the musket took Church by surprise. He thought one of his soldier's guns might have gone off by accident. But other shots soon followed, and he knew the ambush had begun.

In the eastern part of the swamp stood two men, Caleb Cook and the Pocasset Indian named Alderman. They could see an Indian coming toward them. He was running, they later reported, "as fast as he could scamper." He was dressed in only his breeches and stockings. They waited until he had come within range, and now confident that he was one of the enemy, Cook pulled the trigger of his musket. But his weapon refused to fire. It was up to Alderman.

The Pocasset pulled the trigger, and his musket fired two bullets, one of which hit Philip's rapidly beating heart. He fell facedown into the mud with his gun beneath him. The warriors coming up from behind heard the shots and turned in the opposite direction. Hidden in the dark shadows of the swamp and not yet aware of his sachem's death, Annawon could be heard calling out in a booming voice, "Iootash! Iootash!"—"Fight! Fight!"

Alderman and Cook rushed over to Church and told him that they had just killed Philip. He ordered them to keep the news a secret until the battle was over. The fighting continued for a few more minutes, but finding a gap in the English line on the west end of the swamp, most of the enemy, now led by Annawon, escaped.

Church gathered his men on the hill where the Indians' shelter had been built and told them of Philip's death. The army, Indians and English alike, shouted "huzzah!" three times. Taking hold of the sachem's breeches and stockings, the Sakonnets dragged his body through the mud and

◆ *A nineteenth-century engraving of King Philip's death from a shot fired by a Pocasset Indian.*

dumped him beside the shelter—"a doleful, great, naked, dirty beast," Church remembered.

With his men around him and with Philip's mud-smeared body at his feet, Church declared, "That for as much as he had caused many an Englishman's body to lie unburied and rot above ground, that not one of his bones should be buried." He called forward a Sakonnet who had already executed several of the enemy and ordered him to draw and quarter the body of King Philip.

Soon the body had been divided into four pieces. One of Philip's hands had a distinctive scar caused by an exploded pistol. Church awarded the hand to Alderman, who later placed it in a bottle of rum and made "many a penny" in the years to come by showing the hand to curious New Englanders.

◆ ◆ ◆ On Thursday, August 17, Plymouth Pastor John Cotton led his congregation in a day of Thanksgiving. Soon after the end of public worship that day, Benjamin Church and his men arrived with the biggest trophy of the war. "[Philip's] head was brought into Plymouth in great triumph," the church record states, "he being slain two or three days before, so that in the day of our praises our eyes saw the salvation of God."

The head was placed on one of the palisades of the town's one-hundred-foot-square fort, built near where, back in 1623, Miles Standish had placed the head of Wituwamat after his victory at Wessagussett. Philip's head would remain in Plymouth for more than two decades, becoming the town's most famous sight long before anyone took notice of the hunk of granite known as Plymouth Rock.

◆ ◆ ◆ Philip was dead, but Annawon, the sachem's "chief captain," was still out there. Old as Annawon was, the colony would not be safe, Governor Winslow insisted, until he had been taken. There was yet another well-known warrior still at large: Tuspaquin, the famed Black Sachem of Nemasket.

Church was expected to hunt down and kill these two warriors, but he had other ideas. He had recently been contacted by Massachusetts Bay about helping the colony against the Abenakis in Maine, where fighting still raged. With Tuspaquin and Annawon at his side, Church believed, he might be able to beat the mighty Abenakis.

On August 29, he learned that the Black Sachem was in Lakenham, about six miles west of Plymouth. But after two days of searching, he'd only managed to take Tuspaquin's wife and children. He left a message for the sachem with two old Nemasket women that Tuspaquin "should be his captain over his Indians if he [proved to be] so stout a man as they reported him to be." With luck, Tuspaquin would turn himself in at Plymouth, and Church would have a new Native officer.

About a week later, word came from Taunton that Annawon and his men had been seen at Mount Hope. On Thursday, September 7, Church and just five Englishmen, including his trusted lieutenant Jabez Howland, and twenty Indians left Plymouth to hunt for Annawon.

They searched Mount Hope for several days and captured a large number of Indians. One of the captives reported that his father and a girl had just come from Annawon's headquarters. The old man and the girl were hidden in a nearby swamp, and the Indian offered to take Church to them. Leaving Howland and most of the company with the prisoners, Church and a handful of men went in search of the prisoner's father.

That afternoon they found the old man and the girl, each of whom was carrying a basket of food. They said that Annawon and about fifty to sixty men were at Squannakonk Swamp, several miles to the north between Taunton and Rehoboth. If they left immediately, they could be there by sundown. The old man and the girl walked so quickly over the swampy ground that Church and the rest of the company had difficulty keeping up. The old man insisted that since Church had spared his life, he had no choice but to serve him, and if Church's plan was to work, they needed to get there as quickly as possible.

By the time they reached Annawon's camp, it was almost completely dark. Annawon, the old man explained, had set up camp at the base of a steep rock, and the surrounding swamp prevented entry from any other

• *A nineteenth-century engraving depicting Church's capture of Annawon.*

point. In the gathering darkness, Church and the old man crept up to the edge of the rock. They could see the fires of Annawon's people. There were three different groups, with "the great Annawon" and his son and several others sitting nearest the rock. Their food was cooking on the fires, and Church noticed that their guns were leaning together against a branch with a mat placed over the weapons to keep them from getting wet. He also noticed that Annawon's feet and his son's head were almost touching the muskets.

No one in his right mind would dare climb down from the rock to enter Annawon's camp. But if Church could hide himself behind his two Indian guides, who were known to Annawon and his warriors, he might be able to grab the Indians' guns before they realized who he was.

With the two guides leading the way, Church and his men climbed down the rock face, sometimes grasping bushes to keep from falling down the steep descent and using the noise of women grinding corn to hide the sounds of their approach. As soon as he reached the ground, Church walked over to the guns with his hatchet in his hand. Seeing who it was, Annawon's son pulled his blanket over his head and "shrunk up in a heap." Annawon leaped to his feet and cried out "howoh?" or "who?" Realizing that the Englishman could easily kill his son, Annawon sadly surrendered.

Now that he had captured Annawon, Church sent the Sakonnets to the other campsites to inform the Indians that their leader had been taken and that Church and "his great army" would grant them mercy if they gave up quietly. As it turned out, many of the enemy were related to the Sakonnets and were more than willing to believe them. Soon, Church and his company of half a dozen men had won a complete and bloodless surrender.

Church then turned to Annawon and through an interpreter asked what he had to eat—"for," he said, "I am come to sup with you." In a booming voice, Annawon replied, "taubut," or "it is good." Sprinkling some of the salt that he carried with him in his pocket on the meat, Church enjoyed some roasted beef and ground green corn. Once the meal had been completed, he told Annawon that as long as his people cooperated they would all be allowed to live, except perhaps Annawon himself, whose fate must be decided by the Plymouth courts.

As the meal came to an end, Church realized he desperately needed sleep. He'd been awake now for two days straight. He told his men that if they let him sleep for two hours, he would keep watch for the rest of the night. But as soon as he lay down for a nap, he discovered that he was once again wide awake. After an hour or so, he looked up and saw that everyone else was fast asleep, with one exception: Annawon.

For another hour, they lay on opposite sides of the fire "looking one upon the other." Since Church did not know the Indians' language, and, he assumed, Annawon did not know English, neither one of them had anything to say. Suddenly the old warrior threw off his blanket and walked off into the darkness. Church assumed he had left to relieve himself, but when Annawon did not return for several minutes, Church feared he might be up to no good. Church moved next to Annawon's son. If his father should attempt to attack him, he would use the young man as a hostage.

A full moon had risen, and in the ghostly silver light, he saw Annawon approaching with something in his hands. The Indian came up to Church and dropped to his knees. Holding up a woven basket, he said in perfect English, "Great Captain, you have killed Philip and conquered his country, for I believe that I and my company are the last that war against the English, so [I] suppose the war is ended by your means and therefore these things belong unto you."

Inside the basket were several belts of wampum. One was nine inches wide and showed a picture of flowers, birds, and animals. Church was now standing, and when Annawon draped the belt over his shoulders, it reached down to his ankles. The next belt was one that Philip had often wrapped around his head and had streamers that had hung at his back; the third was meant for his chest and had a star at either end. There were also two powder horns and a rich red blanket. These, Annawon explained, were what Philip "was wont to adorn himself with when he sat in state."

The two warriors talked late into the night. Annawon spoke with particular fondness of his service under Philip's father, Massasoit, and "what mighty success he had formerly in wars against many nations of Indians." They also spoke of Philip. Annawon blamed the war on two factors: the lies of the Praying Indians, especially John Sassamon, and the young warriors, whom he compared to "sticks laid on a heap, till by the multitude of them a great fire came to be kindled."

At daybreak, Church marched his prisoners to Taunton, where he met up with Lieutenant Howland, "who expressed a great deal of joy to see him again and said 'twas more than ever he expected." The next day, Church sent Howland with the majority of the prisoners to Plymouth. In the meantime, he wanted Annawon to meet his friends in Rhode Island. They remained in Newport for several days and then finally left for Plymouth.

In just two months' time, Church had brought in a total of seven hundred Indians. Given his efforts toward ending the war, he hoped that Governor Winslow might listen to his pleas that Annawon and, if he should turn himself in, Tuspaquin be granted mercy.

Massachusetts governor John Leverett had requested to meet with him to discuss again the possibility of his leading a company in Maine, and Church quickly left for Boston. But when he returned to Plymouth a few days later, he discovered "to his grief" that the heads of both Annawon and Tuspaquin had joined Philip's on the palisades of Fort Hill.

◆ ◆ ◆ In September of 1676, fifty-six years after the sailing of the *Mayflower* and a month after the death of Philip, a ship named the *Seaflower* left from the shores of New England. Like the *Mayflower*, she carried a human cargo. But instead of 102 colonists, the *Seaflower* was bound for Jamaica with 180 Native American slaves.

More than a thousand Indians were sold into slavery during King Philip's War, with over half the slaves coming from Plymouth Colony alone. But by September 1676, plantation owners in the Caribbean had decided that they did not want slaves who had already shown a willingness to revolt. We don't know what happened to the Indians aboard the *Seaflower*, but we do know that the captain of one American slave ship was forced to venture all the way to Africa before he finally sold his cargo. And so, fifty-six years after the sailing of the *Mayflower*, a vessel from New England completed a voyage of a different sort.

EPILOGUE
The Rock

◆ ◆ ◆

WHEN I BEGAN writing this book, I wanted to tell the story of how the voyage of the *Mayflower* led to the voyage of the *Seaflower*. It would be a very different story from the one I was taught in school about the First Thanksgiving and Plymouth Rock. This is not to say that what I learned as a child was all wrong. As we have seen, the Pilgrims and the Wampanoags did join in a celebration in the fall of 1621, during which they ate ducks, geese, deer, and perhaps turkeys. There is also a boulder beside Plymouth Harbor that is still known today as Plymouth Rock. But unlike the First Thanksgiving, there is no direct evidence connecting Plymouth Rock with the Pilgrims. As it turns out, the story of Plymouth Rock is not about what actually happened in Plymouth Colony. It's a story about how a hunk of granite became one of America's most popular—and powerful—myths.

The Pilgrims never mentioned a rock in their own accounts of their arrival in Plymouth Harbor. Not until 121 years later, in 1741, did ninety-five-year-old Thomas Faunce claim that his father (who didn't even arrive in Plymouth until 1623) told him that the *Mayflower* passengers used a boulder at the edge of Plymouth Harbor as a kind of stepping-stone to America. So was born the legend of Plymouth Rock.

Several decades later, just before the start of the American Revolution, a group of patriots known as the Sons of Liberty decided that the rock was the perfect symbol for their cause. They decided to move the rock from its original location beside the harbor to the center of town. Unfortunately, when the Sons of Liberty pulled the rock from the

◆ *A photograph of Plymouth Rock in front of Pilgrim Hall.*

mud, it broke in half. Leaving half the rock behind, they carted the other half to the town square.

In the years to come, souvenir hunters used hammers to knock pieces from the rock in the center of town until it was about half its original size. In 1834, the Plymouth town fathers decided that they should move what was left of the rock to the front of a newly built museum called Pilgrim Hall. Once again, disaster struck: After being loaded onto a cart, the rock was passing by the town's courthouse when it fell to the ground and broke in two. With the help of some cement, it was put back together and placed in front of the museum.

By 1880, it had been decided to build a fancy monument around the *other* half of the rock, which was still beside Plymouth Harbor. It was also decided that it was now time for the two pieces of the rock to be put back together. That year, the half in front of Pilgrim Hall was moved down to the waterfront (this time without being dropped), and the two halves were finally reunited after more than a hundred years apart.

Today, the town of Plymouth is a place of historic houses, museums, restaurants, and gift shops. A few miles away on the north bank of the Eel River is Plimoth Plantation, a re-creation of the Pilgrim settlement as it looked in 1627, the last year the original settlers all lived within the great wall. The design and construction of the buildings have been carefully researched, and historical interpreters dress and act as if they were English men and women from 1627. Outside the wall is the re-creation of a small Native settlement known as the Wampanoag Homesite. Here the interpreters are busy with the many daily tasks of a typical Wampanoag village in the early 1600s, which includes carving a large log into a beautifully crafted dugout canoe.

Also part of Plimoth Plantation is the *Mayflower II,* a replica of the ship that brought the Pilgrims to America. It is now tied to a dock beside the fancy granite monument that encloses what remains of Plymouth Rock. The monument is large and impressive, but the actual rock is much smaller than most people expect. Some have even claimed that Plymouth Rock is one of the biggest letdowns in American tourism.

And yet, even if the Pilgrims never did set foot on the rock, it is still, I believe, an important part of this story. Plymouth Rock has been broken, moved, chipped away, broken again, and put back together, but in the end it is still there, reminding us that in 1620 something important happened at this spot, something that eventually led to the making of America.

TIME LINE

◆ ◆ ◆

1524 • Italian explorer Giovanni da Verrazano stops at Narragansett Bay.

1602 • English explorer Bartholomew Gosnold visits New England and names Cape Cod.

1605 • French explorer Samuel Champlain explores the Cape and creates detailed maps of the region.

1607 • Jamestown settlement founded in Virginia.

1608 • English Separatists from Scrooby decide to emigrate to more religiously tolerant Holland.

1611 • William Bradford turns twenty-one and becomes a leading member of the Separatist congregation in Leiden, Holland.

1614 • Captain John Smith visits New England and creates maps of the region. Thomas Hunt captures Natives and sells them as slaves in Spain.

June 1619 • John Carver and Robert Cushman secure a patent from the Virginia Company to start settlement in America.

July 1620 • The Pilgrims depart from Delfshaven, Holland, aboard the *Speedwell.*

September 6, 1620 • The *Mayflower* sets out from Plymouth, England, for America.

November 9, 1620 • The *Mayflower* passengers see land on the other side of the Atlantic Ocean.

November 11, 1620 • The *Mayflower* arrives in Provincetown Harbor. Forty-one men sign the Mayflower Compact.

December 1620 • The Pilgrims have the First Encounter with Natives when they meet the Nausets of Cape Cod. The next day they find Plymouth Harbor.

December 15, 1620 • The *Mayflower* leaves Provincetown Harbor to sail for Plymouth Harbor.

December 25, 1620 • First house frame erected.

March 16, 1621 • Samoset, the first Native American to approach the settlement, speaks the now famous words, "Welcome, Englishmen!"

March 22, 1621 • Samoset returns to Plymouth with Squanto. Massasoit visits with his brother Quidequina, and the Pilgrims record treaty negotiations made with the Indians.

April 5, 1621 • The *Mayflower* sets sail for the return trip to England.

April 1621 • Governor Carver dies. William Bradford is elected the new governor.

July 7, 1621 • Edward Winslow and Steven Hopkins arrive back at Plymouth after visiting Massasoit's village on Narragansett Bay.

August 14, 1621 • Hobbamock and Miles Standish lead Pilgrims on a midnight raid to Nemasket.

September 13, 1621 • Nine sachems come to Plymouth to sign a treaty professing loyalty to the English King James.

Fall 1621 • The First Thanksgiving is celebrated.

November 1621 • The English ship the *Fortune* arrives at Plymouth Harbor.

November 1621 • The Pilgrims receive a threatening message from the Narragansetts and decide to build a wall around their village.

Fall 1622 • The Pilgrims build a fort at Plymouth. Thomas Weston's men leave Plymouth to settle at Wessagussett.

February 1623 • Massasoit falls ill; Winslow, Hobbamock, and John Hamden visit and attend to the sachem.

Winter 1623 • Raid at Wessagussett led by Standish.

Summer 1623 • The supply ship *Anne* arrives with sixty passengers.

1625 • Minister John Robinson dies in Leiden.

1626 • Holland purchases Manhattan from the Indians and establishes the colony of New Netherland. The Adventurers in London disband, and members of Plymouth take on the colony's debt.

1630 • Puritans arrive in area of Boston, Massachusetts, and begin the Great Migration.

1636 • Roger Williams founds the colony of Rhode Island.

1637 • The Pequot War.

1639 • Benjamin Church born in Plymouth.

1642 • Miantonomi attempts to persuade the Montauks on Long Island to join the Narragansetts against the English.

1643 • Miantonomi is captured and executed by Uncas and the Mohegans.

September 7, 1643 • The United Colonies of New England is established and meets for the first time.

1646 • Winslow sails to England on a diplomatic mission and never returns to Plymouth.

May 9, 1657 • Governor William Bradford dies.

Fall 1657 • Massasoit signs his last Plymouth land deed.

Spring 1660 • Wamsutta and his brother Metacom officially change their names to Alexander and Philip.

July 1662 • Major Josiah Winslow leaves with ten men to bring Alexander into court for illegally selling land. Alexander dies after being taken by Winslow and his men.

August 1662 • Philip becomes sachem of Mount Hope and appears in Plymouth court.

April 1664 • Philip sells land bordering the towns of Bridgewater, Taunton, and Rehoboth for a record £66 (roughly $12,000 today).

September 24, 1671 • Philip meets Plymouth officials and signs a treaty that results in the confiscation of all of his weapons and a large fine.

1673 • Philip sells the last parcels of land surrounding his territory at Mount Hope. Josiah Winslow becomes governor of Plymouth.

June 1–8, 1675 • Three Indians put on trial for murdering John Sassamon are found guilty and executed.

June 20, 1675 • Indians start burning houses around the English village of Kickemuit.

June 28, 1675 • Major James Cudworth leads English forces against Philip at Mount Hope.

July 9, 1675 • Benjamin Church and thirty-six of his men are caught in the Pease Field Fight.

July 19, 1675 • A combined Plymouth-Massachusetts force engages Philip and Weetamoo in the swamps of Pocasset.

August 6, 1675 • Having escaped to Nipmuck country, Philip meets with three sachems.

August 22, 1675 • Nipmucks attack the town of Lancaster.

August 24, 1675 • Council of War held by the English at Hatfield on the Connecticut River.

September 18, 1675 • The Battle at Bloody Brook takes place just after a day of public humiliation and prayer had been declared in Boston.

October 5, 1675 • Indians attack Springfield.

October 30, 1675 • Hundreds of Praying Indians are confined to Deer Island in Boston Harbor.

December 8, 1675 • Winslow and an army of a thousand men depart Dedham, Massachusetts, for Rhode Island.

December 15, 1675 • Indians attack Bull's Garrison in Narragansett, Rhode Island.

December 19, 1675 • Winslow and his army attack the Narragansetts in the Great Swamp Fight.

January 27, 1676 • Winslow pursues the Narragansetts in what comes to be known as the Hungry March.

February 5, 1676 • Winslow disbands his army.

February 10, 1676 • Indians attack Lancaster for the second time and take hostages, including Mary Rowlandson.

March 4, 1676 • Governor Edmund Andros witnesses the Mohawks' triumphant return to Albany after attacking Philip's forces.

March 9, 1676 • Philip meets Canonchet, leader of the Narragansetts, for the first time during the war.

March 26, 1676 • The English, led by Captain Michael Pierce and his men, suffer one of the worst defeats of the war along the Blackstone River.

April 9, 1676 • Canonchet is caught by Niantic warriors—allies of the English—and killed by a Pequot firing squad.

April 12, 1676 • The Praying Indian Tom Doublet returns to Boston with the news that the Indians will not yet discuss peace, but will consider the possibility of ransoming hostages.

May 16, 1676 • Mary Rowlandson is released at Redemption Rock.

June 9, 1676 • Nipmuck leader Sagamore Sam loses his wife in an English assault, and the Nipmucks decide to make peace with the English.

June 16, 1676 • Philip and his army attack Swansea and burn all but four garrisons to the ground.

June 27, 1676 • Bradford's army arrives at Pocasset.

July 7, 1676 • Church arrives in Plymouth to get permission from officials to enlist the Sakonnet Indians.

July 24, 1676 • Winslow officially gives Church the power to grant mercy to Indians who will fight with the English.

July 30, 1676 • Church is sent to pursue Indians seen on the Taunton River.

August 6, 1676 • Weetamoo drowns while attempting to escape across the Taunton River.

August 12, 1676 • Church and his company attack and kill Philip at Mount Hope.

August 17, 1676 • Church and his company arrive at Plymouth with Philip's head.

September 7, 1676 • Church begins pursuit and eventual capture of Philip's leading warrior, Annawon. By the end of the month, the heads of Annawon and Philip's brother-in-law Tuspaquin join Philip's head on the palisades of Fort Hill in Plymouth.

September 1676 • The *Seaflower* leaves New England for Jamaica with 180 Native American slaves aboard.

1741 • Thomas Faunce, son of a man who arrived in Plymouth in 1623, originates the legend of Plymouth Rock.

MAYFLOWER PASSENGER LIST

◆ ◆ ◆

Transcription of William Bradford's list of original passengers traveling on the *Mayflower,* as found in his account, *Of Plymouth Plantation.*

Mr. John Carver, Katherine his wife, Desire Minter, and two manservants, John Howland, Roger Wilder. William Latham, a boy, and a maidservant and a child that was put to him called Jasper More.

Mr. William Brewster, Mary, his wife, with two sons, whose names were Love and Wrestling. And a boy was put to him called Richard More, and another of his brothers. The rest of his children were left behind and came over afterwards.

Mr. Edward Winslow, Elizabeth his wife and two menservants called George Soule and Elias Story; also a little girl was put to him called Ellen, the sister of Richard More.

William Bradford and Dorothy his wife, having but one child, a son left behind who came afterward.

Mr. Isaac Allerton and Mary his wife, with three children, Bartholomew, Remember and Mary. And a servant boy John Hooke.

Mr. Samuel Fuller and a servant called William Button. His wife was behind, and a child which came afterwards.

John Crackston and his son John Crackston.

Captain Myles Standish and Rose his wife.

Mr. Christopher Martin and his wife and two servants, Solomon Prower and John Langmore.

Mr. William Mullins and his wife and two children, Joseph and Priscilla; and a servant, Robert Carter.

Mr. William White and Susanna his wife and one son called Resolved, and one born a-shipboard called Peregrine, and two servants named William Holbeck and Edward Thompson.

Mr. Stephen Hopkins and Elizabeth his wife, and two children called Giles and Constanta, a daughter, both by a former wife. And two more by this wife called Damaris and Oceanus; the last was born at sea. And two servants called Edward Doty and Edward Lester.

Mr. Richard Warren, but his wife and children were left behind and came afterwards.

John Billington and Ellen his wife, and two sons, John and Francis.

Edward Tilley and Ann his wife, and two children that were their cousins, Henry Sampson and Humility Cooper.

John Tilley and his wife, and Elizabeth their daughter.

Francis Cooke and his son John; but his wife and other children came afterwards.

Thomas Rogers and Joseph his son; his other children came afterwards.

Thomas Tinker and his wife and a son.

John Rigsdale and Alice his wife.

James Chilton and his wife, and Mary their daughter; they had another daughter that was married, came afterward.

Edward Fuller and his wife, and Samuel their son.

John Turner and two sons; he had a daughter came some years after to Salem, where she is now living.

Francis Eaton and Sarah his wife, and Samuel their son, a young child.

Moses Fletcher, John Goodman, Thomas Williams, Digory Priest, Edmund Margesson, Peter Browne, Richard Britteridge, Richard Clarke, Richard Gardiner, Gilbert Winslow.

John Alden was hired for a cooper at Southampton where the ship victualed, and being a hopeful young man was much desired but left to his own liking to go or stay when he came here; but he stayed and married here.

John Allerton and Thomas English were both hired, the latter to go master of a shallop here, and the other was reputed as one of the company but was to go back (being a seaman) for the help of others behind. But they both died here before the ship returned.

There were also other two seamen hired to stay a year here in the country, William Trevor, and one Ely. But when their time was out they both returned.

These being about a hundred souls, came over in this first ship and began this work, which God of His goodness hath hitherto blessed. Let His holy name have the praise.

—William Bradford, *Of Plymouth Plantation*

SELECTED READING

◆ ◆ ◆

Anderson, Robert Charles. ***The Pilgrim Migration: Immigrants to Plymouth Colony, 1620–1633.*** **New England Historic Genealogical Society, 2004.** This detailed and readable work includes biographies of the passengers who came to America on the *Mayflower.*

Arenstam, Peter, John Kemp, and Catherine O'Neill Grace. ***Mayflower 1620: A New Look at a Pilgrim Voyage.*** **National Geographic Society, 2003.** An excellent description of the voyage for young readers that includes beautiful photography of the *Mayflower II,* the replica of the Pilgrim ship.

Cronon, William. ***Changes in the Land: Indians, Colonists, and the Ecology of New England.*** **Hill and Wang, 1983.** This is the definitive account of how the arrival of English colonists impacted on the native people and ecology of New England.

Deetz, James, and Patricia Scott Deetz. ***The Times of Their Lives: Life, Love, and Death in Plymouth Colony.*** **W. H. Freeman, 2000.** A fun, informative, sometimes iconoclastic book about the Pilgrims and Plymouth Colony from a noted archaeologist who helped make Plimoth Plantation the important institution it is today.

Grace, Catherine O'Neill, and Margaret M. Bruchac. ***1621: A New Look at Thanksgiving.*** **National Geographic Society, 2001.** This tells the story of Thanksgiving with the help of photographs taken at Plimoth Plantation; aimed at young readers.

Philbrick, Thomas, and Nathaniel Philbrick, eds. ***The Mayflower Papers: Selected Writings of Colonial New England.*** **Penguin, 2007.** A selection of the original documents used in writing *The Mayflower and the Pilgrims' New World,* with large portions of William Bradford's *Of Plymouth Plantation* and Benjamin Church's narrative of King Philip's War.

Schultz, Eric B., and Michael J. Tougias. ***King Philip's War: The History and Legacy of America's Forgotten Conflict.*** **Countryman Press, 1999.** An accessible and detailed account of King Philip's War that includes directions to the actual places where the war was fought.

Simmons, William S. ***Spirit of the New England Tribes: Indian History and Folklore, 1620–1984.*** **University Press of New England, 1986.** A fascinating compilation of the recorded oral traditions of the native people of New England.

ACKNOWLEDGMENTS

◆ ◆ ◆

Many thanks to everyone at G. P. Putnam's Sons—Nancy Paulsen, Richard Amari, Shauna Fay and especially John Rudolph for a fantastic job of editing. Special thanks to Wendell Minor for the cover art. Many thanks to my agent Stuart Krichevsky for first suggesting that I write for a younger audience. I'd also like to thank my parents, Thomas and Marianne Philbrick, and my in-laws, Marshall and Betty Douthart—educators all and all young at heart—as well as my children, Jennie and Ethan, and especially my wife, Melissa. Lastly, to my middle-school and younger nieces and nephews—Abby, Lilly, Ryan, and Andrew—this book is for you.

PICTURE CREDITS

◆ ◆ ◆

Courtesy American Antiquarian Society: pp. 175, 215, 266; Azel Ames, M.D., *The Mayflower and Her Log, July 15, 1620–May 6, 1621,* Houghton Mifflin and Company, The Riverside Press, 1907: pp. vi–vii; Author's Collection: pp. 197, 200, 211, 221, 234, 282, 292; Illustration courtesy of Marc Castelli: p. 63; Collection Rijksbureau voor Kunsthistorische Documentatie (RKD), The Hague: pp. 18–19; Photographs courtesy of Shauna Fay: pp. 113, 277; Fruitlands Museums, Harvard, Massachusetts: p. 204; Getty Images: pp. 102–103, 240; Courtesy of the Huntington Library, Art Collections, and Botanical Gardens, San Marino, California: p. 188; The John Carter Brown Library at Brown University: pp. iv–v, 161; Courtesy of Caleb Johnson, MayflowerHistory.com: pp. 15, 33; Kellscraft Studio: pp. 49, 76, 93, 118, 145; Library of Congress: pp. 39, 99, 124–25, 272–73, 320; Courtesy of the Little Compton Historical Society, photo by Edward Denham: p. 289; Illustrations courtesy of PD Malone and Patrick Malone: pp. 72, 185; Patrick Malone, *The Skulking Way of War: Technology and Tactics Among the New England Indians,* Madison Books, 1991: pp. 42–43, 239, 242, 250–51, 252–53, 296–97, 311; Massachusetts Historical Society: pp. 1, 8, 11, 52–53, 82–83, 172, 177, 218, 271, 280, 303, 306, 309, 314; Nativestock Pictures: p. 69; Photograph courtesy Peabody-Essex Museum: p. 224; Pilgrim Hall Museum: pp. 12, 21, 40, 88, 91, 126, 131, 139, 168, 186, 194; Courtesy of Plimoth Plantation: pp. 3, 27, 30; Plymouth County Commissioners: p. 190; Courtesy of the State Library of Massachusetts: p. 157; Wikipedia: pp. 7, 58, 97, 108.

DISCUSSION QUESTIONS

◆ ◆ ◆

PART I: DISCOVERY

- Why did the Pilgrims decide to attempt settlement in the New World? Do you think their plan was well made? Why did they finally settle in Massachusetts instead of their intended Virginia? Do you think any group traveling in the 1620s could have done better, given the resources available at the time?

- Why did the Pilgrims and other passengers decide to forge the Mayflower Compact? What is the main objective, or principle, laid out in the Compact?

- What had happened to the Native American population in the years just before the Pilgrims' arrival and how had Europeans contributed to this catastrophe? What questionable actions did the Pilgrims take in trying to establish contact with their Native American neighbors? How did these events affect the early Pilgrim–Native American interactions?

- Compare and contrast the Mayflower Compact with the Pilgrims' initial agreement with Pokanoket sachem Massasoit. How do these texts help readers understand the Pilgrims' attitudes toward the Adventurers and the Pokanokets?

- How does the author's account of the First Thanksgiving differ from previous descriptions you have read? Describe the relationship between the Pilgrims, the Pokanokets and the other denizens of New England at that moment in history.

PART II: COMMUNITY

- Describe at least two ways in which the title of the book's second section can be understood. How did the Pilgrims view themselves and their efforts in the context of Plymouth; of European settlements in New England; and of the New World community, including its Native Americans?

- What roles did Squanto and the Wessagussett community play in the dangerous realignment of colonial and Native American alliances? Who helped to reestablish the Pilgrims' friendship with Massasoit and how did this lead to the attack on Wessagussett? How does this early attack provide a blueprint for the colonial-Indian conflicts of the ensuing years?

- How did the establishment of the Massachusetts Bay Colony and the Great Migration of the 1630s to the New World affect the Pilgrims? What was the importance of the United Colonies of New England? How did Native American leaders, such as Miantonomi, also recognize and attempt to address the need for collective action among their own peoples? What were the results of these efforts?

- How and why did the Plymouth colony begin to spread and disperse during the 1630s? Why did this worry Governor Bradford from a religious perspective? How did he connect this concern to his disapproval of gun sales to the Indians?

- Who were the "Praying Indians"? Were colonial missionary efforts to convert Indians successful? In the many conflicts between colonial and Indian groups, was religion ever the incendiary factor? Why or why not?

- In what ways did the attitudes of Massasoit's sons and of the sons of the *Mayflower* Pilgrims change in similar fashions? Do you think they simply forgot the lessons of history? What other factors may have impacted the viewpoints of these young men?

- How was the death of Alexander a turning point in Pilgrim-Indian relations? Do you think the Pilgrims were right to call Philip (Metacomet) repeatedly into Plymouth courts? What were the charges? Were his punishments just?

PART III: WAR

- How did Native American land sales to colonists affect tribal fortunes? Do you think the colonists made honorable deals for Indian land? How did the land situation contribute to Philip's sense that he was being forced into a war position? What other major factors drove Philip toward a commitment to fighting?

- What were Philip's strategies for amassing a sufficient army to fight the English? Was there agreement among the Indian tribes regarding Philip's plan? Describe the opinions of dissenting sachems such as Awashonks. Describe the various colonies' commitments to the war begun between Philip and the Pilgrims. How and why did these agreements and alliances change during the course of the war?

- How did the colonists' changing attitudes toward Native Americans, particularly the "Praying Indians," help turn the tides of the war? How did Benjamin Church's military strategy help evoke these changing attitudes?

- What were the major Native American victories during King Philip's war? What were the major colonial battle successes? Compare and contrast Indian and colonial war strategies. What led to Philip's ultimate defeat?

- What percentage of Puritan and Native American populations were lost in the war? How was the property ownership map of New England changed by the war?

- Give at least two reasons the departure of the *Seaflower* is a fitting event with which to end this narrative.

POST-READING QUESTIONS

- How might the Pilgrims and Native Americans of 1620 have defined the terms *spirituality*, *prosperity*, *property ownership*, *loyalty*, and *war*? How might their children or grandchildren have defined these notions in 1676? In what ways did these two groups bring about changes to each others' definitions? How do you think these changes affected the land that would, a century later, become the United States of America?

- Why are the stories of the First Thanksgiving and Plymouth Rock, though more legend than fact, still important parts of American history? How does understanding the way these stories evolved into legend help us understand more about American history and culture? Might this change the way you study other famous historical moments?

- In what way has this book affect your understanding of colonial America? How might you tell the story of the Pilgrims' journey to others today?

INDEX

◆ ◆ ◆

Note: Page numbers in *italics* refer to illustrations

TURN THE PAGE FOR A PREVIEW OF ONE OF THE GREAT, HAUNTING TRUE-LIFE ADVENTURE STORIES.

Preface

February 23, 1821

Like a giant bird of prey, the whaleship moved lazily up the western coast of South America, zigging and zagging across a living sea of oil. For that was the Pacific Ocean in 1821, a vast field of warm-blooded oil deposits known as sperm whales.

Harvesting sperm whales—the largest toothed whales in existence—was no easy matter. Six men would set out from the ship in a small boat, row up to their prey, harpoon it, then attempt to stab it to death with a lance. The sixty-ton creature could destroy that boat with a flick of its tail, throwing the men into the cold ocean water, often miles from the ship.

Then came the enormous task of transforming a dead whale into oil: ripping off its blubber, chopping it up, and boiling it into the high-grade oil that lit the streets and lubricated the machines of the Industrial Age. That all of this was conducted on the limitless Pacific Ocean meant that the whalemen of the early nineteenth century were not merely seagoing hunters and factory workers but also explorers, pushing out farther and farther into a scarcely charted wilderness larger than all the earth's landmasses combined.

For more than a century, the headquarters of this global oil business had been a little island called Nantucket, twenty-four miles off the coast of southern New England.

It was a Nantucket whaleship, the *Dauphin*, just a few months into what would be a three-year voyage, that was making her way up the

Chilean coast. And on that February morning in 1821, the lookout saw something unusual—a boat, impossibly small for the open sea, bobbing on the swells. The ship's captain, the thirty-seven-year-old Zimri Coffin, trained his spyglass on the mysterious craft with keen curiosity.

He soon realized that it was a whaleboat—a double-ended and about twenty-five-foot-long boat that the whalers used to row from the ship to catch their prey—but a whaleboat unlike any he had ever seen. The boat's sides had been built up by about half a foot. Two makeshift masts had been rigged, transforming the rowing vessel into a rudimentary sailboat. The sails—stiff with salt and bleached by the sun—had clearly pulled the boat along for many, many miles. Coffin could see no one at the steering oar. He turned to the man at the *Dauphin*'s wheel and ordered, "Hard up the helm."

Under Coffin's watchful eye, the helmsman brought the ship as close as possible to the mysterious craft. Even though their momentum quickly swept them past it, the brief seconds during which the ship loomed over the open boat presented a sight that would stay with the crew the rest of their lives.

First they saw bones—human bones—littering the floorboards, as if the whaleboat were the seagoing lair of a ferocious, man-eating beast. Then they saw the two men. They were curled up in opposite ends of the boat, their skin covered with sores, their eyes bulging from the hollows of their skulls, their beards caked with salt and blood.

Instead of greeting their rescuers with smiles of relief, the survivors—too delirious with thirst and hunger to speak—were disturbed, even frightened. They jealously clutched handfuls of gnawed-over bones, refusing to give them up, like two starving dogs found trapped in a pit.

Later, once the survivors had been given some food and water (and had finally surrendered the bones), one of them found the strength to tell his story. It was a tale made of a whaleman's worst nightmares: of being in a boat far from land with nothing left to eat or drink and—perhaps worst of all—of a whale with the calculating vengeance of a man.

➤ ➤ ➤

The sinking of the whaleship *Essex* by an enraged sperm whale was one of the most well-known marine disasters of the nineteenth century. Nearly every child in America read about it in school. It was the event that inspired the climactic scene of Herman Melville's *Moby-Dick.*

But the point at which Melville's novel ends—the sinking of the ship—was merely the starting point for the story of the real-life *Essex* disaster. Of the twenty men who escaped the whale-crushed ship, only eight survived.

For nearly 180 years, most of what was known about the calamity came from the 128-page *Narrative of the Wreck of the Whaleship* Essex, written by Owen Chase, the ship's first mate, and published with the help of a ghostwriter only nine months after the first mate's rescue.

Then, around 1960, an old notebook was found in the attic of a home in Penn Yan, New York. Not until twenty years later, in 1980, when the notebook reached the hands of the Nantucket whaling expert Edouard Stackpole, was it realized that its original owner, Thomas Nickerson, had been the *Essex*'s cabin boy. Late in life Nickerson owned and ran a boardinghouse on Nantucket. He had been urged to write an account of the disaster by a writer named Leon Lewis, who may have been one of Nickerson's guests. Nickerson sent Lewis the notebook containing his only draft of the narrative in 1876. For whatever reason, Lewis never prepared the manuscript for publication and eventually gave the notebook to a neighbor, who died with it still in his possession. Nickerson's account was finally published as a limited-edition monograph by the Nantucket Historical Association in 1984.

At fourteen, Thomas Nickerson had been the youngest member of the ship's crew, and his account remains that of a wide-eyed child on the verge of manhood, of an orphan (he lost both his parents before he was two) looking for a home. He was seventy-one when he finally put pen to paper, but Thomas Nickerson could look back to that distant time as if it were yesterday, his memories bolstered by information he'd learned in conversations with other survivors. In the account that follows, Chase will get his due, but for the first time his version of events is challenged by that of his cabin boy, whose testimony can now be heard 182 years after the sinking of the *Essex*.